Third Parties, Outsiders, and Renegades

Lexington Studies in Political Communication

Series Editor: Robert E. Denton, Jr., Virginia Tech University

This series encourages focused work examining the role and function of communication in the realm of politics including campaigns and elections, media, and political institutions.

Recent Titles in This Series

Third Parties, Outsiders, and Renegades

Modern Challenges to the Two-Party System in Presidential Elections

Melissa M. Smith

LEXINGTON BOOKS
Lanham • Boulder • New York • London

Published by Lexington Books
An imprint of The Rowman & Littlefield Publishing Group, Inc.
4501 Forbes Boulevard, Suite 200, Lanham, Maryland 20706
www.rowman.com

6 Tinworth Street, London SE11 5AL, United Kingdom

British Library Cataloguing in Publication Information Available

Library of Congress Cataloging-in-Publication Data Available

ISBN 978-1-7936-2072-9 (cloth)
ISBN 978-1-7936-2074-3 (pbk.)
ISBN 978-1-7936-2073-6 (electronic)

Contents

Acknowledgments

In writing this book, I often thought of Dr. Gary Copeland, who enjoyed a good political discussion and whose door was always open. We all miss you.

A special thanks to Dr. Barry P. Smith, who has indulged my obsession with politics for many years. You will never know how much I have treasured our conversations. Here's to hoping that Matthew takes our love and passion for politics into the next generation.

In memory of Charles Jackson Shubert

PART I

Introduction

Chapter 1

Outsiders and their Origins

Americans love underdogs. Pitch the public a narrative outlining someone's rise from rags to standing on the precipice of success, and Americans will most often cheer on that person, almost willing him or her to overcome the odds. Perhaps it stems from the nation's history, which was forged when an upstart group of colonies decided to break away from the British Empire. In that case, the underdog was successful. This support of those who have the odds stacked against them seems to be part of the nation's psyche, often seen in rags-to-riches stories both in entertainment and in real life. Give Americans a Rocky Balboa, a USA hockey team playing against the Soviets in the Olympics, or this year's Cinderella team in the NCAA basketball playoffs, and they will happily cheer them on, despite the overwhelming odds.

A similar phenomenon can be seen in American politics. In general, Americans have never really liked politics—which are usually viewed through the lens of a political party—and for many, political involvement is limited to occasionally voting in a presidential election. Americans also tend to have rather negative views about how effectively the federal government is working. According to a Pew Research report from April 2018, most Americans think that United States democracy is working, but is not really in great shape. Only 18 percent say it is working well, and four-in-10 say it's not working well—or even at all. (Pew 2018). In 2016, a whopping 61 percent of Americans said that neither political party reflected their opinions. (Cooper, Cox, Lienesch, and Jones 2016). The degree of political partisanship in Washington D.C. and politics in general has effectively divided the nation in half. Toss in an economy that has left some people behind, an uncertainty regarding jobs and economic security, or an economy in a state of flux, and the conditions become ripe for a degree of voter rebellion.

It's in this type of crucible—anger toward the political system, a lack of party loyalty, and looming economic challenges—that notable outsiders, third-party candidates, and political renegades are forged and make their way into national politics. From William Wirt in 1932—who carried the state of

Vermont with seven electoral votes—to Wendell Willkie and Ross Perot, the nation has often flirted with the notion of electing a president who was—or was presented as—a political outsider.

But how does one define an outside political candidate? That becomes tricky, because, while some candidates truly have little political experience or hold beliefs outside the political mainstream, for others being a political outsider is more image and narrative than actual reality. Most often those presenting themselves as outside the political mainstream make rhetorical appeals based on political views from outside the Washington D.C. beltway—as those who are just regular people who see the federal government as corrupt, power-hungry, and overstepping its constitutional authority.

Political scholars often categorize this as populism, and oftentimes these candidates do employ populist rhetorical appeals. There is often an overlap between outsider candidates and populist verbiage that seeks to persuade audiences that someone from the "common people" can be more effective than the political elites who are currently in charge. Yet, not all third-party, outsider, or renegade candidates employ populist rhetoric. These types of candidates tend to be challengers rather than incumbents—because it is hard to position oneself as an outsider if he or she is already in office—but for some, their outsider status is related more to their unconventional stands on issues which put them outside the dominant political consensus of the major political parties. Yet their contributions to the evolution of fringe discourse in the United States should not be overlooked.

HISTORY OF CANDIDATES OUTSIDE
THE MAINSTREAM

Many scholars trace the beginning of outsider appeals to the Populist movements in the late 1800s in the United States. While an argument can be made that Andrew Jackson ran as an outside candidate in 1824 and 1828, he actually had been a territorial governor, served in Congress and was a wealthy landowner. However, he did position himself as a "man of the people," and was elected president in 1828.

But it was in the Populist movements in the late 1800s when Americans first began to hear and pay attention to rhetorical appeals similar to the ones we still hear from outsider and fringe candidates. The Farmer's Alliance in the 1870s railed against an ever-more invasive federal government and political power being concentrated in the hands of wealthy elites (Goodwyn 1978).

The Populist Party (or People's Party) was a left-wing revolt against the Democratic and Republican parties by farmers in the South and Midwest who wanted the government to improve conditions for farmers and workers.

It began in 1892, and the party's presidential nominee, James B. Weaver, collected more than one million popular votes. Several party members were also elected to Congress, and three governors rode to victory using populist rhetoric. The movement faded away with the defeat of populist presidential candidate William Jennings Bryan, although many found a political home in the Democratic Party (Harpine 2001).

A similar movement began in 2004 with the Tea Party, a group of candidates—many of whom were already elected—who advocated for a smaller federal government, lower federal taxes and a halt to what they saw as the federal government overstepping its authority in several areas. According to its web site, the Tea Party is a "grassroots movement calling awareness to any issue which challenges the security, sovereignty, or domestic tranquility of our beloved nation, the United States of America. From our founding, the Tea Party represents the voice of the true owners of the United States: WE THE PEOPLE" (Tea Party Website, n.d.). Named in honor of those who dumped British tea into Boston Harbor in 1773, the rhetoric used by Tea Party candidates bears a great similarity to that used by candidates from the Farmer's Alliance and other Populist movements in that it is highly critical of the federal government and the concentration of political power, but this one is primarily a conservative political movement. Williamson, Skocpol, and Coggin (2011) argue that the Tea Party brought together several ideas that were already present in the conservative movement. "More broadly, Tea Party concerns exist within the context of anxieties about racial, ethnic, and generational changes in American society" (26). While the Tea Party claimed membership by those in the Republican and Democratic parties, as well as several others, many saw the movement as an internal threat to the Republican Party. At its most influential moment, the party had sixty members in Congress, many of whom were in Republican leadership positions.

In addition to the populist rhetoric that was introduced to American society in the late 1800s, the country has a history of flirting with various types of outsider political candidates, not all of whom used populist appeals.

Victoria Woodhull was an advocate for women's rights and labor reforms in the years following the Civil War, and she and her sister were the nation's first female stock brokers and formed the first women's-owned brokerage firm on Wall Street. She and her sister established Woodhull and Claflin's Weekly, a newspaper that advocated for radical ideas. It also became the first American newspaper to print the English translation of Karl Marx's Communist Manifesto (Horowitz 2000). Woodhull advocated for "free love," by which she meant a woman's right to marry, divorce, and bear children without the interference of government or being subject to social restrictions. Given her time in history, it is easy to see Woodhull as a true outsider candidate, given that she advocated for social changes that were seen as shocking and outside the mainstream. She was the first female presidential candidate, becoming the nominee for the Equal Rights Party in 1872. However, her presidential campaign was not taken seriously, as women were not given the political space to run for office, vote, or express their ideas at that time. Even her chosen running mate, Frederick Douglass, never agreed to take part in the campaign and never attended any party functions. She did not receive any electoral votes.

Gen. Winfield Scott was someone who presented himself as an outsider candidate in the presidential elections of 1840, 1844, 1848, and 1852. Scott served in the U.S. Army from 1812 until the Civil War, and he oversaw the relocation of the Cherokee people in 1838 and fought in the Mexican-American War, actually capturing Mexico City to end the war. He is ranked by many historians as the best military commander of his time, but he was not well suited to some of the more subtle political etiquette that some presidents expected. Scott's military career spanned fifty years, during which he served under fourteen United States presidents. He was made commanding general of the U.S. Army in 1841. He never served in office, but had somewhat of a national reputation because of his military exploits. However, his bureaucratic struggles with various presidents and other military leaders were also somewhat legendary. "Late in 1847, after the capture of Mexico City, Scott became enmeshed in a web of politically charged quarrels with high-ranking subordinates, arising largely from the publication of reports and letters intended to inflate the officers' contributions in the battles for the Mexican capital" (Skelton 2006, 165). Because of this, overall Army command was divided between Scott and Zachary Taylor, who was the Whig candidate and eventual winner in the 1848 presidential campaign—a campaign in which Scott himself had been a candidate.

During this period in American history, political activity was not discouraged among active members of the military. Scott continued his political efforts until 1852, when he was nominated for president by the Whig Party, becoming its last presidential candidate when he lost to Franklin Pierce. Scott's anti-slavery position caused Whig support to be split between the North and the South, and Pierce won twenty-seven of the thirty-one states. Scott, however, won 43.9 percent of the popular vote. After this defeat, Scott primarily devoted his energies to the military.

Wendell Willkie was perhaps a bit more of an outsider candidate than Scott. He had been a longtime activist in the Democratic Party, but swapped to the Republican Party late in 1939. He did not run in the primaries, but waited for an opportunity should there be a deadlocked nominating convention. When that happened, he became the Republican nominee and ran against Franklin Delano Roosevelt in 1940. The election took place during World War II, which had started in September 1939, but before American involvement, and isolationism became an important campaign issue. While Willkie had not been isolationist before entering the campaign, he moved in that direction to increase his national appeal, and he also condemned Roosevelt's New Deal policies. Despite his success as a Wall Street attorney, Willkie positioned himself as a "simple barefoot, Wall Street lawyer" and touted his Midwestern roots. "That Willkie secured the nomination under such circumstances was generally explained by his curious combination of populist enthusiasm and a gee-whiz folksiness with a solid record as a corporate executive in defending Republican big-business interests against creeping New Deal socialism" (Beidler 1994). Willkie's attempt to position himself as a representative of ordinary Americans was not ultimately successful, as he won only ten states in the general election. His popular vote total, however, set a record for Republican presidential candidates and was not surpassed until Gen. Dwight Eisenhower in 1952.

In more modern times, candidate Lyndon LaRouche, who ran for president eight times, including once from his prison cell, was a presidential candidate as a member of the Democratic and Labor parties who began his political career as a Marxist. He later became a totalitarian, was a Holocaust denier, and he promoted the idea that there was a British conspiracy to have him killed (Severo 2019). He was known for elaborate conspiracy theories, including that the International Monetary Fund was guilty of mass murder by spreading AIDS through its economic development policies. He was sentenced to federal prison for tax evasion, but did not let that stop him from continuing to run for president. He ran for president in 1976, 1980, 1984, 1988, 1992, 1996, 2000, 2004, and 2016, but was never considered a serious candidate.

Of course the ultimate recent outsider candidate was Donald J. Trump, who had never held elective office and was given almost no chance of winning the presidency in 2016. He entered the race during a rare confluence of economic uncertainty, anger with both political parties, and an image that painted him as the only one who could navigate the challenges facing the nation. His unconventional campaign style attracted many supporters who rallied around his shoot-from-the-hip style speeches and events. A later chapter will be devoted to analysis of President Trump and his outsider style campaign.

WHAT MAKES SOMEONE A POLITICAL OUTSIDER?

As you can see from the brief history of selected unconventional U.S. political candidates, it can be difficult to define what makes a candidate a political outsider. Some candidates are truly outside the mainstream in their ideas and political affiliation, while others may have been elected or maintain associations with those in political power. One might try to present him or herself as an outsider, but that might not be enough to convince potential audiences of his or her authenticity. This degree of authenticity is important, as voters ultimately decide if a candidate's rhetoric rings true. Stewart (2018, 107) states that "The win–loss record of outsider candidates in presidential elections reflects a clear advantage for those who can effectively separate themselves from the politics of Washington, D.C." His analysis of presidential debates found that use of outsider appeals and rhetoric has dropped from 1976 levels (a banner year for modern outsider presidential candidates given the aftermath of the Watergate scandal) but has remained at a somewhat consistent level since 1996.

The most simple, and least effective, possible definition of an outsider candidate is one who lacks political experience or connections to those with political power. While this seems like a plausible definition, it overlooks the power of personal narratives in the past and especially in today's online, social media-saturated world. Some candidates, such as Patrick Buchanan, might never have been elected but have rubbed shoulders with the political elite. Yet, his personal narrative when running for president stressed his outsider status because his views were not represented by the dominant political consensus in Washington. Therefore, this definition seems too limiting.

Nor is it fair to say that only one political party is more likely to produce outsider candidates. Bonikowski and Gidron primarily discuss populism in their analysis of United States presidential candidate speeches from 1952 to 1996. Their definition of populism is an accepted one within comparative political science, stated as "a form of politics predicated on a moral vilification of elites and a concomitant veneration of the common people" (Bonikowski and Gidron 2016, 1594). They examine political rhetoric in terms of "a transactional process in which meanings are shaped by relations between actors embedded in social fields" (1594) and looked at political speeches, rather than individual candidates and their political positioning. They found in their analysis that populism is present in both the Republican and Democratic parties, and it is generally a "strategic decision shaped by political opportunity structures" (Bonikowski and Gidron 2016, 1614). Some political challengers simply find it necessary to present populist rhetoric to combat the success-oriented rhetoric of incumbents and to try to forge a space for themselves in the political debate.

Populist candidates tend to be divisive and can attract supporters from opposing political parties, much as then-candidate Donald J. Trump did in 2016. Trump garnered support from blue-collar workers who traditionally would have voted for a Democratic candidate because of his promises of increasing factory jobs and bringing manufacturing back to areas hard hit during the Great Recession. Even President Barack Obama described himself as a populist in a 2003 interview on public-access television, and again in 2016 at a news conference in Ottawa, Canada, based on his desire to provide educational opportunities such as charter schools for children, a progressive tax system, and a desire to help Americans have reliable and effective health care (Von Drehle 2016). While most people would not look at Obama and call him a populist, Obama himself apparently makes a distinction between combative and controversial rhetoric aimed at getting votes and a concern for others that motivates political action.

Many outsider candidates are found running as third-party candidates or independents because their stands on issues are outside the mainstream or they lack access to the power structures within the Democratic and Republican parties. Within the primarily two-party system in the United States, future candidates are groomed and promoted through leadership in the party and election to progressively higher-level offices. This system has been in place for almost as long as the parties have existed, and a candidate running for U.S. president counts on the backing of his or her party when a nomination is secured. Those running on third-party platforms cannot expect as much support, and they must attract voters from the major parties. This often casts a third-party candidate in the role of a "spoiler," rather than a serious candidate. It also often necessitates a reliance on populist rhetoric or controversial statements to attract media and voter attention.

There are also candidates who agitate within a political party, veering toward extreme positions or actions. Those generally are seen as rebelling against the establishment, yet their renegade positions sometimes lead to quite a following during an election, pulling votes away from a more mainstream candidate in the same party.

These candidates all face the same challenge: attract a base of followers who will vote for them and perhaps establish an ongoing movement. While each candidate's methods might be somewhat different, they all face similar barriers. The mainstream media routinely ignores outside candidates, because it tends to focus only on those who are seen as having a realistic chance of winning. Outsider, renegade, and third-party candidates also lack the funding of major-party candidates, and their campaigns are woefully underfinanced. "So severe are these barriers that most minor party candidates abandon hope of winning, aiming instead for the goal of using strategies of agitation to advocate for social and political change" (Neville-Shepard 2014, 215). The need to distinguish themselves from other candidates and deliver messages to large numbers of potential voters requires those outside the political mainstream to be creative in their rhetoric and memorable in their tactics.

METHODOLOGY

Because this book will be considering three different types of candidates outside the political mainstream, the following definitions will be used:

For purposes of this book, *third parties* will refer to political parties other than the Republican and Democratic parties.

An *outsider* presidential candidate will be defined as a candidate who approaches politics from outside the establishment-oriented field of Washington politics. These candidates hold views on economic, social, or legislative issues that are considered outside the mainstream beliefs of Americans at the time. This also includes candidates who are viewed outside the mainstream because of gender or ethnicity.

Renegades will be defined as presidential political candidates who began within a party's establishment but then moved outside that establishment. These candidates reject establishment views on economic, social, or legislative issues and adopt discourse or tactics that position them beyond the boundaries of acceptable establishment beliefs and behavior.

This book's research approach will be presented as a rhetorical history, and it will utilize examples of presidential candidates in the last fifty years to show the evolution of fringe discourse in United States presidential elections.

As a rhetorical history, this text will seek to provide what Michael Tumolo defined as a perspective "in which histories of ideas and events are appropriated to develop a deeper understanding of those contexts and events that resonate as timely and relevant to the contemporary reader" (2011). As humans, we use the past to explore, explain, and predict our current circumstances and events. Bruce E. Gronbeck said rhetorical history "studies describe, explain, account for, and judge a rhetorical artifact or discourser principally by references to the 'real' world outside symbolic manipulations, texts, and subjective feelings about eloquence" (1975, 311). This manuscript will use the discourse, campaign tactics, and issues of several candidates who were on the fringes of the political landscape in the last fifty years to trace the evolution of their ideas in modern presidential politics. As Gronbeck and other scholars (Benson 1967–68, Kellner 1989, Gronbeck 1995, Murphy 2015) have stated, the rhetorical historian can sift through the past to trace the influence of messages on present-day issues. "Ultimately, such studies will help answer questions concerning the roles of rhetors and of discourse as causes among all other causes precipitating historical effects and processes broadly conceived" (Gronbeck 1975, 313).

History unfolds around people all the time, yet it's not seen as history until an undefined amount of time has elapsed. Humans generally look to the past for causes and explanations of current events, and those examinations usually lead to stories about people whose thoughts, lives, actions, and ideas shaped the future. In that respect, this book seeks to discuss how these particular candidates challenged the established political parties and made an impact on future political discourse, campaign tactics, and campaign issues. It will seek to tell their stories—how their political exploits led to the fringe discourse that is seen in American politics today. As Robert J. Connors (1989) said, "Historians are no more or less important than any other researchers. We are your memory. Memory without the ability to test and act on the knowledge it provides is paralyzed; memory without attempts to understand its linguistic or cognitive constituents is stunted; memory without connections to the world of human struggle and contact is isolate and self-referential" (231).

This book will utilize a mixture of scholarly and mass-media articles, as well as personal writings from some of the candidates. This type of interdisciplinary study benefits from a look at not only what scholars have said about a topic in retrospect, but what was being said about a candidate's impact on political policy and institutions in his or her day and time. That generally is gleaned from mass-media sources, and those are utilized in the book. There is also value in examining the candidate's own words, not just in speeches, but in books and other texts that he or she may have written or have taken credit for writing. As Serazio notes, "patterns of discourse are important to chart because they raise concerns about how power is conceptualized and wielded in democracy" (2016, 192). It is with that thought in mind that this text will seek to tell the stories of these candidates and their impacts on the current political system in the United States.

ORGANIZATION

This book is organized into two introductory chapters that provide an overview of fringe rhetoric followed by a grouping of candidates into three sections: Third Parties, Outsiders, and Renegades. Then it moves into a section that considers the implications for outsider candidates following the election of Donald J. Trump. Here is an overview of the chapters:

Introduction: This section will provide a look at early outside presidential candidates, as well as provide definitions and methodology.

Chapter 1: Outsiders and their origins in the United States. This chapter provides an initial look at outside candidates and sets up the definitions and methodology used in the following chapters.

Chapter 2: Populism and its impact on modern fringe discourse. The history of populism will be discussed in this chapter, and the characteristics of populist discourse will be discussed. The definition of populism used in this book will be discussed, as well as three representative populist candidates in the early to mid-twentieth century.

Outsiders Section: This section will look at four outsider candidates and how their discourse, campaign tactics, and issues were received during their campaigns and how they had a lasting impact on modern politics.

Chapter 3: The ideas, rhetoric, and campaign tactics of Shirley Chisholm will be examined. Although she was a marginalized Black woman, Chisholm refused to be silenced, and many of her ideas and thoughts can be seen in today's Democratic Party candidates.

Chapter 4: The campaigns of Jesse Jackson will be analyzed to look at the impact of his campaign discourse, tactics, and issues on modern outsider rhetoric, as well as his role in empowering Black political candidates.

Chapter 5: Former Congressman Ron Paul's presidential campaigns will be examined in light of his political issues and rhetoric that led to a devoted following, especially online, and the development of online campaigning and fundraising.

Chapter 6: The campaign and election of President Donald J. Trump will be examined. Trump is the first true outsider candidate to be elected president of the United States, and his campaign discourse, tactics, and issues will be related to the ideas and discourse of outsider and renegade candidates who came before him.

Third Parties Section: In this section, the campaigns of three notable third-party candidates will be examined to look at how their discourse, campaign tactics, and issues were received at the time of their campaigns and their possible impact on later elections.

Chapter 7: In this chapter, the election campaigns of Ross Perot will be examined. Perot's tactics of going around the mass media will be analyzed in light of modern campaigns, as well as his discourse and issues.

Chapter 8: This chapter will analyze the discourse and issues in the third-party campaigns of Ralph Nader, who was a hero to many people, but is viewed by many as a third-party spoiler.

Chapter 9: The campaigns of Dr. Jill Stein, a medical doctor and activist turned political candidate, will be discussed. Stein, a Green Party candidate, often used guerrilla and activist techniques to gain media attention for her discourse and issues.

Renegades Section: In this section, three candidates who left their party's mainstream will be discussed in light of how they became political renegades and the impact they had on later elections and their political parties.

Chapter 10: The campaigns of George Wallace will be examined in light of how his discourse, tactics, and issues were received in the late 1960s and early 1970s, as well as his ongoing political legacy in current fringe rhetoric.

Chapter 11: The campaign discourse and tactics of Pat Buchannan will be discussed, as well as how his issues and discourse played a role in the 2016 campaign of Donald Trump.

Chapter 12: The presidential campaign of former Congressman Newt Gingrich will be examined, especially in light of impact of the tactics, discourse, and issues he used to reshape the Republican Party and pave the way for future candidate Donald J. Trump.

Implications for Outsiders: In this section, the possible implications of Donald Trump's legacy on outsider candidates will be considered.

Chapter 13: The 2020 defeat of President Donald Trump and its potential impact on outsider candidates will be considered.

Chapter 14: This chapter will consider the future of outsider candidates, given their legacy of fringe discourse and tactics and the current political polarization in the country.

Chapter 15: In this chapter, final thoughts will be made regarding outsider political candidates in the United States.

This is not a text that seeks to look at the impact of outsider rhetoric in an election outcome or in voter preference, other than to relate how each candidate fared in his or her quest for the presidency. As Hinich, Shaw and Huang (2010, 283) ably state, "successful candidates win by effectively positioning themselves vis-à-vis the major party opposition." The candidates highlighted in this compilation are those who attempted to position themselves as being outside and against the Washington political establishment, and, in doing so, laid a foundation for future fringe candidates and discourse.

REFERENCES

Beidler, Philip. 1994. Remembering Wendell Wilkie's One World. *Canadian Review of American Studies* 24 (2): 87–105. Retrieved through Academic Search Complete. June 7, 2021.

Benson, Lee. 1967-68. An Approach to the Scientific Study of Past Public Opinion, *Public Opinion Quarterly* 31 no. 4 (Winter): 522–567.

Bonikowski, Bart and Noam Gidron. 2016."The Populist Style in American Politics: Presidential Campaign Discourse, 1952-1996," *Social Forces* 94 no. 4 (June): 1593–1621. https://doi.org/10.1093/sf/sov120.

Connors, Robert J. 1989. Rhetorical History as a Component of Composition Studies. *Rhetoric Review* 7, no. 2 (Spring): 230–240.

Cooper, Betsy, Daniel Cox, Rachel Lienesch and Robert P. Jones. 2016. "The Divide over America's Future: 1950 or 2050? Findings from the 2016 American Values Survey." PRRI Research. https://www.prri.org/research/poll-1950s-2050-divided-nations-direction-post-election/.

Goodwyn, Lawrence. *The Populist Movement: A Short History of the Agrarian Revolt in America.* 1978. New York: Oxford University Press.

Gronbeck, Bruce E. 1975. Rhetorical History and Rhetorical Criticism: A Distinction. *The Speech Teacher* 24, no. 4 (November): 309–320.

Gronbeck, Bruce E. 1995. The Rhetorics of the Past: History, Argument, and Collective Memory. Paper presented at *Greenspun Conference on Rhetorical History: Rhetoric, History, and Critical Interpretation: The Recovery of the Historical-Critical Praxis, the University of Nevada Las Vegas, 1995.* https://clas.uiowa.edu/commstudies/sites/clas.uiowa.edu.commstudies/files/THE%20RHETORICS%20OF%20THE%20PAST.pdf.

Harpine, William D. 2001. Bryan's "A Cross of Gold:" The Rhetoric of Polarization at the 1896 Democratic Convention. *Quarterly Journal of Speech* 87, (3): 291–304. https://doi.org/10.1080/00335630109384338.

Hinich, Melvin J., Daron R. Shaw and Taofang Huang. 2010. "Insiders, Outsiders and Voters in the 2008 U.S. Presidential Election." *Presidential Studies Quarterly* 402, (2): 264–285. https://doi.org/10.1111/j.1741-5705.2010.03754.x.

Horowitz, Helen Lefkowitz. 2000. Victoria Woodhull, Anthony Comstock, and the Conflict Over Sex in the 1870s. *The Journal of American History* 87, no. 2 (September): 403–434. https://doi.org/10.2307/2568758.

Kellner, Hans. 1989. *Language and Historical Representation: Getting the Story Crooked.* Madison: University of Wisconsin Press.

Murphy, John. M. 2015. Barack Obama and Rhetorical History. *Quarterly Journal of Speech* 101, no. 1 (February): 213–224.

Neville-Shepard, Ryan. 2014. Triumph in Defeat: The Genre of Third Party Presidential Concessions. *Communication Quarterly* 62, no. 2 (April): 214–232.

Pew Research Report. 2018. "The Public, the Political System and American Democracy." April 26, 2018. https://www.people-press.org/2018/04/26/the-public-the-political-system-and-american-democracy/.

Serazio, Michael. 2016. Encoding the Paranoid Style in American Politics: "Anti-Establishment' Discourse and Power in Contemporary Spin. *Critical Studies in Media Communication* 33, no. 2 (May): 181–194.

Severo, Richard. 2019. "Lyndon LaRouche, Cult Figure who Ran for President 8 Times, dies at 96." *The New York Times*, Feb. 13, 2019. https://www.nytimes.com/2019/02/13/obituaries/lyndon-larouche-dead.html.

Skelton, William B. 2006. The Commanding Generals and the Question of Civil Control in the Antebellum U.S. Army. *American Nineteenth Century History* 7, no. 2 (June): 153–172. https://doi.org/10.1080/14664650600809271.

Stewart, Jared Alan. 2018. "In Through the Out Door: Examining the Use of Outsider Appeals in Presidential Debates." *Presidential Studies Quarterly* 48, (1): 93–109. https://doi.org/10.1111/psq.12433.

Tumolo, Michael. (2011). On Useful Rhetorical History. *Journal of Contemporary Rhetoric* 1, (2): 55–62.

Tea Party Website. n.d.: https://www.teaparty.org/about-us/.

Von Drehle, David. 2016. Barack Obama Reveals His Populist Blind Spot. *TIME.* June 30, 2016. https://time.com/4389939/barack-obama-donald-trump-populism/.

Williamson, Vanessa, Theda Skocpol and John Coggin. 2011. The Tea Party and the Remaking of Republican Conservativism. *Perspectives on Politics* 9, (1): 25–43. https://doi.org/10.1017/S153759271000407X.

Chapter 2

The Roots of Populism
in American Politics

In many ways, politics in the United States is still being influenced by a movement that began in response to the economic and banking policies following the Civil War. While most schoolchildren can recite the dates of the Civil War, few people are aware of the collapse of the economic structure of the Southern United States during those years. That collapse led to new, disruptive banking policies after the war that favored the wealthy and kept the poor—especially farmers—in perpetual debt.

Farmers in Midwestern states also felt the crunch of economic factors that led to falling prices for crops, increasing costs of getting crops to markets, and a loss of family owned farmland to increasing foreclosures. A credit crisis in the nation, which was blamed on tying the nation's money supply to the gold standard, led to reliance in both the South and the Midwest on crop liens, which caused most farmers to get ever-deeper into debt.

The frustration that spread among farmers led to market and political alliances, culminating what many call the Populist Movement in the United States. Populist movements have occurred in many nations around the world, but this chapter will be confined to a discussion of the discourse, rhetoric, and issues of the movement in the United States and its impact on the nation's political rhetoric in the twentieth and twenty-first centuries.

WHAT IS POPULISM?

The definition of populism is often debated, although most people agree that it is rooted in opposition to what is seen as a misuse of power or perceived moral failings. Some scholars argue that populism and nationalism should be considered intertwined, while others try to separate out the two, yet look for ways they influence each other. Most political scholars have some level of agreement, though, that populism is rooted in political and class struggle, most often with those who are generally thought of as having less political power, usually referred to as "the people," in opposition to "the elites." The definitions of both "the people" and the "elites" are somewhat prone to vagueness because they can refer to different entities at different times and in differing situations, but the elite are generally characterized as those seen as adversaries by populists (Knott 2020).

Many see in the American populist movement of the 1890s a struggle to regain a cultural and political identity that may or may not have ever been reality, but existed within a shared vision of political liberty. Historian Lawrence Goodwyn relates the efforts of the American populist movement to an attempt to change culture and elevate the status of "the people" in not only importance, but also in self-determination. "Out of their cooperative struggle came a new democratic community. It engendered within millions of people what Martin Luther King would later call a 'sense of somebodiness.' This 'sense' was a new way of thinking about oneself and about democracy" (Goodwyn 1978, XXIV). Although the movement ultimately failed, its legacy and importance is still discussed in American political rhetoric and the concepts of power and persuasion.

A populist approach to politics can be found in many different countries and in greatly contrasting situations. Perhaps this elusiveness of its practice has contributed to the difficulty of defining the term. Scholars have debated the definition and different characteristics of populism, but have come to no consensus regarding how to actually define it.

In Ernesto Laclau's classical theory of populism (1977), those targeted by populist rhetoric are seen as having betrayed some aspect of public trust or principles. "Within this tradition, populism is predicated on a moral opposition between the people, who are viewed as the only legitimate source of political power, and the elites, whose interests are perceived as inherently contrary to those of the populace" (Bonikowski and Gidron, 2016). For Laclau, discourse is performative, and it shapes the social world through power relations and politics. He saw discourse—and populist discourse in particular—as important, for "one needs to know for what one is fighting, what kind of society one wants to establish" (Laclau and Mouffe, 2014, xix). Laclau sees all politics as populist, with some being more populist than others. As Palonen (2020) states "Populism is therefore a process where foundations are challenged, where new dichotomies and divisions are introduced, and where the contingent and ultimately ungroundable figure of the people is performed" (56). Thus, populism is how political meanings are formed.

Cas Mudde is seen as one of the leading contemporary scholars on the subject. He defines populism as "an ideology that considers society to be ultimately separated into two homogeneous and antagonistic groups, 'the pure people' versus 'the corrupt elite,' and which argues that politics should be an expression of the *volonté générale* (general will) of the people" (2004). Mudde and Kaltwasser (2017) identify three key concepts that define populism. Briefly stated, these are: (1) it contains an appeal to "the people," (2) it contains a "denunciation of the elite," and (3) it is a "thin-centered ideology" (2017, 5–6). Mudde does not consider all political actors to be populist at all times.

Brubaker (2020) views populism as a two-dimensional discursive space, embodying both vertical and horizontal oppositions. Vertically, "the people" are defined by their contrast to "the elites," who are seen as as above them and out of touch with the hardships of the ordinary people. Horizontally, populism is more of a contrast between the elites on the outside and "the people" on the inside of a community. "Economic, political, and cultural elites are represented as 'outside,' as well as 'on top' in both left-and right-wing populist discourses. They are seen not only as comfortably insulated from the economic struggles of ordinary people but also as differing in their culture, values or way of life" (Brubaker 2020).

In terms of the characteristics of populism, Knott relies on three elements he argues are common to populism, which he describes as an antagonistic form of politics. First, he argues that populists will "challenge the dominant values of society," which indicates that populism most often appears in times of crisis. The second characteristic he attributes to populism is that it only grows and becomes a movement if there is an audience not only listening, but willing to accept it. The third characteristic is that "there are left and right variants of populism," meaning that it is not an ideology, but "a logic, discourse, style or practice of doing politics" (Knott 2020a). Mudde and Kaltwasser (2017) argue instead that populism is a "thin-centered ideology" that is usually coupled with a more dominant ideology. For instance, a populist who veers to the left of the political spectrum might combine populism with a form of socialism, while those veering toward the right might combine it with some degree of nationalism. The reason it is combined with another ideology, they argue, is that populism doesn't usually offer detailed plans for how to fix what is seen as a problem. By itself, they posit, populism reacts against a perceived injustice or betrayal, but doesn't offer solutions. When paired with a broader ideology, populists can offer remedies for the moral issues at hand.

It should be obvious by now that offering a simple definition to the term "populism" is not easy. Political scholars look at various aspects of populist rhetoric in an effort to better understand its characteristics, but there is often disagreement among those who study the topic. This book will not attempt to provide in-depth conceptualizations of populism, nor will it give a critique on each approach taken to define the concept since the twentieth century.

For the purposes of this book, populism will be defined in a more discursive vein, looking at populism not as an ideology, but as a political discourse characterized by an antagonistic relationship between "the people" and "the elites," and the performance, or public shaping, of populist ideas, messages, and rhetoric. Given the development of mass communication methods and technology in the twentieth and twenty-first centuries, and the propensity of populist candidates to adapt to and rely on such new technology, the performative aspects of discourse will also be discussed. As Moffitt and Tormey (2014) state, political style includes the "repertoires of performance that are used to create political relations" (387). They "acknowledge and highlight the fact that the contemporary political landscape is intensely mediated and 'stylised,' and as such the so-called 'aesthetic' or 'performative' features are particularly (and increasingly) important" (388).

A SHORT HISTORY OF THE POPULIST MOVEMENT

To understand the populist movement in the United States and the rhetoric that characterized its messages, one must have at least a basic understanding of the Agrarian Movement that gave birth to its development.

Following the Civil War, many areas of the South had limited access to banking, and a crop-lien system developed that ensured most farmers would never be able to make a profit, much less pay for items such as food and crop seed which were purchased on credit. Farmers hoping for a good crop would buy their household items on credit, signing a crop lien to the merchant that would be settled once the crop had matured and been taken to market. What most farmers didn't understand was that the prices for goods purchased on credit were always higher than those purchased with cash. By the time the crops were sold, it always seemed there wasn't enough to pay for the goods that had been purchased. Then a lien on the next year's crops was signed, and the cycle continued each year, with farmers becoming deeper in debt.

Goodwyn notes that the conditions for the poor in the South forced men into perpetual servitude. "Farmers learned that the interest they were paying on everything they consumed limited their lives in a new and terrible way: the rates imposed were frequently in excess of 100 percent annually, sometimes over 200 percent" (1978, 22) Some only escaped debts when they died and the debt was written off. Those working their own land often would sell their land to the "furnishing man" to settle debts, which left them as tenant farmers, rather than land owners. The system degraded both white and African American farmers, leaving them in a perpetual cycle of debt and desperation.

For many poor farmers, this never-ending cycle of debt led to a migration West, usually to Texas. It was in Texas that the seeds of what would become the populist movement were born. In the West and Midwest, farmers not only had to deal with crop liens, but also droughts and the problems of transporting farm products to markets. There were various attempts to get farmers to work together to overcome these issues, mainly through the building of associations for the cooperative buying and selling of crops. This Agrarian movement built slowly, spreading east across Texas and back into the Old South and eventually became known as The Farmer's Alliance. The group wanted to give power back to farmers, who they saw as the rightful land owners, by denouncing and ending the crop lien system and reforming the nation's economic policies.

In the Midwest, the center of what Theodore Saloutos and John D. Hicks called the "center of agricultural discontent" included North Dakota, South Dakota, Minnesota, Wisconsin, Iowa, Nebraska, Illinois, Kansas, and Missouri (1951, 5). In this region, the beginning of its Agrarian movement was centered in Chicago, where a farm journalist began the National Farmers' Alliance, which included local chapters from several nearby states. Farmers in this region were seeing more land sink into the hands of landlord investors, and a rising number of tenant farmers were struggling to find enough capital to stay afloat. Railroads were accused of hiking rates for hauling crops, and elected officials were said to show favoritism to railroads and other large companies. For most, the move from being a tenant farmer to actual farm ownership seemed like a far-fetched dream.

African American farmers in the South suffered from similar problems, and had the additional barrier of being denied membership in the regional alliance simply because of their race. They worked together and formed the Colored Farmers' Alliance with similar goals as their counterparts in the Midwest and South.

Thus, many of the farmers in Midwestern and Southern states found themselves in difficult financial positions, and they saw an advantage in banding together to work for better access to capital, lower tariffs, lower interest rates, changes in the income tax rates, and easier distribution of crops. The groups established cooperative mills for the processing of crops, built storage facilities that could help lower the costs of farmers bringing products to market, and they established cooperative stores where farmers could sell their products at less expensive prices than retail stores.

While these were worthwhile advancements, eventually the Agrarian movement recognized that true reform would only come through political action. Goodwyn argues that those in the movement were "engaged in a cultural struggle to redefine the form and meaning of life and politics in America" (1978, 33). By working together to institute change, those in the Agrarian movement found a self confidence that they never experienced on their own. Goodwyn calls this the movement culture of populism, which was a new political vision. By the turn of the twentieth century, this movement was growing, with more than 2 million members in the Farmers' Alliance alone (Gilder Lehrman Institute of American History, n.d.) The Farmers' Alliance members established a third party before the 1892 national election, and it was called the People's Party of the United States, also known as the Populist Party.

POPULIST DISCOURSE

True to its party name, the People's Party saw itself in opposition to those with money and power who they said enacted laws that often crippled the common people. The Agrarian movement had been popularized by a type of "us versus them" rhetoric which they believed would exploit a common bond among farmers, people who operated small businesses, and average workers. "Concentrating on a kind of social dualism that pitted the common people against the hosts of wickedness, party leaders tended to ignore the heterogeneous character of American society" (Glad, 1960, 52). The movement found much support among Midwest and Southern farmers, but less support among small business owners, especially in other parts of the nation. While the movement's rhetoric called for the common, decent people to rise up against the evils of capitalism and the banking system, at its core it was a rebellion against what they saw as a corruption of the nature of the democratic system.

Gerteis and Goolsby are among the scholars who argue that the Populist movement was, at its core, about American identity. "While the movement was built around economic and political grievances of farmers, it was also motivated by a powerful sense that American democracy was being undermined and that the interests of everyday Americans, particularly the farmers, were under attack" (2005). Those in the movement believed "the people" had built the country, but now were suffering economic and political decline at the hands of "the elites."

Populism is not the product of only liberal or conservative parties, but is an approach or appeal that transcends political aggregation. In the case of the Agrarian Movement, it was originally not affiliated with any major party, but developed its own third party. Nadia Urbinati (2013) states that populism is not a revolutionary movement, in that it is not seeking to gain sovereignty for a people, but instead questions the way democracy is currently working. Urbinati argues that populism can actually be detrimental to representative democracy, as a successful movement can lead to an ineffective political reorganization of the state.

Although the populist movement in the United States ultimately failed, it was "an attempt to mobilize American identity—a culturally powerful and broadly unifying thing—in service of economic and political inclusion, but in doing so invoked other forms of exclusion" (Gerteis and Goolsby 2005). The movement has been criticized for excluding minorities and condemning immigration in favor of restoring economic power to poor white farmers. However, many see its criticisms of the banking industry and consolidation of power in the hands of big business as prescient, given the influence of large corporations in the current day. The People's Party collapsed after the defeat of William Jennings Bryan, the Democratic presidential candidate in 1896. The People's Party had grown increasingly internally polarized and did not nominate its own candidate in that election, but endorsed Bryan.

LEGACY OF POPULIST RHETORIC

Even though the Agrarian Movement failed to achieve its goals, the discourse it used to promote change still echoes in United States politics more than 125 years later. One of its lessons is that a populist can only become an effective and powerful political figure if he or she is supported by a great mass of people. The list of well-known politicians in the United States who have employed populist discourse in an effort to stir a nationwide following is impressive, especially given that the original movement was not successful. Here is a representative sample of those who employed populist discourse and rhetoric while seeking elective office in the twentieth century.

WILLIAM JENNINGS BRYAN

William Jennings Bryan, who was known as the "prophet of midwestern moralism" (Glad 1960, 50), was first nominated for president by the Democratic Party in 1896. The People's Party, as mentioned earlier, also supported Bryan for president and did not name its own presidential nominee that year. Bryan, who was born and raised in rural Illinois, had a childhood that centered him around what populists would call "the people." He exhibited the moralism in which he had been steeped as a child and young man, and he was a gifted public speaker. "Whatever Bryan may have been to his contemporaries— devil, saint, or simply a product of the Middle West—his ethical and religious ideas together with their social, economic, and political implications do much to account for his prominence and power" (Glad 1960, 22). As noted earlier, populism is at its root a moral opposition to the elites by the common people. Bryan was known as a defender of the common man and those who described themselves as "the working classes."

Bryan was elected to the U.S. Congress from Nebraska in 1890 and served two terms. In addition to his being the Democratic Party's nominee in 1896, he was also the nominee in 1900 and in 1908. Although populists found in him a kindred spirit, Bryan was a staunch Democrat, and he never endorsed the idea of a third party. He also implored his party to be unified in its quest to elect leaders to the United States Congress. It was his skills as an orator that many say actually won him the Democratic nomination in 1896, in a speech that came to be known as "A Cross of Gold." Most people saw this speech as an endorsement of the free, unlimited coinage of silver, but it was also an argument that the elites were responsible for the nation's problems. "Superficially, bimetallism may appear to be an abstruse economic issue. But Bryan used this issue to symbolize the struggle of the ordinary working Americans" (Harpine 2001).

In comments prior to receiving the party's presidential nomination in 1900, he took the opportunity to castigate the country's leaders for the Spanish-American War and warned against American rule in the Philippine Islands. His comments urged against American Imperialism, which he said would be based entirely on the quest for pecuniary gain, not on the cause of freedom. He also warned of the burden such actions would place on common Americans:

> In addition to the evils which he and the farmer share in common, the laboring man will be the first to suffer if oriental subjects seek work in the United States; the first to suffer if American capital leaves our shores to employ oriental labor in the Philippines to supply the trade of China and Japan; the first to suffer from the violence which the military spirit arouses and the first to suffer when the methods of imperialism are applied to our own government. (Bryan 1900)

As can be seen in this passage, Bryan is arguing that "the people"—here combining farmers and common laborers—will be the first to suffer from these actions, which would be taken by the political elites but backed by industry and banking leaders. His comments also reflect the anti-immigrant comments often found in populist texts. Later in this speech, he intones a glorious vision for the nation "a republic in which every citizen is a sovereign, but in which no one cares to wear a crown." Although Bryan was advocating for the working class, he never failed to pinpoint those who he felt had abandoned their moral principles. "There was little doubt in Bryan's mind that the greatest sores on the body politic resulted from policies advocated by a small group of self-seeking and sinister men and imposed on the people through devious means" (Glad 1960, 100). In Bryan, we can also see a hint of the conspiracy theories which are still prevalent in populism today. In the case of "us" versus "them," it seems the elites were often accused of conspiring against the common man and masking their real intent.

Bryan's greatest accomplishment may have been his control of the Democratic Party for several years, resulting in his three presidential nominations. Although he never became president, he was named Secretary of State by President Woodrow Wilson after the 1912 election. He went on to become known for presiding over the 1925 Scopes Trial, in which he opposed evolution and Darwinism.

HUEY LONG

Huey Long was born in a poor area of Louisiana known for its populist leanings and its Southern Baptists, who were a religious minority in a staunchly Catholic state. While Long may not have exhibited the strict moral behavior of a Southern Baptist boy, growing up as a religious outsider and being a part of the "common people" was ideal for shaping the populist leanings of this future governor and U.S. senator. As with William Jennings Bryan, Long was noted for his oratory skills, which later brought him to state and nation-wide fame. Long was the first politician, outside of President Franklin D. Roosevelt, to realize the power that radio offered in building a national constituency. As a U.S. senator, he would purchase radio time to explain his proposals and ideas to the nation. His broadcasts often took on an almost religious tone, with multiple Bible references and assertions that what he was proposing could be found in God's laws.

Long's speeches were usually delivered with great exuberance and energy, and he was one of the most effective political speakers the nation has ever seen. Many of those who heard him speak were entranced and professed to love him. Yet others developed great hatred for a man they considered quite dangerous. Hogan and Williams described him as "a larger-than-life symbol of alienation and discontent—a dangerous demagogue to some, but a hero and savior to millions of others" (2004). In 1934 Long used his radio program to unveil his "Share Our Wealth" initiative in which America's wealthiest individuals would be limited to $50 million and have any excess finances or property redistributed to poor Americans. He used folksy language to chat with radio listeners about his ideas, rather than giving more formal speeches. In this way, he exhibited an uncanny sense of understanding the difference between an audience moderated by a media platform, rather than an in-person performance.

In his defense of his "Share Our Wealth" speech on the floor of the U.S. Senate in 1935, Long lays the blame for starving Americans at the feet of of the federal government, which had asked farmers to cut back on production in order to drive up prices. "We have brought on the dust storm. Yea, we brought on the dust storm! We brought on the shortages. We brought on the poverty. We aggravated the misery. We promoted the rich to become richer and the poor to become poorer" (Congressional Record 1935). Long also produced a printed pamphlet outlining his "Share Our Wealth" plan, and it contained many references to Biblical passages and principles. In one of his most famous phrases, Long said this program would make "Every man a king, so there would be no such thing as a man or woman who did not have the necessities of life, who would not be dependent upon the whims and caprices and ipse dixit of the financial barons for a living" (Long 1934). He urged individuals to begin "Share Our Wealth" societies in their own communities.

Long's discourse generally fell into the camp of appealing to "the people" to rally against the power that wealth and industry held over the state or the nation. He paid less attention to the politics of race, but instead traded on his image of a man of the people as he shouted and contorted his body while speaking. This sort of performance appealed to the less-educated and more impoverished members of the audience, who were probably more emotionally moved by Long's impassioned speeches. In 1929, while he was governor of Louisiana, the state legislature attempted to impeach him, and in response he went on a speaking tour around the state. Huge crowds turned out to hear him, even though his speeches sometimes lasted more than two hours. He called his enemies names and "cultivated the image of a 'common man' who was also an extraordinary leader—a leader who defied the rules of political decorum, fearlessly confronted the powerful, and intuitively grasped the problems of the 'common people'" (Hogan and Williams 2004).

Long was one of the most accomplished populist politicians in the twentieth century, and possibly in the history of the United States. He served two terms as governor of Louisiana and then three years in the U.S. Senate before his assassination. Many consider him a very productive governor, fulfilling many of the populist promises that were made during his election campaigns.

JOSEPH MCCARTHY

Few twentieth-century politicians left a legacy as chilling as Joseph McCarthy. Known now mainly for his campaigns against pro-Communist Americans, McCarthy presented himself as a country rube and exaggerated his World War II service as "Tail Gunner Joe." Elected to the U.S. Senate in 1946, he served as a Republican senator from Wisconsin until 1957.

McCarthy rose to national prominence when he proclaimed in 1950 that he had a list of names of State Department officials who were Communists. In fact, those who saw the piece of paper that the names were supposedly written on said it actually contained notes on another topic. McCarthy spoke at many events around the country, rallying Americans to the dangers of Communist sympathizers, and even accused President Harry Truman's secretary of defense, World War II hero Gen. George C. Marshall, of being part of a conspiracy involving Communism. When Gen. Dwight Eisenhower was campaigning for president in 1952 in Milwaukee, Wisconsin, he removed a paragraph from his speech to avoid losing the potential votes of McCarthy supporters. The removed paragraph read, in part: "The right to challenge a man's judgment carries with it no automatic right to question his honor." Eisenhower went on to defend Marshall by saying, "I know him, as a man and a soldier, to be dedicated with singular selflessness and the profoundest patriotism to the service of America" (Eisenhower 1952). Even though Eisenhower was said to dislike McCarthy, he did not publicly defend Marshall, and he went on to win the presidential election.

McCarthy's discourse was angry, exaggerated, and usually labeled his real and professed enemies as traitors and anti-Christian, and he often launched into vile personal attacks against them. He sometimes re-arranged the truth to suit his own purposes, and once he found that the comments about a rising Communist threat struck a chord with Americans, he grabbed onto it and never let go. In a speech to the Wheeling, West Virginia, Republican Women's Club in 1950, McCarthy whipped up his rhetoric to invoke fear about the nation's survival: "Today we are engaged in a final, all-out battle between communistic atheism and Christianity. The modern champions of communism have selected this as the time. And, ladies and gentlemen, the chips are down—they are truly down" (Senate 1950). While McCarthy's rhetoric wasn't the same as Bryan's or Long's populist approach, he positioned himself as the one who could root out the Communists and save the nation. His discourse was "the people" against those who were infiltrating American society at all levels and threatening its future.

McCarthyism, as it became known, was exemplified by vicious, unfounded attacks on individuals, and his position as the chair of the Senate's Permanent Subcommittee on Investigations gave him the power to initiate investigations into multiple individuals. His "investigations" were usually prompted by public accusations and characterized by unfair tactics that were sometimes rumored to involve blackmail, especially in the case of homosexual individuals. Some of those who were being investigated committed suicide, while others had their lives ruined. In 1954, during a hearing investigating alleged Communists in the Army, McCarthy appeared drunk during the televised proceedings. After being censured by the Senate later that year, McCarthy's power and popularity faded.

In a letter to a friend, President Eisenhower stated that the average American probably could not understand the tactics some politicians would take in order to gain popularity. "They have learned a simple truth in American life. This is that the most vicious kind of attack from one element always creates a very great popularity, amounting to almost hero worship, in an opposite fringe of society" (Eisenhower 1953). The president went on to compare McCarthy to Huey Long, whose populist rhetoric had swayed many people in the 1930s. McCarthy was one of the first populists to exploit the new media of television, much as Long had taken advantage of radio when it was a new medium. It also became McCarthy's undoing, as it revealed his cruelty and alcoholism to the nation. For a few years, though, McCarthy was one of the most powerful and dangerous men in the nation.

CHARACTERISTICS OF POPULIST DISCOURSE

In just these three examples of very different populist politicians, it can be seen that there are some recurring aspects of populist discourse. One of the most obvious is the reliance on "us vs. them" rhetoric. In the case of populists, "us" is often less definable than "them," as populists usually have alliances with different groups and movements. What is more important is their common enemies. For these three politicians, it is easy to see that the targets of their attacks were very different. "The specific elites targeted by populist claims can vary, from elected politicians and business leaders to intellectuals, but they are invariably portrayed as having betrayed the public trust" (Bonikowski and Gidron 2016). The framing of those charges will be influenced by where a specific politician is located in the current political environment. Most populists are outside the mainstream, so opposition rhetoric makes sense for their political aspirations and possible acquisition of power. It is usually more difficult to determine who "us" might be in this type of discourse. Simply saying populist leaders represent "the people" is a bit vague, but perhaps this is necessary for them, because limiting it to specific groups could possibly eliminate potential supporters. Having people self-identify with a populist candidate because of perceived shared morals, values, or backgrounds is a safer route to accumulating followers and power.

Another recurring aspect of populist rhetoric is its reliance on perceived sincerity and authentic performance. For instance, Huey Long never tried to present himself as anything other than a simple man from a small parish in Louisiana. When he spoke about "the elites," it resonated with others who had similar backgrounds and who appreciated his "authentic" voice. Similar comments could be made about other populists. "Appearing to be close to 'ordinary' people and taking up their concerns against a powerful, privileged and distant elite is another of the characteristics of populist style that has been identified in much political communication research" (Ekstrom and

Morton 2017). Authentic performance is also important, as the way that a person looks or acts also references shared values. When Huey Long went on the radio and spoke with religious fervor and included Biblical references, this resonated with many of the "ordinary" people listening. When Joseph McCarthy expressed such outrage and disgust with those he said were threatening the country, many Americans identified with that outrage because of their shared love of the nation.

In close association with authenticity was the recurrence of storytelling among these politicians. When Huey Long spoke about his upbringing in a small town in Louisiana, or when William Jennings Bryan recounted the stories of America's patriotic heroes (Gardner 2010), they were looking to engage an audience in identification, a rhetorical concept that Kenneth Burke argues is necessary because there are divisions between people. "If men were not apart from one another, there would be no need for the rhetorician to proclaim their unity" (1969, 22). By sharing their personal stories or those which have engaged the nation, a degree of identification was often achieved among the politicians and their respective audiences. Once that identification was achieved, persuasion became more likely because the audience now felt they shared something in common with that person. This contributes to a sense of authenticity, and that often leads to stronger persuasion. The role of myths are important in populism, as well. A myth is generally thought of as a storytelling device that explains a natural or social phenomenon or even introduces a supernatural element to lend explanation to an event. In the realm of politics, myths are narratives that discuss the common bonds among members of a community. "Populist myths belong to the class of political myths, but they are unique in that the commonality between all of those who form the 'us' is anchored in the common feature of having been recently wronged by a nefarious elite" (Casullo 2020, 28). The populist myth stresses the wrongs or betrayals that have happened in the past and then presents a leader who will rise up and give vindication to "the people." Long's stories about his upbringing, McCarthy's appeals to patriotism, and Bryan's celebration of American heroes fit into a populist myth that stresses their commonalities with "the people," and positions them as the hero who will avenge the wrongs.

Another characteristic exhibited by these three men is their reliance on emotional rhetoric and appeals. Bryan could take an issue and use it to exemplify how ordinary Americans were being hurt at the hands of "the elite." Long was able to whip audiences up into emotional lathers by talking about the injustices being heaped upon them because of wealth being accumulated by the top one percent of Americans. McCarthy frightened Americans by claiming that there was a Communist threat within their own government. Ekstrom, Patrona and Thornborrow (2018) argue that populists generally employ a communication style that uses increased emotional appeals, dramatization, and the use of colloquial language. This allows them to often gloss over actual facts and use emotion to connect with their audiences. In this way, McCarthy was able to say that he had the names of Communists within the government, but never actually produce a list. The mere idea that this could be happening in their nation was enough to scare Americans into demanding action, and McCarthy was happy to begin investigating this threat for them.

Another characteristic of populist discourse can be seen in both Long and McCarthy, and that is the early adoption of new technology. Long saw the potential in radio to develop a nationwide following, and McCarthy realized that television would introduce him to the nation in a way that would make him an even more powerful foe for his enemies in Washington. Using the new technologies of the day allowed each one to better mobilize the public to listen and adopt the populist messages. This has continued in the intervening years, both in the United States and in other countries. Nash (2016) noted that "upsurges of populist sentiment have often coincided with innovations in communication technology that rendered the voices of the 'little people' more discernable and easier to mobilize" (12). In their examination of populism, Jager and Borriello (2020) note that more recent populist parties "have leaned on new communication strategies and lay claim to a high online presence" (70). As noted later in this book, recent outsider, third-party, and renegade candidates, including former President Donald Trump, have made use of new and emerging communication technologies.

POPULIST DISCOURSE IN MODERN POLITICS

The following chapters will look at ten United States presidential candidates. Many of them employed some variation of populist discourse, although some can be seen as having stronger populist messages than others. Bonikowski and Gidron argue that "the probability of a candidate's reliance on populist claims is directly proportional to his distance from the center of power (in this case, the presidency)" (2016). While all of the candidates profiled would be considered outside the political mainstream in some way, some are listed as outsiders, some are discussed as third-party candidates, and others are analyzed as renegades, all based on the definitions set forth earlier. For different candidates, the distance from the center of power, or the presidency, might have been longer or shorter, but all of them were campaigning from political points outside the political norms of the day. This led to many of them incorporating populist approaches in their campaign messages. They will each be evaluated in relation to their discourse, campaign tactics, and major issues that were used while laying a political foundation and in their presidential campaigns.

REFERENCES

Bonikowski, Bart and Noam Gidron. 2016. The Populist Style in American Politics: Presidential Campaign Discourse, 1952–1996. *Social Forces* 94, no. 4 (June): 1593–1621. https://doi.org/10.1093/sf/sov120.

Brubaker, Rogers. 2020. Populism and Nationalism. *Nations & Nationalism* 26, no. 1 (January): 44–66.

Bryan, William Jennings. 1900. Imperialism (Flag of an Empire). https://www.americanrhetoric.com/speeches/wjbryanimperialism.htm.

Burke, Kenneth. 1969. *A Rhetoric of Motives*. Berkeley: University of California Press.

Casullo, Maria Esperanza. 2020. Populism and Myth. In *The Populist Manifesto*, edited by Emmy Eklundh and Andy Knott, 9-23. London: Rowman & Littlefield.

Congressional Record. 1935. Share Our Wealth. Huey Long. May 15, 1935. https://www.hueylong.com/docs/cr-speeches/share-our-wealth_cs.pdf.

Eisenhower, Dwight D. 1952. Communism and Freedom. Oct. 3, 1952. https://www.eisenhowerlibrary.gov/research/online-documents/mccarthyism-red-scare.

Eisenhower, Dwight D. 1953. Letter, President Eisenhower to Friend, Swede Hazlett, July 21, 1953. https://www.eisenhowerlibrary.gov/sites/default/files/file/mccarthyism_1953_07_21_DDE_to_Hazlett.pdf.

Ekstrom, Mats and Andrew Morton. 2017. The Performances of Right-Wing Populism: Populist Discourse, Embodied Styles and Forms of News Reporting. In *The Mediated Politics of Europe*, ed. Mats Ekstrom and Julie Firmstone, 289–318. Palgrave Macmillan: Cham, Switzerland.

Ekstrom, Mats, Marianna Patrona and Joanna Thornborrow. 2018. Right-Wing Populism and the Dynamics of Style: A Discourse-Analytic Perspective on Mediated Political Performances. *Palgrave Communication* 4, (83). https://doi.org/10.1057/s41599-018-0132-6.

Gardner, Elizabeth. 2010. William Jennings Bryan, "Imperialism." *Voices of Democracy*, 5: 37–56.

Gerteis, Joseph and Alyssa Goolsby. 2005. Nationalism in America: The Case of the Populist Movement. *Theory and Society* 34, no. 2 (April):197–225.

Gilder Lehrman Institute of American History. n.d. *Populism and Agrarian Discontent*. https://ap.gilderlehrman.org/essays/populism-and-agrarian-discontent.

Glad, Paul W. 1960. *The Trumpet Soundeth*. Lincoln: University of Nebraska Press.

Goodwyn, Lawrence. 1978. *The Populist Movement: A Short History of the Agrarian Revolt in America*. New York: Oxford University Press.

Harpine, William D. 2001. Bryan's "A Cross of Gold": The Rhetoric of Polarization at the 1896 Democratic Convention. *Quarterly Journal of Speech* 87, (3): 291–304. https://doi.org/ 10.1080/00335630109384338.

Hogan, J. Michael and Glen Williams. 2004. The Rusticity and Religiosity of Huey P. Long. *Rhetoric and Public Affairs* 7, (2): 149–171. Accessed through Academic Search Complete. April 27, 2021.

Jager, Anton and Arthur Borriello. 2020. Making Sense of Populism. *Catalyst* 3, no. 4 (Winter): 49–81. https://catalyst-journal.com/vol3/no4/making-sense-of-populism.

Knott, Andy 2020a. Populism: The Politics of a Definition. In *The Populist Manifesto*, edited by Emmy Eklundh and Andy Knott, 9–23. London: Rowman & Littlefield.

Knott, Andy. 2020b. "The New Moving Right Show." *Soundings: A Journal of Politics and Culture* 75 (Summer): 111–123.

Laclau, Ernesto. 1977. Towards a Theory of Populism. In *Politics and Ideology in Marxist Thought: Capitalism, Fascism, Populism*. London: New Left Books.

Laclau, Ernesto and Chantal Mouffe. 2014. *Hegemony and Socialist Strategy: Towards a Radical Democratic Politics*. Second Edition. London: Verso.

Long, Huey. 1934. Share Our Wealth. Feb. 23, 1934. https://www.hueylong.com/programs/share-our-wealth-speech.php.

Moffitt, Benjamin and Simon Tormey. 2014. Rethinking Populism: Politics, Mediatisation and Political Style. *Political Studies* 62, no. 2 (June): 381–397.

Mudde, Cas. 2004. The Popular Zeitgeist. *Government & Opposition*, 39 (3): 541–563. http://works.bepress.com/cas_mudde/6/.

Mudde, Cas and Rovira Kaltwasser. 2017. *Populism: A Very Short Introduction*. Oxford, UK: Oxford University Press.

Nash, George H. 2016. Populism, I: American Conservatism and the Problem of Populism. *The New Criterion* 35, no. 1 (September): 4–14.

Palonen, Emilia. 2020. Ten Theses on Populism—and Democracy. In *The Populist Manifesto*, edited by Emmy Eklundh and Andy Knott, 55–69. London: Rowman & Littlefield.

Saloutos, Theodore and Hicks, John D. 1951. *Twentieth-Century Populism: Agricultural Discontent in the Middle West 1900–1939*. Lincoln: University of Nebraska Press.

Senate, U.S. 1950. Communists in Government Service, McCarthy Says. Feb. 9, 1950. https://www.senate.gov/about/powers-procedures/investigations/mccarthy-hearings/communists-in-government-service.htm.

Urbaniti, Nadia. 2013. The Populist Phenomenon. *Raison Politiques* 51, (3): 137–154.

PART II

Outsider Candidates

Chapter 3

Shirley Chisholm

BLAZING A TRAIL FOR FEMALE AND MINORITY CANDIDATES

Shirley Chisholm was a diminutive figure—barely more than one hundred pounds—but she may have been the scrappiest fighter that the United States Congress has ever seen. The daughter of Barbadian immigrants, in 1968 she became the first black woman elected to Congress, representing New York's 12th congressional district.

But getting there wasn't easy, even for someone as stubborn and determined as Chisholm. She became seriously ill during the race for the congressional seat in 1968 and had to undergo surgery to remove a tumor in her pelvic basin. Chisholm didn't want to have the surgery—she wanted to be out campaigning. But her doctors and her husband disagreed, and she relented. She returned home after the surgery in August, less than three months from the general election, to find that her Republican opponent, a black man named James Farmer, was making an issue of her absence on the campaign trail. He was also telling voters that they should send a man to Congress from the district, not a woman. Chisholm was eager to get back to campaigning, but her doctor told her to stay in bed and give her body time to recover.

Chisholm had never been one to back down from a political fight, and her competitive spirit led her to remark to her doctor "Look, the stitches aren't in my mouth. I'm going out" (Chisholm 1970, 73). She wrapped a beach towel around her hips to keep her clothes from falling off—her weight loss was a side effect of the surgery and hospital stay—and made her way down three flights of stairs to a sound truck outside her apartment building. She had one man walk in front in case she fell, and she had two others hold her so that she could make it to the truck. Once inside, she went into campaign mode and began speaking to her district.

"Ladies and gentlemen, this is Fighting Shirley Chisholm, and I'm up and around in spite of what people are saying," she said into the sound system (Chisholm 1970, 73).

She won a surprise victory over the black Republican opponent by a 2–1 margin.

People should have realized by then that they should never underestimate Shirley Chisholm, who was a fighter for racial minorities and women, those whom she said were often not simply ignored, but exploited by the political system of the day. She was already the first black woman elected from Brooklyn to serve in the New York state legislature, and, when she set her sights on the United States House, not only was it unusual to see a woman in office, but far more uncommon to see a black woman holding elective office.

CHISHOLM'S DISCOURSE

Shirley Chisholm was on the outside looking at politics from a different vantage point from the established political leaders of the day. Her experiences and those of the people in her area confirmed daily that most minorities were living in poverty with dead-end jobs that would keep them in a vicious cycle of debt and inadequate housing. Discrimination was an issue for her and for all the different immigrants who lived in her district. She knew about poverty and discrimination because she had lived it, and she was determined to help those in her district receive help to overcome what seemed like insurmountable odds.

Black women have always faced multiple challenges because they initially were seen only in relation to black men and white women. "Black women have always occupied a tertiary position in the American hierarchy, primarily because Black women exist at the intersection of race and gender. As such, they have constituted a neglected and oftentimes invisible category" (McClain, Carter and Brady 2005, 53) Chisholm faced unusual political obstacles because she was a black woman, and this combination had never been represented in national politics before. Rhetoric scholars see in Chisholm's political messages a Womanist Rhetorical Style which speaks to a particular audience—in her case, black women—or identity. "We have argued that a womanist rhetorical genre is met with blatant rhetorical constraints due to the complexities of race, class, and gender. It must, therefore, work to reclaim the voice and agency silenced, and push forth a trajectory that establishes holistic and whole living for the community" (Watkins-Dickerson and Johnson 2019, 160). Because of the constraints on women, and in particular black women, at the time, Chisholm forged coalitions with other marginalized groups to gain support and to popularize her messages. She was the forerunner of all female presidential candidates who followed, and even for some male candidates, including the Rev. Jesse Jackson, who promoted some of her key issues and met some of the same resistance that Chisholm fought.

By all accounts, Chisholm was a born leader. She bossed her sisters and other children, and even her mother was apparently intimidated by her. She came into politics in the late 1950s and early 1960s, when the Civil Rights Movement was beginning, and when black Americans began to raise their expectations about their lives and political representation.

Early on, Chisholm cultivated the image of a fighter—someone who would fight for her constituents and against discrimination. As a young woman, her heroes were all women who were fighters. She became fascinated by the lives of three particular ones: Harriet Tubman, Susan B. Anthony, and Mary McLeod Bethune (Brownmiller 1970). She devoured information on these women, and it is easy to see the impression that their activism had on Chisholm.

When she ran for president, Chisholm crafted together a coalition of marginalized groups, and she specifically appealed to black women, who appreciated her fight against the power system that existed. Patricia Hill Collins (2000) stressed that individuals should not be placed into generic social groups or categories such as race, class, gender, or sexuality because those are not reflective of the power structures or social inequities that might be intersecting at any one time. Her idea of intersectionality formulated a way to identify particular forms of oppression, which for Chisholm and her fellow black women could have come from within the Black community and from outside that community. This system of power marginalized women, and especially women of color, from active participation in politics. This led to Chisholm's Womanist Rhetorical Style, which encouraged women who had been pushed to the side in American politics. "A womanist rhetorical genre affirms its audience, Black women, by working to reclaim the voice through loving the body" (Watkins-Dickerson and Johnson 2019, 160). There had never been a Black woman—much less a Black female candidate—who spoke as forcefully and with as much energy in American politics as Chisholm.

One of the hallmarks of her campaigns and her elective communication style was her blunt honesty. Those who didn't want an honest answer knew not to ask Chisholm about her opinion. She repudiated black leaders such as George Washington Carver, who she said "cooperated with the white design to keep their people down" (Chisholm 1970, 142), and by the 1970s she proclaimed the Civil Rights Movement a failure. Central to all of her speeches and campaign materials was a focus on moving blacks and other minorities out of poverty and discrimination and into an integrated society in which everyone, regardless of skin color, had the same opportunities. As a woman of color, she knew about discrimination based on both her gender and her skin color. "Of my two 'handicaps,' being female put many more obstacles in my path than being black. Sometimes I have trouble, myself, believing that I made it this far against the odds" (Chisholm 1970, xii).

She said that men always underestimate women, who often head house-
holds, raise families, and vote in large numbers. Women were political organizers, often serving in the background during a political campaign.

> It was not my original strategy to organize womanpower to elect me; it was
> forced on me by the time, place, and circumstances. I never meant and never
> mean to start a war between women and men. It is true that women are second-
> class citizens, just as black people are. Tremendous amounts of talent are being
> lost to our society just because that talent wears a skirt. (Chisholm 1970, 75)

Simien and Clawson (2004) are among the many scholars who study black
feminist consciousness, which stems from the fact that women such as
Chisholm are discriminated against not only because they are black, but also
because they are women. They term this a "double disadvantage faced by
black women" (2004, 808). Their research finds that black men and women
have "similar levels of black feminist consciousness and that the political consequences of this consciousness are fairly comparable across gender" (2004,
808). Given that Chisholm was a formidable black female elected official in
the late 1960s and early 1970s, and this research looked at data from 1993,
it is unclear how much understanding there was about this at the time when
Chisholm was running for president. What is clear is that Chisholm faced
political barriers that were not in place for white men or Black politicians.

Female candidates have always faced a variety of challenges that are
foreign to men who are running for office. Men are not generally viewed
through a lens of physical appearance, held to a higher standard of com-
petence, or seen as needing to spend more time with their young children.
These have been traditional arguments against female candidates trying to
overcome a voting bias toward males. Chisholm, as a black woman, faced
the additional challenge of racial discrimination, both from within and outside of the Black community. She found herself early in her political career
speaking to women, because they were more receptive to her messages, and
they were looking for someone to take on the issues that were keeping them
from moving forward. While these challenges were present in Chisholm's
campaigns, they are still obstacles for female candidates today. "A number
of complex factors are at play from sexism and stereotypes to the lack of
time (the "second-shift" syndrome) and training, to concerns by prospective
female candidates about negative attacks, public scrutiny, and the challenge
of fund-raising, to ongoing double-standards in the socialization of women
toward politics" (Watson 2006, 5). The challenges are still present for Black
women seeking public office, and they still face the double disadvantage
mentioned by Simien and Clawson.

CHISHOLM'S TACTICS

Chisholm's motto became "Unbought and Unbossed." She kept this through-out her Congressional career, and it was found on her presidential campaign posters in 1972. She directly engaged those in her district, often by means of a sound truck that rolled down the street, which was basically a truck with a loudspeaker. She would speak into the sound system, which blared her voice to everyone in the area. She always began with "This is Fighting Shirley Chisholm . . ." and people would often stop and listen to what she was saying.

While politicians now have the ability to directly address those who are likely supporters through mass and social media, Chisholm's choice of directly addressing her voters in this way was both effective and cost-efficient when she was running from her district. She spoke in Spanish to voters whose first language was Spanish. However, in a national election it is much harder to target a message to potential voters. She attempted to pull together black, female and working-class voters, with posters emblazoned "Bringing U.S. Together," and her signature slogan "Unbought and Unbossed." She used the slogan on posters, buttons, and bumper stickers. She chose the colors of red and yellow on her campaign buttons, and they stood out among the traditional red, white, and blue signs used by most candidates. To anyone who was listening or watching, Chisholm announced who she was and why she was running.

But being a fighter wasn't enough in the political atmosphere of the day. Even Black politicians—who were male—were unsure in 1972 if they should run for president and split the black vote or throw support behind a white candidate who might have a better chance of winning. Always the type to take action, Chisholm grew tired of waiting for one of them to enter the race. Instead, she threw her own name into the race. "They were standing around, peeing on their shoes," an unnamed Chisholm aide told *The New York Times*. "So Shirley finally said the hell with it and got a campaign going. If she hadn't, we'd still be without a black candidate" (Landers 2016).

Her entry into the presidential race caused confusion among the Black political groups of the day, many of which were run by men and had little interest in supporting a female presidential candidate, even if she was Black. The media also largely ignored her entry into the presidential race, but she continued anyway.

So, Chisholm campaigned in her own way, and in her own style. She announced her candidacy for president in Brooklyn on Jan. 25, 1972. Her speech echoes her belief that Americans of the day could move past their racist and sexist beliefs and vote for the person, not the skin color or gender. "I stand before you today to repudiate the ridiculous notion that the American people will not vote for qualified candidates simply because he is not right or because she is not male. I do not believe that in 1972 the great majority of Americans will continue to harbor such narrow and petty prejudice" (Chisholm 1972).

She made it clear that she was looking for support from those who felt alienated from political process. "Those of you who have been neglected, left out, ignored, forgotten, or shunned aside for whatever reason, give me your help at this hour. Join me in an effort to reshape our society and regain control of our destiny as we go down the Chisholm Trail for 1972" (Chisholm 1972).

She received no support from her Black male counterparts in Congress, most of whom ignored her presidential run. She was the first woman to participate in a U.S. presidential election debate, but it was only after she was initially blocked from participation. She wrote a letter to the Federal Communications Commission and complained about being left out, despite having met the same required criteria. She then was able to take the stage with Sen. George McGovern and Sen. Hubert Humphrey.

She was viewed as being too far out of the mainstream for most voters, many of whom found her issue positions to be extreme. Her support team members, who went ahead of her to campaign locations, were harassed and often found her materials defaced with racial slurs. She had helped found the Congressional Black Caucus and the National Organization for Women, and neither group endorsed her candidacy. She faced several assassination attempts and had to travel with Secret Service agents to keep her safe (Karger and Fox, 2019).

Chisholm refused to accept the constraints that had been placed on women, and she insisted that women should work together to gain a greater voice and level of power in society. "Women in this country must become revolutionaries. We must refuse to accept the old—the traditional roles and stereotypes" (Chisholm 2012, 35). She equated discrimination with being anti-human, and stated that society needed to work toward the integration of not just black and white, male and female, but, ultimately, human and human.

Her campaign was woefully underfunded. Unlike those who had been elected to Congress for a few years, she did not have a large war chest. Much of the money she used for her campaign was her own. She began the race with just over $40,000, which is a mere pittance in a national contest. The other Democratic candidates spent more money on television ads in battleground states than she had total for her campaign. She received no support from the Democratic Party, and large political donors went elsewhere.

She acknowledged her lack of campaign finances and political support in a television interview. "I don't have money. I don't have endorsers. But I'm still trudging along" (Lesher 1972). Through all of this, she persevered. It was hard to keep Fighting Shirley Chisholm down, even if the odds were stacked against her.

OUTSIDER ON THE ISSUES

Chisholm made it clear in her announcement speech that she was going to be a voice for those who wanted to work for environmental causes, those who wanted to change the nation's Vietnam policies, those who wanted to change federal election laws, and that she would work for freedom from poverty and discrimination for all Americans.

As a member of the New York Assembly, Chisholm had worked to make unemployment insurance for domestic workers a reality, pushed for laws to give college aid to young people from poor backgrounds, and fought for teachers to retain tenure when out on maternity leave. When she got to Washington, she refused to sit by the side and wait for her turn to become one of those with political power. One of her famous quotes is: "If they don't give you a seat at the table, bring in a folding chair."

She approached her presidential race in the same way, forcing her way into discussions with fellow politicians and potential voters, even if they didn't agree with her stands on the issues. Chisholm and other Black members of Congress endorsed a twelve-point Black Bill of Rights that they wanted to push at the Democratic National Convention in Miami. It called for an end to the Vietnam War, for full employment in the United States, and for a $6,500 guaranteed income. It also called upon the party to pursue quality education for all people, even if busing was necessary to achieve that goal (Lesher 1972). Chisholm said that one of her political strengths was her bluntness and willingness to say things that others only thought. She was described as "a passionate and effective advocate for the needs of minorities, women, and children who changed the nation's perception about the capabilities of women and African-Americans" (Grady and LaCost 2005, 1).

She called health a human right, noting that minorities and women had less access to healthcare than those with more privilege. This argument seems very current, but was unusual during the time when she was campaigning. This was noted by Mary T. Bassett in 2017 when she recalled that Chisholm said racism was so prevalent that no one even noticed it. "The conditions of our society are not the outcome of some vague social physics impenetrable to change: they are the product of decisions made at every level of power" (Bassett 2017, 667). These levels of power were impenetrable by women at the time, but Chisholm kept drawing attention to the discrimination and inequities that existed.

Chisholm was accustomed to hard campaigning. To win her Congressional seat, she had walked and talked her way through her district. "Indoors, with a selected audience, you have control. But out on the street corners with the people, in the housing projects, in parks, you are under fire constantly," she said. "If you are insincere or have something to hide, you will be found out" (Chisholm 1970, 69). She utilized the communication tools that she could afford and that gave her the most access to the most voters at one time. Although her finances were meager compared to other candidates, she had something most of them did not: a passionate voice.

She was a gifted speaker, and an even more gifted writer. Her speeches were eloquent, but oftentimes punctuated with raw emotion. She could be feisty in her campaigning, often when talking about discrimination and her own struggles. She was idealistic, but had a streak of pragmatism that could be seen in her approach to some issues, as can be seen in this section of a presidential campaign speech:

> Our will can create a new America in 1972, one where there is freedom from violence and war, at home and abroad, where there is freedom from poverty and discrimination, where there exists at least a feeling that we are making progress and assuring for everyone medical care, employment, and decent housing. Where we more decisively clean up our streets, our water, and our air. Where we work together, black and white, to live in the confidence that every man and every woman in America has at long last the opportunity to become all that he was created of being, such as his ability. (Chisholm 1972)

Yet her anti-authority stances and support for the Equal Rights Amendment always showed through, and that turned off many voters. She said that she would demand a Black on the Democratic ticket, that an American Indian run the Department of the Interior, and that a woman should head the Department of Health, Education and Welfare, all of which seem like very modern expectations (Lesher 1972). For 1972, though, they were very progressive, and unattainable, goals.

As a member of Congress, she had decided to make a speech against funding for the military after President Richard Nixon announced on the same day that he wanted to build an anti-ballistic missile system, and that the Head Start program in the District of Columbia would be cut back for lack of money. In true Chisholm style, she crafted a message stating that "it was wrong to plan to spend billions on an elaborate and unnecessary weapons system when disadvantaged children were getting nothing" (Chisholm 1970, 95). She declared in her speech that she would vote "no" on every bill that came to the House that would provide funds for the Department of Defense. As she walked off the floor, she overheard a fellow member of Congress remark to another "You know, she's crazy!" (Chisholm 1970, 98). This echoes the Womanist Rhetorical Style, which is always in opposition to the status quo and "not seen as fully competent leaders from various perspectives" (Watkins-Dickerson and Johnson 2019, 160). Because Chisholm took a stand against what was seen as "normal," she was thus branded as incompetent or "crazy" by those comprising the status quo who neither understood her concerns nor cared to find out more about why she felt that way.

CHISHOLM'S PRESIDENTIAL CAMPAIGN OBSTACLES

Although Chisholm's anti-military speech drew the attention of many young, anti-war protestors, it did not win her much support among older Americans who might actually have voted in the presidential election. She was asked to speak on many college campuses, but her outspoken personality and intention to use her voice to bring change to the nation turned off many voters, including those who were Black.

In North Carolina, she found opposition from Black political leaders who went so far as to say "a vote for Shirley Chisholm is a vote for George Wallace" (Lesher 1972, Koplinski 2000), meaning that if someone voted for her, it pulled a Black vote away from a more viable Democratic candidate, leaving Wallace with more room to spoil the election.

Her campaign organization was haphazard, possibly even worse than that of Wallace, who was also running a shoestring campaign. Few announcements and little promotion seemed to be done in advance of her arrival. She showed up at events in Florida to find that no one was there, or only a handful of potential voters would eventually make their way to her location. At the University of Miami, her staff got lost in a building while trying to find a political science class she was to address. At the student union at that university, she drew two hundred students at a location where Sen. Edward Muskie had attracted 2,000 (Lesher 1972). She was unable to find support even in Black communities or among locally elected Black officials.

She tried to get every media interview possible, as that was a far more efficient way to reach voters than flying here and there to speak with a handful of people. Yet media interviews were also sparse, as she was not seen as an electable candidate. In the United States, much of what legitimizes a candidate is the amount of money he or she has raised, because that is seen as an indication of support. Chisholm, however, didn't have much money, and from the turnout at her events, it seemed she didn't have much support, either. She became more of a curiosity for reporters than a viable presidential candidate.

Chisholm probably had never seen herself as actually winning the election. While she was idealistic, the pragmatic streak in her realized that her true value would lie in having enough delegates to broker votes at the convention. She might not be able to be the nominee, but if she could get enough delegates, she might be able to influence the Democratic Party platform and even make demands of the eventual nominee—especially if there was a deadlocked convention. With fifteen candidates out there trying to grab votes, it seemed possible that this could happen.

CONTROVERSIAL ISSUES AND BEFRIENDING GEORGE WALLACE

One of Chisholm's personality traits was that of empathy. Letters from female constituents who had been scarred or left sterile by illegal abortions led her to support laws making abortion legal, although that had not been her original stance on the issue. It also was not a popular issue stance for someone who was running for president. This was a controversial issue within the Black community during that time, and it still remains so today.

While there continues to be research into Black attitudes toward legalized abortion, most scholars note that there have traditionally been more abortions in the Black population than in the white. "Studies of fertility behavior have shown that, when ratios are compared, not only do black women have more abortions, but they are more likely than whites to abort after the onset of motherhood and throughout their childbearing years" (Lynxwiler and Gay 1994, 80). It is easy to believe that Chisholm was moved by those who shared their abortion stories and the reasons they felt it necessary to obtain an abortion, whether it was legal or not. Factors such as race, income, and social status are seen as impacting the decision to obtain an abortion, as potential mothers weigh the financial and societal consequences of having a child. Because of discrimination, traditionally lower income levels, and stress on those with already-existing families, Black women often were forced to evaluate having a child as a practical consideration. Several researchers have found race differences in the support for abortion, but there are varying interpretations. Lynxwiler and Gay theorize that black and white women shift their support for abortion over their lifetimes, with white women becoming more supportive of abortion rights as they age, but with the opposite happening in the Black community. "Older white women reported the the strongest pro-choice attitudes while older black women consistently displayed the weakest support for legal abortion" (1994, 78). Others also note changing attitudes toward abortion, but find that Blacks are not becoming more supportive of the right to an abortion (Wilcox, 1990). Simien and Clawson see black feminist consciousness contributing to increased support for abortion (2004). This is another example of how Chisholm was in the forefront of a polarizing national issue that impacted women across the nation and is still a complex social issue for the country.

Education was also an issue that was close to her heart. Pleas from high school students asking for help in getting college scholarships and aid money led Chisholm to fight for college aid for disadvantaged youth. As a former teacher and someone for whom education had been so important, she worked to help students get into college. A program she was instrumental in developing, known as Search for Education, Elevation and Knowledge, or SEEK, still helps CUNY students today (Molloy 2005).

Probably the most controversial act that she took during her presidential race was to visit Gov. George Wallace after the assassination attempt on his life on May 15, 1972 in Laurel, Maryland. The Alabama governor was shot five times, and one of the bullets lodged in his spine, leaving him paralyzed for the rest of his life.

Wallace was running as a Democrat, but his campaign rhetoric was filled with messages supporting segregation, denouncing the Civil Rights Movement, and promoting populist views. In short, he represented the opposite of what she had been promoting. Chisholm stunned most of her supporters when she decided to visit Wallace in the hospital. She temporarily suspended her campaign to make the trip. Rep. Barbara Lee (D-Calif.) was a college student who was running Chisholm's presidential race in northern California. She admits that she initially lost enthusiasm for Chisholm because of this visit. She asked Chisholm why she would want to visit the avowed racist. This is her recollection of her conversation with Chisholm about the incident:

> She said, "Little girl," she says, "C'mon now, you're working with me in my campaign, helping me," she said. "But sometimes we have to remember we're all human beings, and I may be able to teach him something, to help him regain his humanity, to maybe make him open his eyes to make him see something that he has not seen." She said, "So you know you always have to be optimistic that people can change, and that you can change and that one act of kindness may make all the difference in the world," she said. "So yes, I know people are angry," — it wasn't just me. She says, "I know people are really angry," she said, "but you have to rise to the occasion if you're a leader, and you have to try to break through and you have to try and open and enlighten other people who may hate you." And that's what she taught me. (Lee, 2019)

Peggy Wallace Kennedy, who was sitting by her father's side when Chisholm arrived, said there was great surprise when the congresswoman came to visit. When her father asked Chisholm what her supporters would say, Kennedy said that Chisholm replied, "I know what they're going to say, but I wouldn't want what happened to you to happen to anyone." Daddy was overwhelmed by her truth, and her willingness to face the potential negative consequences of her political career because of him—something he had never done for anyone else" (Peggy Wallace Kennedy 2019).

In the future, Wallace would ask forgiveness from the Black community that he had so maligned during his previous campaigns. Kennedy said the seeds of that search for forgiveness were sown during Chisholm's visit to his hospital room, with one outsider candidate befriending another, radically different, outsider candidate.

ELECTION RESULTS AND LEGACY

Chisholm had difficulty getting on ballots in many states, but eventually campaigned for votes in fourteen states. Her largest number of votes came from the California primary, where she finished fourth. She won a total of twenty-eight delegates in the primaries. At the Democratic Convention in Miami, Vice President Hubert Humphrey was blocked in his attempt to keep Sen. George McGovern from being the nominee. Humphrey then released his Black delegates to Chisholm, which gave her a total of 152 delegates. This placed her fourth in the roll-call tally, furthering her legacy as the first Black and female candidate to seek the nomination of a major party for president.

She paved the way for later presidential campaigns by African American candidates such as the Rev. Jesse Jackson and Sen. Barack Obama, as well as female candidates such as Sen. Hillary Clinton and Sen. Kamala Harris. "Altogether, Chisholm understood the needs, hopes, and desires of the Black community, along with the struggles of women" (Watkins-Dickerson and Johnson 2019, 163). She was an early voice attacking the status quo for its powerful hold over women and minorities, which she saw as choking off not only opportunities for individuals, but also robbing the nation of those people's contributions to society. While black women have made progress, they are still underrepresented in elective offices across the nation (Darcy, Hadley and Kirksey 1993).

In 2019 the city of New York opened Shirley Chisholm State Park, which is the largest state park in the city. Plans are underway for a public monument to her in Brooklyn, which would make her the first historical female figure to be honored by the area in this way. Discussions are taking place regarding a statue of Chisholm in the U.S. Capitol building. These are in response to the 50th anniversary of her election to Congress, and a salute to the legacy that she left behind for women and minorities.

Shirley Chisholm blazed a political trail that opened up new opportunities for women and minorities willing to travel that road. It was thirty-six years later when Barack Obama was elected president, an achievement for which she had laid the early groundwork. As an outside candidate, she fought for positions on issues that were neither popular nor politically safe during her time in office. But Fighting Shirley Chisholm was out to change the nation, not just represent her district. Her legacy continues as more women than ever are running for and being elected to political offices across the nation, and many of them look back and credit Chisholm for breaking racial and gender barriers. When she took the oath of office as Vice President of the United States in 2021, Kamala Harris wore purple as a nod to Chisholm and the inspiration she sparked in young women of color.

REFERENCES

Bassett, Mary T. 2017. Public Health Meets the Problem of the Color Line. *American Journal of Public Health* 107, (5): 666–667. 10.2105/AJPH.2017.303714.

Brownmiller, Susan. 1970. *Shirley Chisholm*. Doubleday & Company Inc.

Chisholm, Shirley. 1970. *Unbought and Unbossed*. Boston: Houghton Mifflin Co.

Chisholm, Shirley. 1972. Announcement Speech. http://www.4president.org/speeches/shirleychisholm1972announcement.htm.

Chisholm, Shirley. 2012. Race, Revolution, and Women. *The Black Scholar* 42, (2): 31–35.

Collins, Patricia Hill. 1990. *Black Feminist Thought: Knowledge, Consciousness and the Politics of Empowerment*. Boston: Unwin Hyman.

Darcy, R., Charles D. Hadley, and Jason F. Kirksey. 1993. Election Systems and the Representation of Black Women in American State Legislatures. *Women & Politics* 13 (1): 73–89.

Grady, Marilyn L. and Barbara Y. LaCost. 2005. Shirley Chisholm Had Guts. *Journal of Women in Educational Leadership* 3, no. 1 (January): 1–2.

Karger, Fred and Peter Fox. 2019. "Shirley Chisholm's Historic Campaign for President Cannot Be Erased." *The Advocate*. Aug. 8, 2019. https://www.advocate.com/commentary/2019/8/08/shirley-chisholms-historic-campaign-president-cannot-be-erased.

Kennedy, Peggy Wallace. 2019. Voices of the Movement, *The Washington Post Podcast*, Cape Up with Jonathan Capehart. Episode 6. May 16, 2019. https://www.washingtonpost.com/opinions/2019/05/16/changed-minds-reconciliation-voices-movement-episode/.

Koplinski, Brad. 2000. *Hats in the Ring: Conversations with Presidential Candidates*. North Bethesda, MD: Presidential Publishing.

Landers, Jackson. 2016. "'Unbought and Unbossed' When a Black Woman Ran for the White House." SmithsonianMag.com. https://www.smithsonianmag.com/smithsonian-institution/unbought-and-unbossed-when-black-woman-ran-for-the-white-house-180958699/.

Lee, Barbara. 2019. Voices of the Movement, *The Washington Post Podcast*, Cape Up with Jonathan Capehart. Episode 6. May 16, 2019. https://www.washingtonpost.com/opinions/2019/05/16/changed-minds-reconciliation-voices-movement-episode/.

Lesher, Stephen. 1972. "The Short, Unhappy Life of Black Presidential Politics," *The New York Times*. June 25, 1972, Section SM, p. 12.

Lynxwiler, John and David Gay. 1994. Reconsidering Race Differences in Abortion Attitudes. *Social Science Quarterly* 75, no. 1 (March): 67–84.

McClain, Paula D., Niambi M. Carter, and Michael C. Brady. 2005. Gender and Black Presidential Politics: From Chisholm to Mosley Braun. *Journal of Women, Politics & Policy* 27, (1): 51–68.

Molloy, Aimee. 2005. Shirley Chisholm's Legacy. *The Brooklyn Rail*, February 2005. https://brooklynrail.org/2005/02/express/shirley-chisholms-legacy.

Simien, Evelyn M. and Rosalee A. Clawson. 2004. The Intersection of Race and Gender: An Examination of Black Feminist Consciousness, Race Consciousness, and Policy Attitudes. *Social Science Quarterly* 85, no. 3 (September): 793–810.

Watkins-Dickerson, Dianna and Andre Johnson. 2019. "Fighting to be Heard: Shirley Chisholm and the Makings of a Womanist Rhetorical Framework." In *Gender, Race, and Social Identity in American Politics: The Past and Future of Political Access*, edited by Lori Montalbano, 155-167. Lanham, MD: Lexington Books.

Watson, Robert P. 2006. Madam President: Progress, Problems, and Prospects for 2008. *Journal of International Women's Studies* 8, no.1 (November): 1–20. http://vc.bridgew.edu/jiws/vol8/iss1/1.

Wilcox, Clyde. 1990. Race Differences in Abortion Attitudes: Some Additional Evidence. *Public Opinion Quarterly* 54: 248–255.

Chapter 4

Jesse Jackson

EMPATHETIC OUTSIDER STRUGGLING TO BREAK THE COLOR BARRIER

In a speech at the 1988 Democratic Convention in Atlanta, the Rev. Jesse Jackson said "I'm a working person's person, that's why I understand you whether you're black or white" (Jackson 1988). While he professed to understand working people, Jackson has been harder for the public—and the Democratic Party—to understand. His motives for running for president were questioned, as well as the wisdom of a Black man pursuing such a goal. The Democratic Party, while not dismissing Jackson, never totally embraced him, either.

Although Jackson had been in the public eye since his involvement with the Civil Rights Movement in the 1950s and 1960s, his presidential campaigns in 1984 and 1988 were viewed with skepticism from both whites and African Americans. For those involved in the Civil Rights Movement, Jackson was a polarizing figure. Andrew Young, Coretta Scott King, and Julian Bond all refused to endorse him. Others feared that he would divide the Democratic Party, which depended on the tenuous working coalition between whites and Blacks, and that he might possibly damage the party's ability to elect down-ballot candidates. Some considered the campaigns an exercise in futility, as they saw him as an unelectable candidate because they believed the nation would not vote for a Black presidential candidate. It would be twenty-four years before that would happen, when Barack Obama was the first Black man elected president.

JACKSON'S DISCOURSE

As Rep. Shirley Chisholm found in her presidential campaign in 1972, there was still much racial prejudice in the nation, and it was hard for Jackson to secure support even from some prominent Black leaders, especially in his 1984 campaign. They feared that he would siphon votes away from an electable white candidate who might be sympathetic to the needs of the Black community. For his part, Jackson sought to unify African Americans and

49

mold them into a formidable voting bloc. He explained it this way: "My campaign changed the form of politics because, historically, Whites voted for Whites without apology, and Blacks voted for Whites, and nobody was left to vote for Blacks. This time around, with the Whites voting for Whites, Blacks voting for me, they had to share the power" (Bennett 1984).

Pushing for change always came easily to Jackson. Born to a teenage mother in a slum area in Greenville, S.C., he has stated that expectations for him were quite low. He learned about work at an early age, and he saw the conditions that kept many Black Americans in a cycle of poverty and shame. As he grew older, he gravitated toward voices that promised change, eventually helping the Rev. Martin Luther King Jr. as he led the Civil Rights Movement. Himself a minister, Jackson developed a rhetorical style that was familiar to religious African Americans and became a charismatic figure in the continued fight for Civil Rights. In 1971 he formed PUSH, People United to Save Humanity (later changed to People United to Serve Humanity). The organization was founded to improve economic conditions of Black Americans.

While Chisholm's rhetoric was feisty and challenging, Jackson's has proven to be more emotional and hopeful. A gifted speaker, he has delivered speeches in great auditoriums and in small venues, both with equal fervor. "My constituency is the damned, disinherited, disrespected and the despised. They are restless and seek relief. They've voted in record numbers. They have invested the faith, hope and trust that they have in us. The Democratic Party must send them a signal that we care. I pledge my best not to let them down" (Jackson 1984).

Jackson's familiarity with the vocal patterns of a preacher influenced his oral speaking patterns, and it helped to establish a link between himself and his supporters. "Jackson's discourse is vivid and strongly peppered with metaphors, rhyme, repetition, narrative, imagery and the juxtaposition of opposing terms. This witting use of repartee is part of Jackson's charm in identifying with his audience" (Walker and Greene 2006). Jackson also leaned heavily on narratives from his own life and those of his supporters. He spoke of common struggles facing oppressed minorities, and he reminded them of the values and morals that they shared.

Walker and Greene also argue that Jackson embraced an Afrocentric speaking style that used recognizable communicative stylistic devices common to Black culture.

Jackson appeals to his audience by building upon the familiar, shared human needs and concerns, as opposed to differences. He uses all-embracing language, and at times targets scapegoats upon which to blame current conditions and attitudes, thus strengthening the bond between himself and the audience and validating his cause as right and just. (2006, 65)

One of the characteristics of Afrocentric style is a rejection of Western imperialism, and that is also evident in Jackson's messages. However, he counters that rejection with an appeal for the embracing of and coexistence with the different ethnic and cultural groups in the nation. "Outlining the positive attributes of a diverse society and the negative components of a Western ideal, Jackson appeals to common human elements" (Walker and Greene 2006, 69).

Jackson's rhetoric had populist tones, mainly because in his messages he challenged the power structure and warned that the nation was abandoning crucial moral virtues. His discourse was centered around those who felt disenfranchised or forgotten by those with privilege and power, which is another trait of populist rhetoric. His background was important to his populist discourse, as Bonikowski and Gidron state ". . . populism is primarily a strategic tool of political challengers, and particularly those who have legitimate claims to outsider status" (Bonikowski and Gidron 2016).

No one could argue against Jackson's legitimate outsider status. But Jackson faced a dilemma that was uncommon to most political candidates: he was a minister who was hoping to win the highest office in the nation. For many Americans, politics and religion are two topics that don't mix well. "Whether it is Jerry Falwell, Pat Robertson, the Catholic bishops, or Jesse Jackson, religious leaders enter public life knowing that society's expectations make much of the population wary of either direct religious involvement in politics or explicit, detailed comment on political issues" (McTighe 1990, 593–594). Jackson attempted to bring religion into politics, and, in doing so, sought to be the candidate promoting a moral vision for the nation.

He offers a vision of how America should be, and plunges into the political arena to initiate the changes which will bring the vision closer to reality. It is his facility at combining the prophet's thoroughgoing critique of current society with the politician's adeptness at maneuvering and negotiation that makes Jackson unique. (McTighe 1990, 585)

In using rhetoric that combined Afrocentric elements and populism, Jackson tried to form an appeal to both Blacks and religious white voters. Most populist messages are negative, outlining problems and railing against those who are seen as causing or contributing to them. But Jackson's discourse was more uplifting and embracing than the loud, rough, and often bombastic messages common to Huey Long or George Wallace. In Jackson, the populist message was critical of the nation and its history of broken promises, but also hopeful that it could come together and repair itself. But the challenge he faced as a

Black candidate was something that neither Long nor Wallace ever had to deal with in politics.

CAMPAIGN TACTICS

Jackson knew that he would need to get his messages to a particular demographic in order to be successful. He was very familiar with the strategies used in the Civil Rights Movement, which encouraged non-violent actions to provoke social and governmental change. That approach worked for the Civil Rights leaders and participants in the movement, and it eventually led to the Civil Rights Act that was signed into law. However, the non-violent approach is a long-term plan of action and is not usually a successful political strategy, so he decided to take a different approach in his political campaigns.

Jackson needed to gain political traction and leverage by mobilizing African Americans and other minorities in sufficient numbers to make the Democratic Party share power with him, and by extension, his constituency. This had not been done by Black politicians before. In the past, Blacks had worked within the Democratic Party to support white candidates who were supportive of their issues. As Shirley Chisholm discovered, chipping away at that system was difficult, because Blacks feared it might decrease their power to influence the Democratic Party platform and its candidates for president. "Direct intervention in the political system and the explicit use of political power were, therefore, new tactics designed to influence the means by which social resources are allocated" (Craigen 1986, 595). Jackson was able to encourage large numbers of Blacks to vote who had not registered to vote before, and his messages were also well received by many other minority groups. While he was most successful in the South, Jackson also received significant support in other parts of the country.

Jackson campaigned hard in 1984, and he received more votes than people expected. In early primaries in Iowa and New Hampshire, he finished in single digits, which was not unexpected. Those states have a lower percentage of African Americans than those of the Southern states, where Jackson demonstrated his ability to attract the Black vote. His campaign won the majority of the Black vote in Florida, Georgia, and Alabama. He went on to win the Louisiana and District of Columbia primaries, although the Louisiana primary saw its lowest voter turnout in history, with only 15 percent of voters participating. Louisiana Gov. Edwin Edwards, a Democrat, refused to vote in the primary after the state's legislature tried to cancel the election, but was rebuffed at the federal level. Jackson supporters successfully had the primary re-instated after they filed in federal court to have it reversed because, they argued, it was a violation of the federal Voting Rights Act (Gailey 1984).

After these successes, the Democratic Party opened a conversation with Jackson regarding what he might call for at the party's convention, including the elimination of runoff primaries in the South, which was a controversial topic. Jackson had implied that his support of the eventual Democratic nominee might hinge on political concessions, and, with him gathering a significant number of Black votes, the party saw value in trying to negotiate with Jackson's campaign.

During his first presidential campaign, Jackson took an unorthodox break in late December 1983 and flew with a group of ministers to Syria to negotiate the release of an American military pilot who was taken prisoner after his plane was shot down over Lebanon. Jackson and the rest of the delegation prevailed, and Navy Lt. Robert Goodman was returned to the United States on January 3, 1984. This prompted then-President Ronald Reagan to invite both Jackson and Goodman to the White House for a news conference. Jackson felt this garnered him national respect and acclaim as a negotiator who could work with foreign governments when the U.S. government could not. He used his negotiation skills several times, including a 1985 trip to Beirut to free Americans that was financed by future presidential candidate Ross Perot.

Despite Jackson's success in Syria and his ability to capture much of the Black vote, especially in the strategically important South, the Democratic Party chose former Vice President Walter Mondale as its presidential nominee. Jackson was disappointed, but saw his presidential campaign as a step forward.

At the party's national convention in San Francisco in 1984, Jackson gave a lengthy and rousing speech. It was optimistic, but also hard hitting. He talked about the Rainbow Coalition, a political movement he founded that was made of different ethnicities and races and sexual orientations, but with one goal: that of justice, which he saw as "the requirement for rebuilding America." He used the phrase "our time has come" no less than six times, and he referred to his coalition as having "raised the right issues." (Jackson 1984a). He seemed to be lauding the impact that his campaign had on the political process, despite his not being the presidential nominee. Indeed, his campaign spearheaded a massive voter registration campaign across the nation, and almost one million new voters were added, with most of those being African American.

But it was still a bitter defeat. In an interview with Ebony's senior editor after the election, Jackson lamented that he could have won. "If, in addition to our numbers, if our leadership had cashed in our political IOUs and challenged the White liberals who benefited from us, and women and Hispanics, we could have won the entire process" (Bennett 1984). He blamed the loss on both white-controlled media and Black leaders who refused to give him full support because of fears he might divide the Democratic Party.

Some scholars agree that white-owned mainstream media were a barrier for Jackson in his presidential campaigns. Arnold Gibbons (1993) asserts that the media reflected society's racist sentiments in news stories by focusing heavily on Jackson's race, thereby conditioning the public to think of him first as a Black man. This potential media priming activated existing racial biases in the voting population. Research into the prominence of racial content in newspaper stories in the 2008 presidential election found that "the presence of one or more racial minorities in the stories increased the likelihood and presence of racial references found in the story" (McIlwain 2011, 386). Access to mainstream media is always a struggle for outsider candidates, and especially those who are minorities. When a minority's race or ethnicity is focused on in a disproportionate way, it can serve to marginalize that candidate and create another barrier to electoral success.

THE RAINBOW COALITION AND THE 1988 CAMPAIGN

Jackson's impact on the 1984 election was intensely debated after the campaign ended. A record number of Black voters participated in the election, but pundits questioned if they were involved because of Jackson or because President Ronald Reagan was viewed as a major threat to the Black community. Another question was Jackson's impact on Democratic activists in the South, a region that seemed to support Jackson, but which was also entangled in a delicate balance between the whites who controlled the Democratic Party and African Americans who were seeking a change in Black political representation. While Jackson seemed to have been an agent for change in the region, many saw him as a threat to local political systems that relied on a fragile balance of white and Black cooperation. Charles L. Prysby found in his 1989 study that white Democratic Party activists in North Carolina "almost unanimously were not Jackson supporters. However, while they did not prefer Jackson over other candidates, most of the white delegates did not feel that his candidacy was especially harmful to the party" (Prysby 1989, 308).

As noted earlier, Jackson founded the National Rainbow Coalition, which opposed President Ronald Reagan's economic and social programs. It was an attempt to unite politically progressive Americans to seek justice for minorities. Jackson said the coalition would work for people of all races to be better represented in local, state, and national offices. "The Rainbow constituency must continue to be built, and I want to do that. Also, people might have to go into the courts and the streets to get the Voting Rights Act enforced—that's the trigger law to our empowerment process. We should have the broadest based and most unified effort we've ever had in history to register another couple of million Blacks" (Bennett 1984).

To the surprise of almost no one, Jackson declared his candidacy for the 1988 election on October 11, 1987. Because President Ronald Reagan could not run for another term, the race was wide open among Democrats and Republicans. There were eight candidates seeking the Democratic Party nomination. An ABC News-Washington Post poll showed Jackson with 23 percent of the Democratic vote in September 1988, which was higher than Gov. Michael Dukakis, who was the eventual Democratic nominee. Jackson won 55 percent of the vote in the Michigan primary, which temporarily positioned him as the front runner. Dukakis then began a string of primary victories which led to his eventual party nomination.

However, Jackson did better in his second presidential race than in the first. He raised more money and ran a more professional campaign, all the while promoting very left-leaning issues. The Rainbow Coalition of minorities that he sought to build supported his candidacy, but proved too few to overcome the support for Dukakis. Because of Jackson's success—he won almost 7 million votes and won eleven primary contests—his supporters called for him to be Dukakis' running mate in the general election. Instead, Dukakis chose Sen. Lloyd Bentsen of Texas.

Despite his accomplishments, there was still a lukewarm response on the part of many elected Black politicians, who saw Jackson as a potential threat, and there was a backlash against Jackson by many elected white Democrats who used his campaign as a way to solidify their support among the more racist members of their districts. There were also charges of anti-Semitism because Jackson had poked fun at Jews by calling them "Hymies" and referred to New York City as "Hymie-town." He apologized for the comments and asked for forgiveness. He also had to deal with questions about Louis Farrakhan, a Muslim minister and friend of Jackson's, who made anti-Semitic remarks that drew much backlash from both Democrats and Republicans. Both of these instances had the potential to stop Jackson from taking part in the Democratic National Convention. Jackson repudiated Farrakhan's comments and said he disavowed such comments and thoughts.

In a way, Jackson's campaign strategy was successful. The Democratic Party did recognize that Jackson had significant support from the working class and poorer segments of the nation, and leaders within the party looked for a compromise that would allow them to retain the support of these groups, but not award significant power to Jackson. The compromise in both 1984 and 1988 was to allow Jackson a prime speaking slot at the convention, but water down his proposals for the party's platforms. Although it wasn't what he had hoped for, Jackson accepted the opportunity to address the convention--and the nation through the televised event--and to advocate for greater unity and encourage African Americans and other minorities.

On July 20, 1988, Jackson once again addressed the Democratic Party at its nominating convention, and once again, he was not the nominee. This convention was held in Atlanta, a city he called "the cradle of the Old South, the crucible of the New South." Two themes from that speech are "common ground" and "never surrender." He related the different backgrounds of himself and Dukakis, but noted the common ground that Americans have, despite their histories, their occupations, or their religions. "Tonight we choose interdependency in our capacity to act and unite for the greater good," he told the party faithful. "The common good is finding commitment to new priorities, to expansion and inclusion" (Jackson 1988). He argued that if an issue is morally right, then it will eventually be a political issue. This has been somewhat borne out, as many of the societal issues that he addressed in the 1984 and 1988 elections are current political issues facing the nation.

He spent the last part of his address to the party encouraging young people to not give up their dreams. "You must never stop dreaming. Face reality, yes. But don't stop with the way things are: dream of things as they ought to be." He shared his personal story, of being born to a teenage mother who was herself born to a teenage mother, and of the financial hardships of his life. "I'm a working person's person, that's why I understand you whether you're black or white," he said. "I was born in the slum, but the slum was not born in me. And it wasn't born in you, and you can make it . . . Don't you surrender. Suffering breeds character. Character breeds faith. In the end, faith will not disappoint." In closing, he used a phrase that has become closely associated with Jackson over the years. "America will get better and better. Keep hope alive. Keep hope alive. Keep hope alive. On tomorrow night and beyond, keep hope alive" (Jackson 1988).

In this speech, Jackson used his oral skills to present the case for civil and human rights, and to encourage those in the audience to join him in seeking a society that is just for all people, no matter their color, gender, or sexual orientation. Although his speeches and speaking performance often referenced Black culture and values, he is ultimately a populist candidate speaking to a diverse society about developing leadership to solve the problems and issues common to the disenfranchised of the nation. He presented himself as the person who can both see the errors of the past, as well as seek a common path for the future by embracing and reinvigorating a shared vision of American values.

JACKSON'S CAMPAIGN ISSUES

While on the campaign trail, Jackson's rhetoric specifically targeted minorities, but also sought to provide hope to lower-class white Americans. An article in Ebony magazine in 1988 recounted Jackson's campaign stops in Mississippi and Memphis, Tenn. "Together we can change the course of the nation," he told those in Corinth, Miss. "The others have forgotten you. I have not." At a Teamster's meeting in Memphis, he said, "Oppression is too great a thing to war against alone" (Randolph 1988, 161). Jackson's message was that he shared much in common with them, and he was inviting them to help push the nation in a different direction. He admonished Americans to dream, to "face pain," and allow their dreams to help them rise above the pain. As mentioned earlier, his dynamic speaking style was emblematic of Black ministers, and many found it encouraging and moving.

Jackson touted himself as an advocate for those who were the "locked out and forgotten" (Jackson 1984b). The issues he worked to bring to the forefront during both of his presidential races reverberated with minorities, the poor, and working-class people. Many of those issues are still being debated today, while some have found their way into national legislation. Among those issues were creating a single-payer universal system of health care in the United States, cutting the military budget, providing free community college to all, and providing jobs to all Americans through a new Works Progress Administration-inspired program.

Jackson pushed for a recognition of women's rights through the ratification of the Equal Rights Amendment, for equal pay for comparable jobs, and for progressive child and day care, most of which were issues also raised by Shirley Chisholm. He also campaigned for greater employment opportunities, for the enforcement of the Voting Rights Act, and for what he called Strength Through Peace, which was an approach to foreign policy that was based on negotiation to reduce tensions throughout the world.

In a campaign brochure from his 1984 presidential race, Jackson also pushed for government action on the environment. "The plain truth is what politicians like to call environmental issues are a matter of life and death. Not a matter of priorities. Not a matter of budgets. Not a matter of bureaucracy. But a master of life as in life, liberty and the pursuit of happiness. It can be done. It must be done. And if I am your President, it will be done." This issue is one that is still hotly debated in the United States Congress, and Jackson was one of those who worked to bring it to the forefront for Americans to consider.

It is easy to see that Jackson's issues separated him from much of the Democratic Party establishment at the time. James Craigen writes that

Jackson never backed off from fights within the party or with those linked to the Democratic Party. "He opposed existing elitist values, such as the sanctity of the profit motive, class differences and the unequal allocation of opportunity, goods, and power, and the consequences of those values on the lives most directly and adversely affected by the social practices which emanate from such values" (594). Yet, Jackson's rhetorical style and issues are hard to separate. His speeches were optimistic and hopeful while also discussing difficult issues that were creating problems in the areas of crime, mobility, and education for those with less opportunities because of their race, ethnicity, or gender. He urged young people to not give up, but to work hard and participate in politics through voting and political action.

IMPACT ON BLACKS AND MINORITIES

Many people have debated the impact that Jackson had on Black voter participation in the United States. Jackson himself claimed that his campaign helped register one million new voters for the 1984 election and another 2 million in 1988. In some primaries, such as New Jersey, the number of Black voter participation increased dramatically in 1984 from 1980 numbers, and Jackson sparked grassroots voter registration movements among both Blacks and other minorities in a number of states. But the question remained: Did Jackson succeed in bringing more Black voters into the national elections?

After his 1984 campaign, Jackson took credit for substantially increasing Black participation in that election. Scholars and political pundits wondered if that was because of Jackson, or if there was some other cause. Katherine Tate looked into the factors that contributed to a rise in Black voter participation in 1984, which was a then-peak of 55.8 percent. This reversed a twenty-year trend of declining Black participation and was the highest rate until the 2008 and 2012 elections, in which more than 60 percent of Blacks voted in the presidential elections. She examined Black electoral participation in both the 1984 and 1988 campaigns, and her analysis showed that Jackson supporters were more likely to vote in the general election in 1984, but not in 1988 (Tate 1991). In both general elections, Jackson was not on the ballot, having not been named the Democratic nominee.

Tate found that, in addition to Jackson's candidacy in 1984, the re-election campaign of President Ronald Reagan was a factor that increased Black voter participation. Reagan was very unpopular with the Black community, and large numbers of Black voters turned out in November to try to block his re-election. She found that in the 1984 campaign, Black primary voters were better educated and affluent, and they were more interested in the campaign. Older Blacks were more likely to vote than their younger counterparts, but there did not appear to be a gender gap in turnout. Black participation in 1988 fell by 4 percentage points, and Tate's analysis found that Jackson's candidacy was not directly related to Black participation in the presidential primaries, as it had been in 1984. In the general election, it seems that Jackson supporters were less likely to vote for Dukakis in 1988 than they had been to vote for Walter Mondale in 1984. "The disappointment felt by blacks over Jackson's second failed attempt may have been much greater than the disappointment felt over his initial failure in 1984, and Democratic leadership may have been held accountable for their disappointment" (Tate 1991, 1172). She also noted that overall voter turnout was lower in 1988 than in 1984, indicating less enthusiasm for the Democratic nominee among both Blacks and whites.

A research study conducted during the 1988 presidential campaign found that religious variables contributed to Jackson's support among Blacks in Washington, D.C. "These results suggest that those who frequently attend pentecostal or charismatic churches where politics was preached from the pulpit were significantly warmer toward Jackson than were other blacks in the District" (Wilcox 1990, 393). The study also found that Jackson was rated more warmly by those who described themselves as charismatics or Pentecostals. Research showed that religion, and the Black church in particular, was a "positive force in black political mobilization" (387). While it is unclear if the Black church across the country felt the same, there is little doubt that Jackson sparked interest and votes among many religious African Americans in both 1984 and in 1988.

It is interesting to note that Jackson was not the only religious leader running for the presidency in 1988. Pat Robertson, a white Charismatic church leader known for establishing the Christian Broadcasting Network and the 700 Club television program, was a candidate in the Republican presidential primary that year. Some have noted that both Jackson and Robertson invoked populist rhetoric and their campaigns shared some similarities. Hertzke (1993) in particular argues that many of Robertson's supporters viewed Jackson more favorably than other Republican candidates in the primary. A significant percentage of Robertson's supporters—19 percent—had switched from the Democratic Party, and 16 percent labeled themselves independent before the 1988 election (Green and Guth 1988). This does not imply there was any cross-over voting, yet it does point out that there were apparently some common religious and populist components of both campaigns. For those willing to embrace the combination of politics and religion, Jackson apparently presented a compelling mixture of populism, optimism, and a call to return to morals and beliefs that some believed would strengthen the social fabric of the nation.

JACKSON'S LEGACY

For his part, Jackson said that his campaigns paved the way for future Democratic candidates, including President Barak Obama, and brought progressive issues to the forefront. "Obama himself once told Jackson that after watching him debate in 1984, he knew it was possible for a black candidate to win" (Cobble 2018). Jackson said his campaigns also stretched Americans' ideas of an electable candidate. "When I ran in '84, it was like an absurd idea. It was just crazy. Scholars were writing articles" (Meyer and Dardick 2004).

Others point to his legacy of activating those who had not been involved in politics before. Butch Wing, who eventually worked with Jackson's Rainbow/PUSH organization in California, said the Jackson presidential campaigns brought him into political activism. "The Jackson presidential campaign provided a vehicle to combine the grass-roots organizations with an electoral campaign," he said. "He brought in people like myself who never really envisioned ourselves being involved in electoral politics at the national level" (Meyer and Dardick 2004).

Shirley Chisholm promoted many of the same issues as Jackson, but their legacies are different. She was an outside candidate who fought for positions on issues that were neither popular nor politically safe during her campaigns, and thereby paved the way for Jackson. She also brought awareness and a sense of political belonging to women. Many credit Jackson with expanding the Democratic Party and helping to change its rules to make its delegate selection more proportional. Both Chisholm and Jackson were instrumental in pushing the Democratic Party to embrace more liberal policies and ideas, many of which are still being discussed today. The party has become more diverse, moving away from one dominated by white Southern politicians to one with both white and minority membership, making it more of the Rainbow Coalition that Jackson envisioned.

Jackson was a populist outsider political candidate who had little chance of winning, but who may have been one of the most influential by helping to change the nation's ideas about what a presidential candidate looks like, talks like, and how he or she empathizes with the American people.

REFERENCES

Bennett, Lerone Jr. 1984. "I Could Have Won: Candidate Evaluates Historic Campaign and Calls for New Crusade for 'Equity and Parity.'" *Ebony*, August 1984.
Bonikowski, Bart and Noam Gidron. 2016. The Populist style in American Politics: Presidential Campaign Discourse, 1952-1996. *Social Forces* 94, no. 4 (June):1593–1621. https://doi.org/10.1093/sf/sov120.

Cobble, Steve. 2018. "Jesse Jackson's Rainbow Coalition Created Today's Democratic Politics." *The Nation*. October 2, 2018. https://www.thenation.com/article/archive/jesse-jackson-rainbow-coalition-democratic-politics/.

Craigen, James. 1986. "The Influence of Rev. Jesse Jackson's Candidacy for President on Pluralistic Politics: Implications for Community Action." *The Journal of Sociology & Social Welfare,* 13, no. 3, article 12: 591–598.

Gailey, Phil. 1984. "Jackson takes Louisiana Vote in Low Turnout." *The New York Times,* May 6, 1984.

Gibbons, Arnold. 1993. *Race, Politics, and the White Media: The Jesse Jackson Campaigns*. Lanham, MD: University Press of America.

Green, John C. and James L. Guth. 1988. The Christian Right in the Republican Party: The Case of Pat Robertson's Supporters. *The Journal of Politics* 50, no. 1 (February): 150–165.

Hertzke, Allen. 1993. *Echoes of Discontent: Jesse Jackson, Pat Robertson, and the Resurgence of Populism*. Washington: CQ Press.

Jackson, Jesse. 1984a. Democratic National Convention Address. July 18, 1984. https://www.americanrhetoric.com/speeches/jessejackson1984dnc.htm.

_____ 1984b. Jackson Campaign Brochure. http://www.4president.org/bro-chures/1984/jessejackson1984brochure.htm.

_____ 1988. Democratic National Convention Address. July 19, 1988. https://www.americanrhetoric.com/speeches/jessejackson1988dnc.htm.

McIlwain, Charlton D. 2011. Racialized Media Coverage of Minority Candidates in the 2008 Democratic Presidential Primary. *American Behavioral Scientist* 55, (4): 371–389.

McTighe, Michael J. 1990. Jesse Jackson and the Dilemmas of a Prophet in Politics. *Journal of Church & State* 32, no. 3 (Summer): 585–607.

Meyer, Gregory H. and Hal Dardick. 2004. "Jackson, Fans Reflect on Legacy of '84, '88 Bids." *Chicago Tribune*. June 27, 2004. https://www.chicagotribune.com/news/ct-xpm-2004-06-27-0406270320-story.html.

Prysby, Charles L. 1989. "Attitudes of Southern Democratic Party activists toward Jesse Jackson: The effects of the local context." *The Journal of Politics* 51, (2): 305–318.

Randolph, Laura B. 1988. "Can Jesse Jackson Win? Unprecedented Presidential Campaign Gains Momentum and Raises Big Questions about Race and Politics." *Ebony*. March 1988.

Tate, Katherine. 1991. "Black Participation in the 1984 and 1988 Presidential Elections." *The American Political Science Review* 85, (4): 1159–1176.

Walker, Felicia R. and Deric M. Greene. 2006. Exploring Afrocentricity: An Analysis of the Discourse of Jesse Jackson. *Journal of African American Studies* 9, no. 4 (Spring): 61–71.

Wilcox, Clyde. 1990. Religious Sources of Politicization Among Blacks in Washington, D.C. *Journal for the Scientific Study of Religion* 29, no. 3 (September): 387–394.

Chapter 5

Ron Paul

OUTSIDER WITH LIBERTARIAN SENSIBILITIES DEFENDING THE CONSTITUTION

It is fair to call Ron Paul both an outsider and a political renegade. As a congressman from Texas and a three-time presidential candidate, Paul never really followed the rules or fully embraced the Republican Party. In fact, his first presidential campaign was as the Libertarian Party nominee, while the last two were as a Republican candidate.

The seeds of his conflicted nature regarding the Republican Party were sown early, when he was exposed to the economic theories of Ludwig von Mises and the leading thinkers of the Libertarian movement in the 1960s. He took a great interest in economic theory and thought it a national catastrophe in 1971 when President Richard Nixon removed the United States from the gold standard. "That was the moment I knew something very strange was going on in the government establishment" (Altman 2011, 43), he said of that event, and it prompted him to consider how to share his concerns with others.

RON PAUL'S DISCOURSE

Ron Paul was a successful obstetrician-gynecologist in south Texas after serving as an Air Force flight surgeon during Vietnam. He delivered a lot of babies, which a Democratic opponent said created much name recognition and goodwill for Paul (Goodwyn 2007). In 1974 he ran for Congress, but lost. Two years later, he won the seat. He served in the House of Representatives from the area from 1976–1977, from 1979–1985, and from 1997–2013. In all of that time in Congress, he never stopped abiding by the core principles put forth by von Mises, which are that governments should not intervene in free markets and that increasing the size of government or its services leads to less freedom. He championed a return to the gold standard, allowing states to legalize drugs, and pushed for a reduction in the size of government and its federal safety nets. He argued for a non-interventionist foreign policy and always championed the liberty of individuals. He never voted for a tax increase. He hated unbalanced budgets. He was rarely on the winning side of Congressional votes, but was always principled in his approach to federal government issues. To him, the answer always could be found in the Constitution. "It cannot be emphasized enough that we are a republic, not a democracy and, as such, we should insist that the framework of the Constitution be respected and boundaries set by law are not crossed by our leaders" (Paul 2012a).

For Paul, that meant a return to a more hands-off foreign policy. In his 2008 presidential campaign, he rankled the other Republican candidates by stating in a debate that the United States' actions in the Middle East had sown the seeds of 9–11. Rather than assume a military stance in other nations, he advocated diplomacy and other approaches, instead of a military intervention. Paul tied this into his overall narrative that the Republican Party—and the nation—had strayed away from the founders' intentions and the boundaries of the Constitution. "There's a strong tradition of being anti-war in the Republican party. It is the constitutional position. It is the advice of the Founders to follow a non-interventionist foreign policy, stay out of entangling alliances, be friends with countries, negotiate and talk with them and trade with them" (Paul 2007a). This was a popular issue for Paul, especially among younger voters who were concerned about the war dragging on and possibly triggering a national draft. "Paul's rhetoric cast a negative light on an interventionist foreign policy, setting the stage for a different foreign policy vision to be offered that would make the American people safer and restore the nation's foreign policy traditions" (Edwards 2011). Paul traced the United States' involvement in international affairs to World War I, which he said had triggered the nation's quest to control global economic interests, mainly to support its growing dependence on oil (da Fonseca 2014–2015). This, he argued, led to the nation's involvement in the Middle East and its eventual participation in wars in that area of the world. Anti-establishment appeals address the anxieties of people who have lost faith in government or who are feeling vulnerable and anxious (Serazio 2016), and Paul offered a different approach that many found compelling.

Paul was never a rousing speaker. In fact, some compared his speeches to a college professor giving a lecture. But this seemed to be part of his appeal—so much that one college newspaper derided young people's "dangerous affinity for Ron Paul" (Morano 2012). While that affinity may have stemmed more from his stance on legalizing drugs and arguing against military involvement around the world, he also seems to have truly inspired great fervor among many young people. He cared less about being a politician than in furthering his ideas, which he also promoted in several authored books and even scholarly academic articles. Yet, he sparked what many call a revolution. Brian Doherty (2012) examined Paul's enthusiastic supporters and the movement he started and came to the conclusion that part of Paul's allure was his consistency on the issues. He attracted a grassroots following that made him into one of the best-known politicians in the nation.

Paul's concerns went far beyond international relations. He was in favor of cutting the size of government, changing the nation's laws regarding abortion, repealing drug laws that negatively impacted African Americans, and in returning the nation to prosperity for all people. "The free society is the only society that can provide goods and services and distribute them in the most fair manner. And that is the society that I would advocate and argue for and believe it's available to us" (Paul 2007b). He often cited statistics about minorities being unfairly punished by the war on drugs, which he advocated ending. "We don't have to have more courts and more prisons. We need to repeal the whole war on drugs. It isn't working" (Paul 2007b). Paul's libertarian sensibilities often rose to the surface in his speeches and debates, giving voice to those outside the mainstream who wanted changes to take place within the Republican Party, as well as in the nation. For this reason, it might be argued that he had populist tendencies.

Some note the influence that the works of writer and philosopher Ayn Rand had on Paul's beliefs and discourse. While rarely quoting her works outright, Paul often infused his speeches and writings with ideas from libertarian and objectivist literature, such as this: "Once government gets a limited concession for the use of force to mold people's habits and plan the economy, it causes a steady move toward tyrannical government. Only a revolutionary spirit can reverse the process and deny to the government this arbitrary use of aggression" (Paul, 2012a). Rand's character of Ragnar the Avenger in "Atlas Shrugged" reverses the Robin Hood legend and instead returns money to those who produce it, and Paul seemed to agree with this philosophy. He criticized government programs and handouts and questioned not only their morality, but their effectiveness. "Paul's mystique, as a product of his embodiment of Randian heroism, contributes to an explanation for the enthusiasm of his supporters. For his most devout fans, Ron Paul's mind is uniquely vested with the wisdom required to articulate, inspire, and legislate the libertarian revolution" (Waldenmaier 2013, 45). For those who share his belief in limited government and personal liberty, Paul became a hero and the leader of a movement.

Paul relished his role as an outsider, and he often expressed his out-of-the mainstream beliefs and issues through books and newsletters. He has published at least nine books, some with provocative titles such as "The Revolution: A Manifesto," and "End the Fed." All of the books deal with government, individual liberty, and economic policies. He is one of the most prolific of all the candidates profiled in this book, with only Ralph Nader and Pat Buchanan possibly having written more books and articles. The dedication of the book "Liberty Defined: 50 essential issues that affect our freedom," is written to "the great intellectuals of freedom who taught and inspired me and so many others: Ludwig von Mises, F.A. Hayek, Leonard E. Read, Murray N. Rothbard, and Hans F. Sennholz" (2012b). This book contains essays on topics ranging from abortion to envy to insurance and surveillance. All of them express a consistent theme: keeping the government out of people's lives. While these books are more dense reading than most of the titles published by presidential candidates—which tend to be outlines of policy initiatives—his discourse and consistent beliefs built much support for Paul during his presidential campaigns.

PAUL'S CAMPAIGN TACTICS

Presidential Campaign in 1988

Ron Paul ran for Senate in 1984 and lost. He then decided to pursue a presidential bid within the Libertarian Party. He was not seen as a true-blue Libertarian because of his stance against abortions, and he faced a bit of opposition within the party from Native American activist Russell Means. Paul obtained the nomination and ran for president in 1988 as the Libertarian Party's candidate. He was excluded from all presidential debates, but did have the advantage of beginning his campaign several months before nominees for the Democratic and Republican parties were selected. He visited numerous college campuses and found young people interested in hearing more about his ideas regarding the war on drugs and a foreign policy that would take the United States out of the Middle East and other world hotspots. His appeal seemed greatest among younger people who were embracing the new computer and online technologies. Paul was on the ballot in forty-six states in the general election, and he finished third in the popular vote.

In most respects, it was obvious that Paul did not see himself being elected president in 1988. "He knew he had no chance of winning, but welcomed the opportunity to promote his view that the modern version of the federal government was radically different from that envisioned by the Founding Fathers" (Human Events 1998). Paul knew that having access to a national audience was ultimately another way to get his ideas and discourse in front of the American people and to possibly win more converts to his proposals.

Paul did well as a third-party candidate in fundraising, with $2 million collected during the race. His son Rand Paul, later a U.S. Senator from Kentucky, worked on the campaign with his father, and reported that $500,000 of that money was spent on ballot access for the party. The campaign did not achieve the voter success that it had hoped, gaining less than one-half of one percent of the national vote, although it did collect more votes than the Libertarian

Party ticket in 1984. Paul said the party received numerous calls from Americans who wanted to know more about libertarian beliefs and who were looking for an alternative to the Republican and Democratic nominees. In that respect, the campaign was successful.

PRESIDENTIAL CAMPAIGN 2008

Paul returned to the Republican Party and was re-elected to his seat in Congress in 1996. He resumed his previous voting habits and continued to argue against measures he saw as unconstitutional or economically dangerous. He announced his second run for president in 2007, and this one was for the Republican Party nomination. It was quickly obvious that Paul had quite an online following of especially raucous supporters. Although he rarely got higher than single digits in scientific polls, he routinely topped other Republican candidates in online polls. His YouTube channel was viewed more than a million times, and his supporters sent angry messages to news sites demanding they give more coverage to Paul's campaign.

Those who were not on Paul's bandwagon grew tired of what they saw as overzealous supporters. "The 2008 Paul campaign was a ragtag coalition of anarchists, antiwar activists, goldbugs, paleoconservatives, hard-core libertarians and conspiracy theorists" is how a Time Magazine writer described the Paul supporters (Altman, 2011). The campaign raised large amounts of money—setting two fundraising records in the process. His campaign scored the highest single-day donation total among Republican candidates, raising $4.3 million on November 5, 2007. His campaign had another money bomb on the anniversary of the Boston Tea Party, with more than $6 million coming in from supporters on December 16, 2007. By the end of December 2007, Paul's campaign had raised more than $28 million. All of his donations during the campaign came from individual donors, and he received more donations from members of the military than any other candidate in 2007.

A combination of the money bombs, which were mainly fueled through online donations and gimmicks, such as a blimp that flew around to advertise Paul, led people to compare Paul's supporters with those of Howard Dean in 2004. Dean and his campaign worked hard to use the Internet as a rallying and planning vehicle for supporters. Those watching the Paul supporters saw a major difference between them and those who supported Dean. "But the Ron Paul frenzy seems to have sprung from the internet itself. Paul's libertarian message—he is against big government, the war, and pretty much anything that costs taxpayers money—has attracted a group of anti-establishment, tech-savvy supporters who have taken everyone by surprise" (Spiegel 2007). Perhaps this should not have surprised political observers, because cyber-libertarianism was known to be prevalent on the Web and celebrated "the technologically enabled autonomy and resourcefulness of a liberal-individualist DIY citizen-consumer" (Dahlberg 2010, 348), and their abilities to network and promote libertarian interests online.

It didn't seem to bother Paul that his supporters were orchestrating over-the-top events, such as re-enacting the Boston Tea Party, in cities around the country, or that online sites had come to dread receiving messages from his passionate fans. "Paul was almost a passive figurehead in that spectacle, putting his message ahead of campaign tactics" (Altman 2011). Paul continued to talk about the issues that he found most important, such as his anti-interventionist stand on foreign policy, changing the nation's monetary policies, and balancing the budget. Meanwhile, his grassroots support increased, as well as the number of individually made signs, local events, and online fundraising.

Paul's staff embraced new technology that functioned to give supporters a voice and place in his campaign, as well as raise money. This allowed engagement of the grassroots support that characterized his presidential campaigns and mirrored the changes taking place in people's individual online experiences. "Although campaigns in the 1990s might have shied away from online opportunities for fear of losing control, campaigners in the twenty-first century have been adapting to that interactive unpredictability: working through user-generated content by seeding campaign messages and monitoring the opposition through cutting-edge technological means" (Serazio 2015, 1921). Paul's supporters were rowdy and vocal, and many of them were younger voters who adapted quickly to online technology and who put their skills to work on his behalf.

Chamberlain (2010) argues that Paul's 2008 campaign should be considered a third-party run within a major party. His argument is that the Paul campaign received support in 2008 from many voters who supported him in his Libertarian bid. The initial Libertarian campaign elevated Paul's name recognition and provided him with a base of voters who then supported him in 2008, even though he was not the Libertarian candidate. Chamberlain observed that "After 20 years, which included the addition of large numbers of voters who would have been unable to vote in 1988, those states that had voted for Paul in higher percentages during his third-party run remained his strongest supporters in his Republican primary campaign" (112). It was this support base, Chamberlain argues, that helped set fundraising records and fueled the online money bombs.

One bump along the way was an examination of newsletters that had been published in Paul's name in the 1980s and 1990s that were said to include racist comments and sympathy for militia movements and conspiracy theories. Paul denied writing the newsletters, and said he had not even read all of them. He dismissed the controversy, and he refused to send back a $500 donation from a Florida white supremacist group, calling it "pandering" to return money to people or groups with whom you disagree (Gibson 2011). "I didn't write them, didn't read them at the time, and I disavow them. That is the answer," (Bohn 2011) Paul said to CNN's Gloria Barger in a 2011 interview, clearly irritated that the topic continued to dog him in his 2012 presidential campaign.

In his 2008 primary campaign, Paul was able to participate in at least twelve debates with other Republican candidates. He finished in the top five in several early primaries, and then on Super Tuesday he received 4 percent of the popular vote among all states participating. He continued to pull enough votes to place in the top five in most state contests, with his best numbers coming in the Idaho Republican primary, where he received 24 percent of the vote. He finished fourth in the Republican primary. He was not allowed to speak at the Republican convention, so instead hosted a three-day rally a few miles away from the site of the convention in Minneapolis, Minnesota, which he said attracted 12,000 people. Paul received fifteen delegate votes at the convention, compared to McCain's 2,343.

While his stands on many issues appealed to younger voters and those with libertarian leanings, the campaign failed to translate his exuberant online support into votes. Most political analysts agree that Paul's outsider status kept him from attaining more success. "Still, his distance from the political mainstream, while it helped shake up an otherwise sleepy primary season, kept him from mounting a serious bid for the GOP nomination" (Burns 2012).

PRESIDENTIAL CAMPAIGN 2012

It was not much of a surprise when Paul announced that he would again seek the Republican Party nomination in the 2012 campaign. He made the announcement in May 2011, and in July of that year, he announced that he would not be seeking another term in the House of Representatives. Instead, he made the presidential campaign his focus for the next year.

As a politician, Ron Paul's stands on issues were once again seen as too far from the mainstream for most voters. His stump speeches were more similar to college lectures than emotional rallies, and yet crowds at his stops were enthusiastically supportive. He began the race as a longshot candidate, and even acknowledged along the way that Mitt Romney would eventually be the Republican nominee. Alex Altman of Time Magazine recounted that Paul's 2008 warnings about potential economic chaos and the dangers of military intervention around the world had inspired some Republicans to brand his ideas "kooky." Altman acknowledged that Paul was lacking as a serious candidate. "But as a prophet, he is still defining the GOP race," (2011). Perhaps that was Paul's real intention—to change the direction of the Republican Party.

Paul said that he was in the race to win, but many suspected it was to win more people to libertarian ideas, not necessarily to win the presidency. "I do what I do because I believe that truth wins out in the end" (Altman 2012). He continued to attract young voters with his rhetoric, as it appealed to their concerns about the economy and other possible wars.

Sometimes Paul himself seemed to struggle to answer why younger voters were supportive of his candidacy. "I don't know the exact reason for it. I defend the Constitution constantly in Washington, and that's very appealing to young people. Sometimes the two parties mesh together, and it's not too infrequent that I feel obligated to vote by myself. And when [young people] see that, they say, 'He won't go back and forth and will always stick to principle'" (Blakeslee 2012).

In early straw polls, Paul was at the top or near the top of contenders, and he did well in early polls that were taken in fall 2011. His campaign once again proved adept at fundraising, with several money bombs, and eventually raised more than $38 million. The media, however, seemed to often ignore his campaign, which became a source of frustration for his supporters, and even late-night talk show host Jon Stewart, who shared a collection of video clips that showed Paul being ignored by mainstream media. During a Fox News interview in August of 2011, Paul said the media should be reporting on his campaign because it was raising money, had a good organization, and had just won the Iowa straw poll. "I know how the system works, and I know what I'm trying to do, because it's not like I'm just trying to win and get elected," he said. "I'm trying to change the course of history and our history in this country hasn't been good for the past one hundred years" (O'Connor 2011).

The Pew Research Center agreed that mainstream media were less likely to cover Ron Paul's campaign than those of other Republican hopefuls. Pew noted that Paul had "an energized online following," (Wormald 2011) and was the only candidate who generated more positive comments than negative ones on social media, online blogs, and in news coverage. Yet, in mainstream news media coverage, Paul ranked next-to-last among Republican candidates in amount of news coverage received. Baym (2013) researched Paul's appearances on four different television programs—Meet the Press, The Tonight Show, Hannity, and The Daily Show—for insight into how different types of journalistic public-affairs programs combine interviews and entertainment with journalistic accountability. He found that Paul was faced with an alternating mix of traditional news interviews as well as post-modern infotainment, and that most of the interviews, all done just before the Iowa caucus, featured questions and/or skepticism about his radical suggestions about what was necessary to "fix" the nation. It can be surmised that he was invited to these television programs because he was polling well just before the Iowa caucus, as the interviews by mainstream media outlets were somewhat sporadic even after he came in second in Iowa. This led an NPR reporter to declare that Paul might well be wearing an "invisibility cloak" in regard to media coverage (James 2011).

During fall 2011, Paul participated in at least four debates or forums, and he finished in the top tier of several straw polls. An analysis of participants watching the January 26, 2012, Republican primary debate found that Ron Paul made the greatest gains in image evaluation of any of the candidates, and he was the top-ranked vote choice following the debate (McKinney, Houston and Hawthorne, 2014). Before the debate, participants ranked him third in their voting choices. Paul was also the subject of more tweets than any other debate participant and captured the positive attention of those following the debate. One finding from the research was that, "While our participants' support for Ron Paul is in line with his wider appeal to youth and college-age voters who were attracted to his campaign's more libertarian message of individual rights and personal freedoms, less government involvement and anti-military views, Paul's gains in popularity among our participants is clearly a function of their social watching behaviors during this primary debate" (569). Once again, Paul's messages appealed to younger people, and their political information was now often coming online through social media, rather than more traditional media offerings. This research points out the quick development of digital politics and its growing impact on candidate popularity. This would become even more apparent in the 2016 race when Donald Trump's social media campaigns made up the bulk of his campaign messaging.

Paul finished third in the Iowa caucuses, second in the New Hampshire primary, and fourth in the South Carolina primary. He came in third or fourth in several other state primaries, but he seemed to follow a strategy of attempting to gather support from delegates from individual states, rather than attempting to win each contest outright. He skipped states with a "winner take all," such as Florida, where he knew that his resources would probably be wasted. He remained active in the race until the Republican convention, but effectively shut down his presidential campaign in May 2012 as his organization struggled to raise money. He finished with 118 delegates, which was far more than the fifteen he received in 2008, and he finished fourth in the delegate count at the convention.

In his statement regarding the suspension of his campaign, he noted that his pursuit of the presidential nomination had been about much more than politics. "It has been part of a quest I began forty years ago and that so many have joined. It is about the campaign for Liberty, which has taken a tremendous leap forward in this election and will continue to grow stronger in the future until we finally win" (Reeve 2012). While he may have hoped for a better outcome, Paul seemed to feel that more people than ever had been supportive of the ideas and principles espoused by his campaign, and he hoped that would bring about change within the Republican Party.

PAUL'S CAMPAIGN ISSUES

It has always been somewhat difficult to figure out where to place Ron Paul within the Republican Party. He represents a more libertarian wing of the party, but has also been described as a very strong conservative. On the political spectrum, he sits in an unusual spot in which those with more left-leaning ideas mingle with his pro-liberty and anti-intervention stances. "Paul occupies that space where the libertarian right curves around and meets the anti-corporate, anti-authoritarian left," is how Texas Monthly described him (Blakeslee 2012). Dissent calls it "that twilight zone in American politics where Left and Right mingle uneasily" (Burns 2012). Whatever it is called or labeled, it has earned him a solid base of support for many years.

It is easy to see why Paul was a consummate outsider candidate. His stands on common issues were outside the mainstream—after all, what other candidates would dare to argue that Social Security should be phased out over time—and he brought other, more primary issues, to the forefront.

His insistence that the nation follow the Constitution and its narrow list of government duties, as well as his concern for individual liberty, often confused his fellow members of Congress and oftentimes left him as a lone "no" vote. In fact, it earned him the nickname "Dr. No." During his time in Congress, there were more than 675 times when he cast a lone vote against legislation or was one of ten or fewer House members to vote against a measure (Stein 2011). While this might have won him supporters who saw this as a principled stand, it did not not win him supporters within the Republican Party. "Ron Paul was his own island. Leadership tried not to visit and rarely had to. Sometimes we sailed through," said a Republican leadership aide (Stein 2011).

He voted against farm subsidies and flood insurance, against aid for Hurricane Katrina victims, against recognizing the fortieth anniversary of the passage of the Civil Rights Act of 1964, and opposed congressional medals for Rosa Parks, Ronald Reagan, Pope John Paul II, and Mother Teresa (Altman 2011). One of his guiding principles seems to be the libertarian belief, by way of John Stuart Mill, that the only reason to restrict the actions of an individual is to prevent harm to others. This leads to his belief that drugs should be legalized, but that children should be protected from them because they cannot yet make good judgments about drug use. He also believed that prostitution should be made legal and that government cannot "legislate virtue." Both of these issues, he said, are matters for states to discuss, not the federal government.

He was also not a fan of bipartisanship, especially when the legislation being debated was what he saw as bad policy. "People often say that what this country needs is for people to Washington to stop fighting and just get the job done. To achieve that, we need more 'bipartisanship.' I don't agree. If two parties with bad ideas cooperate, the result is not good policy but policy that is extremely bad" (Paul 2012b, 20). Paul basically summarizes his position as this: "When the ideas of both parties are bad, there is really only one hope: that they will continue fighting and not pass any new legislation. Gridlock can be the friend of liberty" (Paul, 2012b, 20).

One of the issues that is usually in the Libertarian Party platform, but which causes some differences within the party, is that of abortion. Paul was pro-life his entire political career, but did say that abortion and gay marriage, if they are to be regulated, are matters for state governments to determine. He delivered a speech during his 2012 presidential campaign in which he outlined his reasons for being anti-abortion. He argued the main reason for having government is to protect liberty and life, and he counts the unborn as life. Most presidential candidates try to avoid making statements on social issues that are this controversial, but Paul chose to include the topic in a speech in Ames, Iowa (Burns 2012). In that same address he also mentioned several of his usual stump speech issues, including his opposition to the wars in Afghanistan and Iraq, and his usual comments against the Federal Reserve.

It was perhaps those last two issues that attracted Paul the most supporters. His outsider belief that the United States should be non-interventionist resonated with younger people who had concerns about a draft and about a long, drawn-out war, and his concerns about the economy resonated with those who held similar fears about a meltdown in the economy because of government meddling. Paul is no fan of a national military draft, and has strong words for what he sees as the American government attempting to justify its actions. "We also need to stand firmly against moral relativism, recalling that actions do not become moral just because our government performs them" (Paul 2008). He also railed against the United State's banking system, and in particular against the Federal Reserve, which he said had taken the nation in the wrong direction.

We have a financial system that pretends to be capitalism but which actually encourages dependence on Washington. By undermining the long-term economic thinking that goes into building strong marriages, families, churches, and voluntary organizations, as well as businesses, the economy of easy money and bigger government uproots the institutions that have defined American life. (Paul 2010, 472)

His comments may have resonated with those who were still struggling to regain a financial foothold after the Great Recession, although he offered no easy solutions and certainly no offer of financial assistance from the government. In the same article, Paul repudiated stimulus packages and low interest rates, which are two of the government's usual remedies during financial downturns. Despite this "tough talk," his supporters still remained dedicated to Paul and the movement that he spearheaded.

THE HAPPY OUTSIDER

Ron Paul seemed to relish the role of the outsider candidate—the one who stood alone in Congressional votes, the one who talked about philosophy and economic ideology, the one who tried to push an entire party in a more libertarian direction. Even though he was an elected official for many years, he was an outsider the whole time.

He was probably the most anti-war candidate in any of the presidential elections in which he participated, and he provoked gasps from audiences when he blamed 9–11 on American foreign policy. He never gave up on his quest to end the Federal Reserve and take the country back to the gold standard, which was the issue that initially prompted him to enter politics.

Paul elevated the conversation about economics, personal freedom and constitutional governance. He drew upon history and those he saw as leading thinkers in these areas, and he seemed to truly believe that if more Americans could understand and accept these ideas, then there would be a new revolution in the United States. "Fortunately, this revolution is under way, and if one earnestly looks for it, it can be found. Participation in it is open to everyone. Not only have our ideas of liberty developed over centuries, they are currently being eagerly debated, and a modern, advanced understanding of the concept is on the horizon. The Revolution is alive and well" (Paul 2012b, xvii).

As many other outsider candidates, Paul seemed to count his victories as something other than what was stuffed into ballot boxes. His legacy seems to be more of a prophet for a change and a testament to the power of ideas, rather than accumulation of power. He acknowledged this in one of his books: "If we want to live in a free society, we need to break free from these artificial limitations on free debate and start asking serious questions once again. I am happy that my campaign for the presidency has finally raised some of them. But this is a long-term project that will persist far into the future. These ideas cannot be allowed to die, buried beneath the mind-numbing chorus of empty slogans and inanities that constitute official political discourse in America" (Paul 2008, introduction xi). In his farewell speech to Congress, which was full of discourse about personal liberty and how the United States government has moved far beyond what its creators intended, Paul places his hopes on the American people: "The #1 responsibility for each of us is to change ourselves with the hope that others will follow. This is of greater importance than working on changing the government; that is secondary to promoting a virtuous society. If we can achieve this, then the government will change" (Spiering 2012).

Part of Paul's legacy is the ability to harness online political support even before it became commonplace among candidates. While Shirley Chisholm and Jesse Jackson relied on more limited technology—trucks with PA systems and mainstream media interviews—Paul's campaigns led the way in gaining supporters across the nation through the Internet. The ability to do this led to some of the first successful attempts to create large groups of unified supporters online who then rallied and worked on behalf of a candidate in their own communities. While this is now commonplace, it was relatively new when pioneered by Paul's campaigns, and he paved the way for more mainstream candidates such as Barack Obama to raise large amounts of money through online donations. It also began a trend that has benefited outsiders and third-party hopefuls, as it allows a candidate's message to spread virally throughout the entire country without a commitment to expensive travel or advertising. The embracing of social media has also benefited outsider candidates, as evidenced by the political rise and election of Donald J. Trump.

REFERENCES

Altman, Alex. 2011. "The Prophet." *TIME* magazine. Sept. 5, 2011.

Baym, Geoffrey. 2013. Political Media as Discursive Modes: A Comparative Analysis of Interviews with Ron Paul from Meet the Press, Tonight, The Daily Show, and Hannity. *International Journal of Communication*, 7 (2013): 489–507.

Bohn, Kevin. 2011. Ron Paul Defensive Over Past Newsletters. *cnn.com*, Dec. 21, 2011. https://politicalticker.blogs.cnn.com/2011/12/21/ron-paul-gets-defensive-over-past-newsletters/.

Blakeslee, Nate. 2012. "The Swan Song of Ron." *Texas Monthly*. February 2012. https://www.texasmonthly.com/politics/the-swan-song-of-ron/.

Burns, Alexander. 2012. "Ron Paul Delivers Strongly Anti-Abortion Speech." *Politico*. Aug. 13, 2011. https://www.politico.com/story/2011/08/ron-paul-delivers-strongly-anti-abortion-speech-061296.

Burns, Jennifer. 2012. "Ron Paul and the New Libertarianism." *Dissent*. Summer 2012. https://www.dissentmagazine.org/article/ron-paul-and-the-new-libertarianism.

Chamberlain, Adam. 2010. An Inside-Outsider or an Outside-Insider? The Republican Primary Campaign of Ron Paul from a Third-Party Perspective. *Politics & Policy* 38, (1): 97–116.

da Fonseca, Alexandre M. 2014-2015. "War Is a Racket!" The Emergence of the Libertarian Discourse About World War I in the United States. *Janus.Net: e-Journal of International Relations* 5, no. 2 (Nov. 2014-April 2015): 45–58.

Dahlberg, Lincoln. 2010. Cyber-Libertarianism 2.0: A Discourse Theory/Critical Political Economy Examination. *Cultural Politics*, 6, no. 3 (November): 331–356.

Doherty, Brian. 2012. *Ron Paul's rEVOLution: The Man and the Movement He Inspired.* New York: Broadside Books.

Edwards, Jason A. 2011. Debating America's Role in the World: Representative Ron Paul's Exceptionalist Jeremiad. *American Behavioral Scientist* 55, (3): 253–269. https://journals.sagepub.com/doi/pdf/10.1177/0002764210392162.

Gibson, Ginger. 2011. "6 Comments Ron Paul Has to Explain." *Politico.* Dec. 22, 2011. https://www.politico.com/story/2011/12/6-statements-ron-paul-needs-to-explain-070798.

Goodwyn, Wade. 2007. Paul Has Long Drawn Support from Unlikely Places. *All Things Considered.* NPR. Oct. 7, 2007. https://www.npr.org/templates/story/story.php?storyId=15016924.

Human Events. 1998. "Paul vs. Sneary." June 26, 1998. http://search.ebscohost.com/login.aspx?direct=true&db=a9h&AN=772974&site=ehost-live&scope=site.

James, Frank. 2011. Ron Paul Wears Invisibility Cloak In News Media's Eyes. *NPR.* Aug. 16, 2011. https://www.npr.org/sections/itsallpolitics/2011/08/16/139669952/ron-paul-wears-invisibility-cloak-in-medias-eyes.

McKinney, Mitchell, S., J. Brian Houston and Joshua Hawthorne. 2014. Social Watching a 2012 Republican Presidential Primary Debate. *American Behavioral Scientist* 8, (4): 556–573. https://doi.org/10.1177/0002764213506211.

Morano, Malcolm. 2012. Ron Paul: A Dangerously Appealing Renegade to Students. *The Observer.* Feb. 22, 2012. https://fordhamobserver.com/9782/opinions/ron-paul-a-dangerously-appealing-renegade-to-students/.

O'Connor, Patrick. 2011. "Ron Paul: Media Are Frightened By Us." *Wall Street Journal.* Washington Wire. Aug. 16, 2011. https://blogs.wsj.com/washwire/2011/08/16/ron-paul-media-are-frightened-by-us/.

Paul, Ron. 2007a. Republican Presidential Candidates Debate at University of South Carolina. May 15, 2007. https://www.presidency.ucsb.edu/documents/republican-presidential-candidates-debate-the-university-south-carolina.

Paul, Ron. 2007b. Republican Candidates "All-American Presidential Forum" at Morgan State University in Baltimore. Sept. 27, 2007. https://www.presidency.ucsb.edu/documents/republican-candidates-all-american-presidential-forum-morgan-state-university-baltimore.

Paul, Ron. 2010. The Banks Versus the Constitution. *Harvard Journal of Law and Public Policy* 33, no. 2 (Spring): 465–473.

Paul, Ron. 2008. *The Revolution: A Manifesto.* New York: Grand Central Publishing.

Paul, Ron. 2012a. Daily Paul. Sept. 12, 2012. Website no longer available.

Paul, Ron. 2012b. *Liberty Defined.* New York: Grand Central Publishing.

Reeve, Elspeth. 2012. "Did Ron Paul Campaign's Influence Anything?" *The Atlantic*. May 14, 2012. https://www.theatlantic.com/politics/archive/2012/05/did-ron-paul-campaign-influence-anything/328147/.

Serazio, Michael. 2015. Managing the Digital News Cyclone: Power, Participation, and Political Production Strategies. *International Journal of Communication* (9): 1907–1925.

Serazio, Michael. 2016. Encoding the Paranoid Style in American Politics: "Anti-Establishment' Discourse and Power in Contemporary Spin. *Critical Studies in Media Communication*, 33, no. 2 (May): 181–194.

Spiegel, Brendan. 2007. "Ron Paul: How a Fringe Politician Took Over the Web." *Wired*. June 27, 2007. https://www.wired.com/2007/06/ron-paul/.

Spiering, Charlie. 2012. Transcript: Ron Paul's Farewell Address to Congress. *Washington Examiner*, Nov. 15, 2012. https://www.washingtonexaminer.com/transcript-ron-pauls-farewell-address-to-congress.

Stein, Sam. 2011. "Ron Paul's Remarkable No Votes: Holocaust Memorial Funding, Ethics Offices, Civil Rights Bills." *HuffPost*. Dec. 28, 2011. https://www.huffpost.com/entry/ron-paul-voting-record_n_1173255.

Waldenmaier, Jacob. 2013. Mystique of the Intellectual: Heroes of Ayn Rand's Dystopias and the Ron Paul Revolution. *Jefferson Journal of Science and Culture* 3 (November): 35–62.

Wormald, Benjamin. 2011. "The Candidates on Twitter." Pew Research Center. Journalism & Media. Dec. 8, 2011. https://www.pewresearch.org/2011/12/08/twitter-and-the-campaign/.

Chapter 6

Donald J. Trump

THE FIRST POLITICAL OUTSIDER PRESIDENT

When Donald J. Trump was elected president in 2016, pundits, scholars, and millions of Democrats were caught off guard. After all, this was the bombastic billionaire whose most recent claim to fame was the American TV show "The Apprentice," on which he got to judge the business skills of several people vying for the chance to win a contract to promote one of Trump's properties. His signature statement, "You're Fired" became a well-known phrase in American culture, and Trump's unusual communication style generated enough viewership for him to be featured on the show for fourteen years.

It wasn't necessarily surprising that he decided to run for president in 2016, but when he announced his candidacy, it was unthinkable that he might become the Republican nominee. To see how he got to that point, one must go back in time a few years.

Trump is a consummate outsider, someone who understands celebrity, who has an appreciation for pivotal moments in culture, and who believed that his business background would make him the ultimate president. But he has never been the ideal political candidate. He has bounced around between the Democratic, Reform, and Republican parties. He has flirted with and then embraced many of the ideas promoted by Pat Buchanan, a man who Trump once described as a "Hitler lover." Buchanan's ideas and rhetoric are discussed later in the Renegades section of this book. Trump embraced several issues touted by Buchanan, but also took cues from Ross Perot and even George Wallace, both of whom are also discussed later.

Trump began thinking somewhat seriously about seeking the presidency in 2000, when he and Buchanan both sought to win the Reform Party's nomination. Many saw Trump's short-lived presidential campaign as a sign that he was simply playing around with politics. A British reporter at the time described his quest as "toying with politics . . . a plaything for a brash property magnate consumed with the importance of his own celebrity" (Helmore 2017).

But was it? Or was it a trial balloon, so to speak, or a testing of the waters? Did he discover something missing from his portfolio that might be important in a future quest for the presidency? He told Dan Rather that "Being good on television doesn't necessarily make you a good president, but if you're not good on TV, you're not going to be president" (Helmore 2017). In 2004, "The Apprentice" debuted on NBC, and Trump struck gold. According to Trump, he earned more than $200 million from the show, but he also earned something else that no one expected: a following based on his persona that made him known by most Americans.

A television game show may seem to an unlikely place to forge a political personality, but this particular show was well suited to Trump and his form of populism. It portrayed him in a role that promoted his company, his business savvy, and his "straight-shooter" personality. In short, it honed his performance style and earned him a fandom through which he achieved political credibility. This sort of fandom is new to American politics, and some argue it needs further study to understand the intersection of discourse and performance:

> The art of politics becomes the art of performance, the art of being a celebrity. It is important, therefore, to develop the concepts and tools that enable us to understand better how political ideas are enacted, and how audiences—"the people"—are created in the act of performance. And how, in turn, the passions of the citizen-fan are elicited and orchestrated. (Street 2019)

A recurring aspect of populist rhetoric is its reliance on perceived sincerity and authentic performance. A populist can only become a powerful political figure by being supported by a great mass of people. Trump's performance style—which promoted the idea that he was rich and powerful and somehow exceptional—set in motion a relationship between him and his political base.

A Gallup tracking poll in 2015 found that 92 percent of Republicans or Republican-leaning independents were familiar with Trump. He was the best-known Republican candidate in the race (Gass 2015). It's hard to imagine that what he might have gained the most from the TV show wasn't money or business success, but becoming a household name. That's something that most outsider candidates never achieve, even if they have been political pundits or part of a regular television talk show.

TRUMP AS DIFFERENT KIND OF OUTSIDER CANDIDATE

In many ways, Trump is the culmination of two hundred years of outsider presidential candidates paving the way for the one who would actually get elected. But he is decidedly different from almost all those who came before him. Many outside candidates have populist tendencies that they employ during political campaigns. In the rhetoric used, the issues selected, and in the performance of those messages, populist candidates tend to position themselves as saviors who gather followers by attacking "the elites" (Mudde 2004). A populist seeks to build alliances with "the people" by stressing shared values and common enemies. It's easy to see those tendencies in Trump, as well.

But what is different about Trump is that, unlike most outsider candidates, he is not dedicated to a particular ideology. Teun A. van Dijk (1998) developed the concept of ideology as serving as "the interface between social structure and social cognition" (8). In his definition, ideologies are the "basis of the social representations shared by members of a group" (8). While most outsider candidates have an ideology that is expressed through populism or a similar appeal, they don't generally have a real expectation that they will win the presidency. They run to promote their ideas and issues and further a particular agenda. For instance, Ron Paul was a Libertarian-leaning idealist. He wanted to make significant changes in the way the United States government functions. He had specific ideas, and he hammered on those ideas every time he ran for president. The same can be said for Ross Perot, a third-party candidate with remarkable outsider credentials. Who can forget his charts and infomercials dramatizing the nation's debt and economic issues? He approached the nation's problems from the standpoint of a businessman—not unlike Trump—but he was urging the change to a different ideology that he thought would save the country from itself. Trump even adopted Perot's way of approaching American voters by going around mainstream media and taking the message directly to them. For both of these candidates, their ideology framed the basis of their beliefs about how government should operate.

For Trump, though, the quest has never been about the ideology. It seems to have always been about celebrity and power, about developing a political following, and about furthering the value of the Trump brand. While he might have been separated from his company while in office, he was never far removed from it, as it's his name on the hotels and golf courses and other products. Some dispute if Trump is truly a populist, as many of his policies seemed to favor big business and industry, but his rhetoric is fully situated in the traditional populist vein, promoting him as the outsider who understands and is working hard for "the people."

In many ways, Trump's ideology seems to elude categorization. He was a cheerleader for the nation, a trait shared by most who have held the office. At times his ideology seemed paleoconservative and far-right, while other times it seemed more pragmatic. It seemed to reflect the decision-making process of someone accustomed to running his own company, rather than someone driven to find a solution through a particular set of ideological beliefs. Sometimes his ideology gets overlooked because of his lack of political correctness and the polarization that his comments often provoked in the nation.

Because of this, he may be more reminiscent of George Wallace than most of the other outsider candidates in this book. That is not to say that Trump is a racist or segregationist. Although some of his comments have invited comparison with far-right political agendas, he has not embraced those issues as Wallace did in the 1960s. But they do share a combative campaign style, a tendency to say provocative things, and both campaigned with a populist message of taking charge of a country that "needed" to be turned around. Neither stressed a particular ideology, but traded heavily on personality and combative politics. Both also expressed a dislike of the media for its many perceived failings.

Trump seems to have had good political instincts about choosing the timing of his presidential campaign. He apparently considered running for president in 1988, but decided against it. He dipped his toes into the water in 2000 when he put together an exploratory committee to seek the nomination of the Reform Party, but he eventually dropped out of the race. He sat out the presidential elections in 2004 and 2008. He spoke to CPAC (Conservative Political Action Conference) in 2012, and once again talked publicly about running for president. However, he ultimately decided not to pursue a campaign that year. In both 2008 and 2012 he endorsed the Republican candidate for president.

But in 2016, he decided it was time to make a run for the Republican nomination.

TRUMP DISCOURSE IN 2016 CAMPAIGN

Unlike many outsider candidates, Trump was not an unknown figure when he entered the 2016 presidential contest. As noted earlier, he was actually the best-known Republican candidate in the race. However, no one gave him much chance of becoming the Republican nominee. He was generally seen as a bit of a political gadfly, as he regularly attacked Republican Party leadership, including Sen. John McCain, and was known as a "birther" who questioned the legitimacy of President Barack Obama's birth certificate. In fact, among the seventeen people seeking the nomination, he was given some of the lowest odds of actually making it through the primary process. It became obvious, though, that his name recognition and his messaging were more popular than expected, leading to a situation in which he was polling better than established politicians such as former New Jersey governor Chris Christie, Sen. Marco Rubio, and former Florida governor Jeb Bush. An article in The Observer in January 2016 stated that "no one thought his popularity would last but Trump has proven to have incredible staying power and his message has proven to resonate with the public" (Alfaro 2016).

He was not supported by the Republican establishment, who thought his comments about minorities would damage the party's attempts at inroads into those communities. They were also concerned about his insulting comments and actions regarding women, especially given that Hillary Clinton would probably be the Democratic nominee. Trump was anti-immigrant, anti-globalization, anti-Obama, and pro-American, which resonated with many voters.

Trump seemed to tap into a reservoir of anger and distrust that many Americans felt toward the federal government. His bases of support included white American males, people over the age of forty-four, and those without college degrees (Elving 2016). He was politically incorrect, and many voters seemed to like that. He was not a professional politician, which also seemed to resonate with this group and made him seem more genuine in their eyes. Issues that were important to his supporters were immigration, keeping a conservative U.S. Supreme Court, reversing the Affordable Care Act (known as Obamacare) and trimming the size of government. They also seemed to want to replace those who had spent a career in Washington, D.C. with new blood, calling it "draining the swamp" of those with ethical lapses. It is interesting to note that his supporters felt that Trump—a self-confessed billionaire— understood them, despite their obvious differences in social ranking. This is not uncommon in the case of populists because the "distinction between the elite and the people is not based on how much money you have or even what kind of position you have. It's based on your values" (Friedman 2017). Trump's base saw him as a charismatic outsider who could give voice to their grievances about being overlooked, taken for granted, and disrespected. They established a bond with him, primarily through his populist discourse and performance.

Trump's combative nature—often a characteristic of populist performance—was a dividing line for many voters, with his supporters usually energized by Trump's verbal assaults and sparring. Others, however, were offended and repulsed by his behavior.

For instance, more than a dozen women accused him of sexual misconduct, and a video surfaced of him on a hot mic before a 2005 interview with "Access Hollywood." He was caught on tape saying that, because he was famous, women "will let you do anything." He went on to use crude slang about how he would sexually violate them, and how most of them would allow him to do so. These comments were seen as offensive by many Americans, and Trump issued an apology, saying the comments did not reflect who he had become since then. He characterized the comments as "locker room banter," and said that former President Bill Clinton, husband of Trump's opponent Hillary

Clinton, had said worse to him on a golf course. He then deflected criticism to the former president's history of infidelities (Taylor 2016).

He also criticized Fox News Host Megyn Kelly for her questions during a presidential debate, saying that she had "blood coming out of her wherever." He also verbally attacked actress Rosie O'Donnell as a "pig," with a "fat, ugly face" (Taylor 2016).

These and other similar comments were widely reported by the mainstream media, yet Trump made no sweeping apology or admission of guilt. He occasionally said he was sorry that people were offended, and, for some of his supporters, that seemed to be enough. Some scholars argue that Trump exercised a type of discourse that, while seen as coarse to some, was seen as authentic and sincere by those who saw him as a "voice of the people." Martin Montgomery makes the point that Trump's rhetoric was appealing and valid for many:

> "It seems, however, that there were not simply two different kinds of public into which Americans were divided as they went to the polls, but two competing universes of discourse. Within one universe of discourse much of what Trump said—its misogyny and boastfulness—was shocking. To those enfolded within his discourse of vernacular folksiness, however, this discourse was acceptable." (2017, 636)

One unusual characteristic of Trump's communication style was his reliance on short, punchy sentences that were relatively simple in nature. Most politicians have historically spoken at a higher reading or comprehension level, but Trump seems to aim his communication at a lower grade level. One academic study found that his language during his 2016 campaign was accessible to a wider audience because his comments averaged a fourth-grade comprehension level (Kayam 2018). This means that roughly 93 percent of Americans understood what he was saying, as opposed to other politicians who talk at a higher comprehension level. For instance, this same study found that Hillary Clinton's average grade level for her communication was the tenth grade, meaning that fewer Americans might be able to fully comprehend her comments and statements (Kayam 2018). This made Trump stand out in a field of candidates heavily populated by college-trained attorneys and professionals, and it differentiated him from political candidates in the past. It also reinforced his image as a non-politician who spoke from the hip and was "honest" with the American public, and it was anti-intellectual in nature.

This could be an artifact of his reality television show experience, as television thrives on short, punchy communication. Television news media rely on sound bites, which are snippets of video showing an individual speaking on camera. Political candidates are coached in how to speak in short sentences, because news organizations are using ever-shorter sound bites. The average sound bite in U.S. presidential election campaigns had decreased from 40 seconds in the 1960s to less than ten seconds by 2015 (Bas and Grabe 2015). This is sometimes attributed to the public having a shortened attention span, but is also indicative of a faster-paced style of modern journalism and narrative storytelling. Trump seems to have mastered the art of speaking in short sentences and using colloquial language. He also tends to repeat short sentences or words for impact. He often ad libs, rather than sticking to teleprompter or pre-written speeches, usually adding short snippets for emotional impact (Montgomery 2017).

For example, take these comments from his speech announcing he was entering the presidential race in June 2015. "And our real unemployment is anywhere from 18 to 20 percent. Don't believe the 5.6. Don't believe it. That's right. A lot of people up there can't get jobs. They can't get jobs, because there are no jobs, because China has our jobs and Mexico has our jobs. They all have jobs." You can see the short sentences at play in this excerpt, as well as repetition in "Don't believe," and in "can't get jobs." He also takes care to get jabs in at China and Mexico, two countries with whom he went on to threaten or impose economic sanctions and renegotiate trade agreements.

This tendency to speak in short, punchy sentences and repeat some phrases seemed to work well during his rallies, and it also provided short sound bites for news organizations. Oftentimes his ad-libbed statements seemed to be added for impact during rallies, with Trump simultaneously feeding off the energy created during the events and creating more passion in the crowd at the same time. "Trump's repetitions, however, are the building blocks of extended speech, composed extempore and as such they reinforce a sense of someone speaking directly to his audience" (Montgomery 2017). He seemed drawn to large rallies and usually left the events smiling, energized, and positive about his campaign.

Trump's Campaign Tactics

The coalition that Trump pieced together during the campaign was an interesting assortment of groups—evangelical Christians, Second-Amendment supporters, those who were pro-life and those those who had not yet recovered economically from the Great Recession. Most shared a sense that they were being ignored or that they were in danger of being cast aside by "the establishment." In Trump, they seemed to find a candidate for whom they could overlook moral missteps and instead focus on the issues that they found most compelling and the values they seemed to share. For instance, many evangelical Christians are pro-life, making them more likely to support a candidate who vocally opposes abortion. They were also more likely to be concerned about keeping a conservative U.S. Supreme Court, partially because they wanted the court to be ready when the next anti-abortion court case landed on its docket. In short, many of his supporters were willing to look the other way when he made comments that others found offensive or combative.

This confounded the media, which kept up a steady barrage of negative stories about Trump, some of them spurred by the candidate himself. One crisis management expert said that Trump's unconventional campaign changed the rules governing his presidential campaign. "Trump is immune to the laws of political physics because it's not his job to be a politician, it's his job to burn down the system," said Eric Dezenhall (Benac & Woodward 2017).

The negative media attention and Trump's combative campaign style combined to give him some of the highest negatives of any nominee for president. Both Trump and Hillary Clinton had historically high unfavorability ratings among voters. Pollsters noted their historically negative ratings among voters. "Donald Trump and Hillary Clinton head into the final hours of the 2016 presidential campaign with the worst election-eve images of any major-party presidential candidates Gallup has measured back to 1956" (Saad 2016). On Gallup's ten-point favorability scale, Clinton scored an unfavorable rating of 52 percent. Trump, however, scored an unfavorable rating of 61 percent.

October 2016 seemed to be a significantly difficult month for the Trump campaign. It is commonly expected that there will usually be an "October surprise" during a presidential election, as it is the month before the election and prime time to reveal something negative about an opponent. The first surprise came on Oct. 1 with the anonymous release of Trump's 1995 tax returns, which showed that he lost $916 million, which probably allowed him to not pay any taxes for several years. He had just been through the first of the presidential debates, which he was judged to have lost. On the campaign trail he often intimated that Hillary Clinton was suffering from some sort of mysterious illness, instead of the pneumonia-related health issues that had been reported. Onstage at a rally in Pennsylvania, he mocked her physical and personal behavior. "Hillary Clinton's only loyalty is to her financial contributors and to herself," Trump said of the first female major party presidential nominee. "I don't even think she's loyal to Bill, you wanna know the truth. And really folks really, why should she be, right? Why should she be?" (Sarlin & Seitz-Wald 2016).

During October he was also forced to defend his comments about former Miss Universe Alicia Machado regarding her weight gain during her reign, and he sent out several late-night tweets to his 12 million followers slamming Machado. There were media allegations of illegal company dealings in Cuba, more reports of him criticizing women as being unattractive, an unclear position on nuclear weapons during a debate, and a media investigation into

Trump's charitable foundation that alleged he used the foundation to pay off lawsuits against his company. It was a steady drone of negative news stories and allegations against him until Oct. 28, when then-FBI director James Comey announced that the agency was pursuing a separate case that could have bearing on Hillary Clinton's use of a private email server, which had previously been investigated. Trump was elated to have some of the media focus move from himself to his opponent. He immediately began to praise the agency for "having the courage" to address her "corruption." The chant "Lock Her Up" was often heard at Trump's rallies, and was a nod to her email server scandal. The month ended with this new development roiling the political waters just a few days before the general election. Rolling Stone magazine later published a story recounting the "23 October surprises" of the 2016 election.

During the campaign and even after he was elected, Trump returned over and over to Twitter, his social media platform of choice. He would often send tweets in the wee hours of the morning, dredging up images of him slipping away to a private location to converse with his supporters. In some ways Trump's use of social media was reminiscent of how Ross Perot used television infomercials to bypass traditional media and take messages straight to voters. Trump had more than 22 million followers on his combined social media accounts, which included Twitter, Instagram, and Facebook. While several candidates made use of extensive social media, none received the attention that Trump garnered from his social media messages. The Pew Research Center found that Trump had an outsized response from the public, compared with the other candidates. "While the candidates' level of posting was about the same, public response was far from equal. In every measurable category of user attention—Facebook shares, comments, and reactions, as well as Twitter retweets—the public responded to Donald Trump's social media updates more frequently on average than to either of the other candidates' posts" (Pew Research Center 2016). Trump's tweets were consistently retweeted more than the other candidate's Twitter messages.

While Clinton was trying to reinforce a softer image through her social media, it was used for a different purpose by Trump. Instead, he used social media "for highly personal statements, immediate reactions, and personal engagement with supporters." (Denton, Jr., Trent & Friedenberg 2019, 313). According to Denton, Jr., Trent and Friedenberg, Trump used social media to attack opponents, as well as the media, and those attacks often dominated the news cycles of mainstream media. In essence, making social media his personal megaphone drowned out many of his opponents' messages, and it provided an umbilical cord of sorts with his supporters.

In this way, Trump's rhetoric—bombastic, populist, combative, and highly unusual for a presidential candidate—ensured that he would usually dominate the news cycle for mainstream media, as well as be an important online source for the almost 25 percent of Americans who said they looked to social media posts to find out news about the election (Shearer 2016). The rhetoric itself became a feature of the campaign, sort of a reflection of the candidate of change that many American voters seemed to be seeking. "The unorthodox nature of Trump's freewheeling rhetoric increased its entertainment value and potential newsworthiness and, with them, the likelihood that ratings-driven cable networks would carry his primary campaign speeches and that cable and Sunday morning network hosts would take his calls on air" (Jamieson, Taussig 2017, 622). By constantly pumping out tweets, Trump guaranteed that he would be a major focus of the news media and control the news cycle on many days.

While Trump often complained about the amount of negative press he received, he frequently provoked that coverage through his unconventional comments during rallies, debates, and social media. Some scholars argue that this rhetoric is the equivalent of his political brand. "Just as a golden, block-lettered "Trump" expressed his brand in business, this spontaneous, Manichean, evidence-flouting, accountability-dodging, institution-disdaining rhetoric serves as his signature in politics" (Jamieson, Taussig 2017, 649).

Trump also utilized a phrase in the 2016 campaign that has had a lasting impact on American media. The phrase "fake news" may or may not have originated with him, but it became one of his signature phrases, and it filtered out into generalized use in society. The term can be used to describe social media or news media stories that are deliberately falsified, or it can refer to sensationalized or speculative stories from online websites. Trump, in particular, used the term to refer to what he called a biased press that collectively wanted to see Hillary Clinton elected. Studies have shown that falsehoods spread more quickly on social media than factual stories. In one study done by researchers at MIT, it took the truth six times as long as a falsehood to reach 1,600 people (Vosoughi, Roy and Aral 2018; Fox 2018). Studies have also found that some individuals have have a more difficult time distinguishing between true and false information. In fact, false information can continue to influence a person's beliefs even after it has been proven to be a lie. Hasher and Zacks (1988) proposed the idea that some people are less likely to be able to discard information that is not relevant to their goals or personal experience, or to the task they are currently performing. While Trump was slamming the media for what he termed fake news, he was also benefiting from it on social media, where false stories about Hillary Clinton were shared by his supporters.

Campaign Issues and Election Fallout

In his speech announcing his candidacy, Trump referenced a number of issues, including violence aimed at police, Obamacare, the dangers of immigration, and China's unfair trade policies. He also called out the other Republican candidates, saying they didn't understand the economic issues facing average Americans, positioning himself as the only one who understood what was happening with "the people." "I watch the speeches of these people, and they say the sun will rise, the moon will set, all sorts of wonderful things will happen. And people are saying, "What's going on? I just want a job. Just get me a job. I don't need the rhetoric. I want a job" (Trump 2015). The Trump campaign expertly drew upon the anxiety of the white working class, many of whom were still feeling the effects of an extended recession, had not seen significant wage increases in several years, and who increasingly felt that the nation's best days were in the past, not in the future. Trump's slogan, "Make America Great Again," embodied that sentiment and became emblazoned on caps and shirts and posters, and was evocative of buttons produced by Ronald Reagan in 1980 that said "Let's make America great again," and Pat Buchanan's campaign slogan, which was "America First." The idea that the nation has fallen on hard times and needs to be reclaimed is a familiar populist narrative. "The appeal to 'the way things were' *against* 'the way things are' is in keeping with a right-wing populism. This rejects the present and mobilises the past against it—although it is an idealized past culled from a historical high point" (Knott 2020, 110). For Trump supporters, who feared losing their own importance and way of life, a call to reclaim the glory days of the past was especially captivating.

Trump also made various promises, including one that would become a familiar issue—and chant—on the campaign trail: "I would build a great wall, and nobody builds walls better than me, believe me, and I'll build them very inexpensively, I will build a great, great wall on our southern border. And I will have Mexico pay for that wall. Mark my words" (Trump 2015).

While Trump was promising a new wall, to put Americans back to work, and to end Obamacare, there were some traditional Republican issues that Trump either ignored or only mentioned in passing. Perhaps that was a recognition that his base voters didn't seem to get energized about some of the party's traditional core issues such as lowering taxes, reducing the size of government, or even free trade, which had been a central value for the Republican Party for years. But, as was pointed out earlier, Trump never seemed to have a great attachment to a particular political ideology. Instead, he seemed to theme his rallies to issues that energized a crowd and were easily understandable.

Trump also used scapegoating to lay the blame for some of the nation's problems at the feet of other countries. For instance, he said trade deals needed to be renegotiated because those who had crafted NAFTA in 1994 had not done a good job. As a self-described master negotiator, Trump cast himself in the role of the one who could "fix" NAFTA and protect the country. He pounded on issues such as making Mexico pay for building a wall to limit immigration, increasing border security, improving the economy, and ensuring the U.S. Supreme Court had more conservative justices. As Clare Malone wrote on FiveThirtyEight: "Rather, [Trump supporters] connected with the cultural signifiers the party had so cleverly carved out: guns, political incorrectness, anti-abortion sentiment, etc. Trump won the GOP primaries by giving the people what they wanted" (Malone 2020).

Trump campaigned for tax relief for middle-class Americans, and he pledged to create jobs for those who were suffering during a period of slow economic growth. He also called for simplifying the tax code. Trump supported gun rights and Second Amendment issues and the right of Americans to defend themselves, which helped earn him an endorsement from the National Rifle Association.

Trump defied the expectations of political pundits, party officials, and political scholars by winning the 2016 campaign. Although Hillary Clinton won the popular vote, Trump won 304 electoral votes to Clinton's 227. Almost every nationwide poll predicted that Clinton would win, leaving her supporters in shock after Trump's victory. There were protests against the outcome, as well as calls for recounts in some swing states. Reform candidate Jill Stein collected contributions and began the recount process, which was eventually stopped by a federal judge. (More on that is included in the chapter on Jill Stein in this book.)

It is unknown whether most of Trump's voters arrived at their voting locations having already made up their minds about who should receive their votes. A study by Kleinnijenhuis, van Hoof, and Oegema (2006) found that "citizens accrue information on a daily basis but that they will often not update their summary evaluation, for example, their intention to cast a vote for a specific party, until the moment of decision" (101–102). Trump won 81 percent of the votes of white, born-again Christian voters and defeated Clinton by a margin of almost 49 percent in the category of white males who did not have college degrees. Exit polls showed that when voters thought that the candidates were equally good or bad, they voted for change, and most of them gave their votes to Trump (Jacobson 2017). As noted before, Trump was the candidate of change for many people, and they voted accordingly.

To say that Trump's election was a surprise is an understatement. As noted before, almost all nationwide polls showed Clinton with a lead, and it was thought that Trump had fallen behind in advertising and messaging. What was unknown at that point was the amount of messaging the Trump campaign placed on social media, which reached a level never before seen in a U.S. presidential election.

Trump generated more than $250 million through online fundraising, and his campaign spent about $90 million on digital advertising. Trump's digital director, Brad Parscale, said the majority of that money went to Facebook, which is still one of the most commonly used social media sites. "Facebook and Twitter were the reason we won this thing. . . . Twitter for Mr. Trump. And Facebook for fundraising" (Lapowsky 2016). Trump's campaign poured money into Facebook advertising in a way that no candidate had ever done before, and it utilized multiple variants of advertising messages seeking the most effective ones for targeted groups of people. On any given day, "the campaign was running 40,000 to 50,000 variants of its ads, testing how they performed in different formats, with subtitles and without, and static versus video, among other small differences. On the day of the third presidential debate in October, the team ran 175,000 variations" (Lapowsky 2016). While Hillary Clinton was focusing much of her messaging on more traditional one-way media platforms, Trump's team was interacting with supporters and starting conversations with them. Supporters often shared campaign messages, pushing them through different social media outlets and into various, but sometimes overlapping, fragmented audiences. The adoption of new communication technologies is another characteristic of populist candidates, as they often come from outside the mainstream and are looking for ways to get their messages to a wider audience in a less expensive fashion. This was certainly the case for Trump, who placed most of his messages on social media.

The role of Russia in creating and distributing divisive messages to Americans during the 2016 election has been a topic of much debate. Evidence has been found that Russian trolls sponsored a disinformation campaign aimed at the U.S. presidential election. A cybersecurity firm analyzed almost 10 million tweets from that time period and found the group used Twitter accounts to push out fake news that looked as if it had originated from regional news outlets or political organizations (Dilanian 2019). The messages originated from a St. Petersburg, Russia based company called Internet Research Agency. U.S. intelligence agencies said the messages may have been a Russian-government sponsored campaign designed to help Trump get elected. Researchers found that propaganda efforts were aimed at both conservative and liberal Americans in an attempt to influence potential voters.

While Trump may have gained the upper hand in using social media and new technology, his rhetoric still caused divisions in the country. Democratic reaction to his election was swift and negative, and for many Americans it never gave way to acceptance of the election's outcome. Many Clinton supporters believed that Trump was elected with the help of Russians through social media manipulation, while others argued that any impact the Russian interference might have produced would have resulted in a minimal influence on the election itself. Nate Silver of FiveThirtyEight said following the election that actions such as the FBI letter regarding Clinton's email server at the end of October probably had more influence on the election's outcome, given the messages from Russian trolls actually seemed to be consistent with the reasons Clinton lost (Silver 2018).

Lasting Changes?

One of the questions remaining from Trump's 2016 election is whether it will spark lasting changes in the way candidates campaign for president, or if this election will be viewed as an aberration. It seems very likely that a greater reliance on social media will become normal in presidential campaigns, especially given Trump's ability to raise money through that medium. Another thing that makes social media so attractive is that it is relatively inexpensive, especially compared to television advertising. One of the current challenges in political campaigns is the fragmentation of the advertising market. A candidate can no longer assume that a message on television will reach a cross section of potential voters. More people than ever have decided to use streaming entertainment and rarely, if ever, watch broadcast television. The numbers for cable television are also falling, although television might be a decent alternative if a candidate is looking to reach older voters who might not have a social media presence. However, putting messages online will become the best way to reach most Americans, partially because it is so much easier to target groups of people with similar ideas, beliefs, and interests.

The question of whether future candidates will adopt a similar rhetorical approach is more difficult to answer. Trump's rhetoric is, essentially, Trump. It is difficult to imagine another candidate being as blunt, bombastic, and combative as Trump. But it does seem likely that Trump has ushered in an era in which presidential candidates can swear, antagonize, and "shoot from the hip" in an effort to seem authentic. In the 2020 presidential campaign, there were instances in which former Vice President Joe Biden used colorful language, subtly attacked Trump's children, and was accused of running a racist ad in which he said Trump was too soft on China in regard to COVID-19, implying that the Chinese were untrustworthy.

Later chapters will look more closely at how the discourse and tactics of renegades George C. Wallace and Pat Buchanan and of third-party candidate Ross Perot may have influenced Trump. He also inherited a GOP that had been trending more conservative, thanks to Newt Gingrich, which will also be discussed. While both Shirley Chisholm and Jesse Jackson were outsiders who exerted pressure to move the Democratic Party to the left, Trump was an outsider who pushed the Republican Party to the right.

As the first true outsider elected president of the United States, Trump's legacy will be complicated. He will probably bring changes to the campaign process in the nation, but his political baggage could pose a danger to future outsider and populist candidates.

REFERENCES

Alfaro, Alyana. 2016. "Will Christie Drop Out After New Hampshire?" *Observer*. Jan. 28, 2016. https://observer.com/2016/01/will-christie-drop-out-after-new-hampshire/.

Bas, Ozen and Maria Elizabeth Grabe. 2015. "Sound Bite." ResearchGate. https://www.researchgate.net/publication/283494592_Sound_Bite.

Benac, Nancy and Calvin Woodward. "Trump Campaign Created Own Rules on Sexual Harassment." *Associated Press*. Nov. 19, 2017. https://apnews.com/d861d0dab11447f08f532d066be5a59c.

Denton, Robert Jr., Judith S. Trent, and Robert V. Friedenberg. 2019. *"Political Campaign Communication, Principles and Practices, 9th Edition."* Lanham, MD: Rowman & Littlefield.

Dilanian, Ken. 2019. "Russian Trolls Who Interfered in 2016 U.S. Election Also Made Ad Money, Report Says." *NBC News*. June 5, 2019.

Elving, Ron. 2016. "Trump Confounds the Pros, Connects With Just the Right Voters." *NPR.org*. Elections. Nov. 9, 2016. https://www.npr.org/2016/11/09/501387988/trump-confounds-the-pros-connects-with-just-the-right-voters.

Friedman, Uri. 2017. What Is a Populist? And is Donald Trump One? *The Atlantic*, February 27, 2017. https://www.theatlantic.com/international/archive/2017/02/what-is-populist-trump/516525/.

Fox, Maggie. 2018. "Fake News: Lies Spread Faster on Social Media Than Truth Does." *NBC News*. March 8, 2018. https://www.nbcnews.com/health/health-news/fake-news-lies-spread-faster-social-media-truth-does-n854896.

Gass, Nick. 2015. "Trump Dominates GOP Field in Name ID." *Politico*. July 24, 2015. https://www.politico.com/story/2015/07/poll-gop-2016-name-recognition-donald-trump-jeb-bush-120573.

Hasher, Lynn and Rose Zacks. 1988. Working Memory, Comprehension, and Aging: A Review and New View. In *The Psychology of Learning and Motivation: Advances in Research and Theory*, edited by G. H. Bower, 193–225. New York: Academic Press.

Helmore, Edward. 2017. "How Trump's Political Playbook Evolved Since He First Ran for President in 2000." *The Guardian*. Feb. 5, 2017. https://www.theguardian.com/us-news/2017/feb/05/donald-trump-reform-party-2000-president.

Jacobson, Gary C. 2017. "The Triumph of Polarized Partisanship in 2016: Donald Trump's Improbable Victory." *Political Science Quarterly* 132, (1): 9–41.

Jamieson, Kathleen Hall and Doron Taussig. 2017. "Disruption, Demonization, Deliverance, and Norm Destruction: The Rhetorical Signature of Donald J. Trump." *Political Science Quarterly* 132, (4): 619–650. https://doi.org/10.1002/polq.12699.

Kayam, Orly. 2018. "The Readability and Simplicity of Donald Trump's Language." *Political Studies Review*, 16, (1): 73–88.

Kleinnijenhuis, Jan, Anita M. J. van Hoof and Dirk Oegema. 2006. Negative News and the Sleeper Effect of Distrust. *The Harvard International Journal of Press/Politics* 11, 2 (Spring): 86–104.

Knott, Andy. 2020. A Manifesto and Populism? In *The Populist Manifesto*, edited by Emmy Eklundh and Andy Knott, 107–122. London: Rowman & Littlefield.

Lapowsky, Issie. 2016. "Here's How Facebook Actually Won Trump the Presidency." *Wired*. Nov. 15, 2016. https://www.wired.com/2016/11/facebook-won-trump-election-not-just-fake-news/.

Malone, Clare. 2020. "How Trump Changed America." FiveThirtyEight. Nov. 7, 2020. https://fivethirtyeight.com/features/how-trump-changed-america/?utm_source=pocket&utm_medium=email&utm_campaign=pockethits.

Montgomery, Martin. 2017. Post-truth politics? Authenticity, Populism and the Electoral Discourses of Donald Trump. *Journal of Language and Politics* 16 (4): 619–639.

Mudde, Cas. 2004. The Popular Zeitgeist. *Government & Opposition* 39, (3): 541–563.

Pew Research Center. 2016. "Election 2016: Campaigns as a Direct Source of News." July 18, 2016. https://www.journalism.org/2016/07/18/candidates-differ-in-their-use-of-social-media-to-connect-with-the-public/.

Saad, Lydia. 2016. "Trump and Clinton Finish With Historically Poor Images." Gallup. Nov. 8, 2016. https://news.gallup.com/poll/197231/trump-clinton-finish-historically-poor-images.aspx.

Sarlin, Benjy and Alex Seitz-Wald. 2016. "Analysis: Trump May Have Had the Worst Week in Presidential Campaign History." *NBC News*. Oct. 1, 2016. https://www.nbcnews.com/politics/2016-election/analysis-trump-may-have-had-worst-week-presidential-campaign-history-n658071.

Shearer, Elisa. 2016. "Candidates' Social Media Outpaces Their Websites and Emails as an Online Campaign News Source." Pew Research Center. July 20, 2016. https://www.pewresearch.org/fact-tank/2016/07/20/candidates-social-media-outpaces-their-websites-and-emails-as-an-online-campaign-news-source/.

Silver, Nate. 2018. "How Much Did Russian Interference Affect the 2016 Election?" FiveThirtyEight. Feb. 16, 2018. https://fivethirtyeight.com/features/how-much-did-russian-interference-affect-the-2016-election/.

Street, John. 2019. What Is Donald Trump? Forms of 'Celebrity' in Celebrity Politics. *Political Studies Review* 17, no. 1 (February): 3–13. https://doi.org/10.1177/1478929918772995.

Taylor, Jessica. 2016. "You Can Do Anything: In 2005 Tape, Trump Brags About Groping, Kissing Women." *NPR*. Oct. 7, 2016 https://www.npr.org/2016/10/07/497087141/donald-trump-caught-on-tape-making-vulgar-remarks-about-women.

Trump, Donald. 2015. "Here's Donald Trump's Announcement Speech." *TIME.com*. June 16, 2015. https://time.com/3923128/donald-trump-announcement-speech/.

Van Dijk, Teun A. 1998. *Ideology*. London: SAGE.

Vosoughi, Soroush, Deb Roy and Sinan Aral. 2018. "The Spread of True and False News Online." *Science* 359, 6380. DOI: 10.1126/science.aap9559.

PART III

Third-Party Candidates

Chapter 7

Ross Perot

"CRAZY" OUTSIDER TAKES MESSAGE DIRECTLY TO AMERICA

Henry Ross Perot was a political fireball from Texas—a self-made billionaire who became one of the most successful outside presidential candidates in history. Perot both regaled and amused audiences with his simple, business-like political presentations that were heavy on charts and graphs, including thirty-minute infomercials in which he would use a pointer to direct viewers' attention to pie charts and bar graphs.

Perot made his money through founding and building Electronic Data Systems, known as EDS, a company that provided data processing services for other companies. He took the company public in 1968 and then sold controlling interest to General Motors in 1984 for $2.4 billion. In 1988 he and a group of investors then established Perot Systems, an information technology services provider. In 2009, the company was sold to Dell, Inc. for just under $4 billion.

Perot approached the nation's problems from the standpoint of a business-man, which was something he knew and understood. He had already been involved in U.S. foreign policy before he entered politics. A graduate of the U.S. Naval Academy, he made several trips to foreign nations on behalf of the U.S. government, including meeting with North Vietnamese officials in 1969. He was involved in the issue of prisoners of war and soldiers who were missing in action in Southeast Asia, and he opposed the United States entering the Gulf War in 1990. When the Iranian government captured and arrested two of his employees in 1979, Perot financed a rescue mission to get them back to the United States. This was recounted in the book "On Wings of Eagles" by Ken Follett and made into a television miniseries in 1986. This reinforced Perot's reputation as a person of action and a man of principle who understood loyalty to his employees.

In 1992, George H.W. Bush was running for re-election, but was facing competition within his own party from conservatives because of what was seen as his reneging on his promise of no new taxes. On the Democratic side, there was competition between Gov. Bill Clinton, former California Gov. Jerry Brown, and Massachusetts Sen. Paul Tsongas. When Perot saw the

United State's national debt rising while the growth in business productivity declined, he became alarmed. In February 1992, he appeared on Larry King's CNN show and said that he would run for president if volunteers could get him on all 50 state ballots. They did, and he began his first quest for the White House, which became the most successful independent or third-party presidential campaign since Teddy Roosevelt ran as the Bull Moose candidate in 1912.

PEROT THE "CRAZY" OUTSIDER'S DISCOURSE

Ross Perot began the 1992 race with an unprecedented show of support from grassroots America. This ragtag group of volunteers was able to get his name on the ballot as an independent candidate in all fifty states, and that's something that had not happened in seventy years. According to a Washington Post story that ran after his death in 2019, Perot hired the Home Shopping Network to deal with the huge number of calls from volunteers for his presidential campaign (Mele, Rapoport and Stone 2019). HSN had 1,200 phone lines, and after one appearance on "The Phil Donahue Show," a quarter of a million people called his toll-free number to volunteer to help with the campaign. These were not seasoned political operatives, either. It was reported that two-thirds of the callers had no experience as a volunteer for a political candidate or any experience with a political party. In short, they were political newcomers who were eager to support this candidate who seemed to speak frankly and directly to them.

Perot's populist rhetoric seemed to appeal to a variety of potential supporters: both blue-collar workers and social moderates, as well as social conservatives and anti-NAFTA (North American Free Trade Agreement) voters. He railed against economic policies and illegal immigration, advocated cutting the defense budget and raising taxes on gasoline, all in an effort to work down the national deficit. He said the wealthy should pay a higher tax rate, and that legislators should hammer out balanced budgets. He said the country had been betrayed by the elites, which is a classic populist argument (Mudde 2004). The future of the country was at stake, he said, and only the people of this nation could stave off disaster.

His homespun delivery delighted some people, while making others cringe. He railed about the national debt, saying this in his book "United We Stand, How We Can Take Back our Country": "The debt is like a crazy aunt we keep down in the basement. All the neighbors know she's there, but nobody wants to talk about her. If we allow the debt to grow, however, we are impoverishing ourselves" (Perot 1992, 8). This sort of discourse made audiences smile, but it also described a serious issue in terms that were understandable to many voters. Ton and Endress (2001) characterize this sort of rhetoric as "folk criticism," a form of discourse identified by Kenneth Burke (1937) that refers to experiences transferred from one area of life and used as metaphors for another area. "Indeed, among the most salient features of Perot's talk was his couching of political issues in the metaphors of down-home, everyday life: sports, illness, family relationships, and domestic chores like car repair, cooking, and housework" (Ton and Endress 2001, 289). They also noted his tendency to use humor and self-deprecating comments, which they argue helped him build trust with potential voters.

His folksy discourse, however, was also a constant reminder that he was an outsider to Washington--someone who hadn't been corrupted by the processes or political deals. He often repeated "I'm not a politician," ostensibly as a way to reinforce his populist credentials. He also often referred to "going to Washington," which reminds voters that "he is spatially and temporally separated from the locus of political control, and thus, by extension, not privy to its influences" (Livengood 1997). Perot used a variety of rhetorical appeals that are common to populists, including self-deprecation, presenting a rough-around-the-edges persona, and frequent reminders that he is the person who can wrestle control back from "the elites" who are running the country without consulting "the people." In some ways, he was reminiscent of Huey Long, but with a more "Aw, shucks" kind of personality. This emphasis on the leader is important, as this person must appear to be "uncontaminated by politics as usual" (Casullo 2020, 28). As Casullo points out, a populist leader communicates to "the people" that he or she is only in politics because the people have been betrayed.

Perot often told his listeners that he wasn't the smartest person in the world, but he was good at finding smart people to work with him, as he did in this speech to the Reform Party in 1996 when accepting its nomination for president: "It's important all of you to know that I am a very ordinary person of average intelligence, and all of my success has come from surrounding myself with people who are far more intelligent than I am, and they have carried me from victory to victory to victory to victory" (Wall Street Journal 1996). He makes a pledge to those in attendance that demonstrates his belief that he has become a spokesperson for "the people." "I'm here today because I am absolutely determined to keep the dream alive and we will pass on a better, stronger country to the next generation." This intimates that Perot considered himself the one person who could "fix" the problems that had beset the country.

Perot's rhetoric always approached the national government as if it were a business, and running a business is what he excelled at, so he could assume the standpoint of an expert. In his 1992 book, he also stated: "The United States is the largest and most complex business enterprise in the history of mankind. Elected officials like to say that government can't be run like a business. I can see why. In business, people are held accountable. In Washington, nobody is held accountable" (Perot 1992, 11). He referred to Americans as the "owners" of the nation, and said the the owners of the country were the only ones who could make America strong again. What was needed was a new CEO, and he offered himself up as an alternative to politics as usual. This approach would later be echoed by Donald J. Trump when he ran for president in 2016 as a political outsider.

Perot and Trump shared a number of rhetorical approaches. Perot was fond of saying that he sacrificed time with his family to run for office, and that, while he had been fortunate in business, he was a billionaire. Trump echoed these same comments while running for president, and even while he was in office. He often reminded people that he gave up a nice life in order to go to Washington and work for them. Perot may have been the originator of those comments, but they also suited Trump's personality and discourse. Another common metaphor that Perot and Trump shared was the focus on the American Dream. Even though Perot was probably the most wealthy candidate in the presidential race, he was careful to remind people that he came from a modest background and had achieved the American Dream. "The 'American Dream' is made a tangible reality, for Perot, a self-made man untainted by governmental influences, paints himself as the flesh-and-blood metaphor for Everyman or Everywoman, and thus a man particularly suited to oversee a true democracy" (Livengood 1997). Similar comments were made by Trump, who intimated that he had worked hard and built up his companies, which was, in effect, the culmination of the American Dream.

CAMPAIGN TACTICS

The matter-of-fact comments made by Perot seemed to speak directly to concerns shared by many Americans, even those who identified with one of the major political parties. During his 1992 presidential campaign, there was less of a partisan divide than now exists in the United States, and a more neutral attitude toward the Republican and Democratic parties. "Although there was no sudden change in the electorate's attitude toward the parties, there is ample evidence to suggest that compared to the 1950s and 1960s, Americans were indeed more neutral toward the major parties, and that this neutrality allowed a candidate such as Ross Perot to win a substantial share of the vote" (Gold 1995, 768). Distrust of the government was found to be significantly related to support for Perot's presidential campaign, but it is unclear if that was the main basis of support for Perot (Gold 1995).

Millions of Americans saw Perot's political messages, but they often took a different form than previous political communication. Perot pioneered the political use of what we now call "infotainment" when he used thirty-minute and sixty-minute commercials to speak directly to the American people. This format fit well with his folksy way of addressing issues and explaining how they could be solved. Devlin (1997) found that Perot's strategy in both 1992 and 1996 was to use time slots on major networks. For instance, in 1992, Perot purchased eleven half-hour and four one-hour time slots. In 1996, the time slots he was offered were different and more expensive, so he instead purchased nine half-hour and only one sixty-minute time slot. In these infomercials, he was often sitting next to charts holding a pointer and speaking—without a teleprompter—about what he saw as the nation's problems. Thousands of Americans watched his ads and bought his book, "United We Stand," which he published in 1992. The political establishment, though, was not impressed.

"He was kind of like a huckster or a medicine man or a guy throwing elixirs out the window—and then he brought out his charts," was how Alan Simpson, a former Republican senator from Wyoming, described Perot's rhetoric (USA Today 2012). Simpson had reason to dislike Perot, as his campaign likely pulled votes from incumbent president George H.W. Bush. Larry Sabato, the director of the Center for Politics at the University of Virginia, agrees that Perot damaged the elder Bush's re-election campaign early in the race, which helped Bill Clinton on his path to victory, but also says that Perot took votes from both of those candidates (Sabato and Kondik 2015).

Perot made several appearances on the "Larry King Live" show, often encouraging viewers to send him $5 to help finance his campaign. He rejected financial donations for more than that amount, and reportedly spent more than $400,000 of his own money the first month. He utilized infomercials and free TV time, such as that on national talk shows, and gave speeches that aired on C-SPAN to leverage his money. Those running the campaign lamented that he was unwilling to spend the millions of dollars on advertising that they advised was necessary to win the race. Gold (1995) argues that Perot's willingness to spend his own money — $69 million in the 1992 race—was "the single most important factor in explaining the Perot phenomenon" (770). Much of the money was used to buy advertising time which allowed Perot to keep his messages in front of the American people. Other third-party candidates in the race did not have access to a similar amount of money.

The media landscape was changing in the early 1990s, as Perot demonstrated with his straight-to-the-people informercials. Bypassing the mainstream media allowed Perot to speak directly to the American public, which was a novel idea at the time. The news media was blamed by both Republicans and Democrats as being unfair (Dalton, Beck and Huckfelt

1998), which is perhaps not an uncommon claim for politicians. But there was also a rise in alternative media, especially in the number of political talk shows on radio. In particular, Rush Limbaugh, who had a syndicated radio show with 15–20 million listeners every week (Kurtz 1996), was exerting an unknown degree of impact on elections. Some scholars labeled the new paradigm of mass media that was unfolding at the time "constructionist," meaning that people construct meanings about events from a wide variety of media choices (Barker and Knight 2000; Neuman, Just and Crigler 1992). This was destined to continue, as the expansion of the Internet and World Wide Web continued and social media emerged as an influence on politics in the twenty-first century. News media in particular have become less objective and instead have returned to a more partisan brand of journalism. Barker and Knight found that Limbaugh's radio show may have exerted a degree of influence over how Perot was viewed by some parts of the public. "Habitual Limbaugh listening is associated with a substantial drop in affect toward Perot" (2000, 163). Given that they state almost one-fifth of American voters in 1994 listened to Limbaugh's show on a regular basis, the impact of his negative comments regarding Perot is worth consideration.

In June 1992, Perot was at the top of a Gallup poll with 39 percent of the vote. He was leading both Clinton and Bush in the polls. But by mid-July, the numbers were slipping, and Perot seemed preoccupied. In July, just before the Democratic National Convention, Perot unexpectedly dropped out of the race. He initially cited his belief that the Democratic Party had been re-energized and that attention of both parties was now focused on the economy, which was his main concern. However, he jumped back into the race 11 weeks later. After his return in October—only one month before the national election—he announced that Admiral James Stockdale, an American war hero and former POW in Vietnam, would be his official running mate, and he began spending millions of dollars on television ads.

The eleven-week break cost him dearly. When he returned to the race, he had lost much of his initial momentum, and many of his supporters had migrated to other candidates. Yet, his TV infomercials still pulled in viewers. He aired one in early October, the month before the election, in which he lectured the American people on economic policies and problems. More people watched this ad than the major-league baseball game that followed it. He used his homespun anecdotes and snappy sound bites to tell Americans what needed to be done.

Some argue that choosing Stockdale as his running mate was a decision that cost Perot many voters. Stockdale took part in the vice presidential debate, and most termed his performance disastrous. He apparently only had one week's notice about the debate, and he had no formal preparation for the event. "Indeed, in his brief televised appearance, Stockdale prompted many citizens to reassess their earlier thinking regarding the merits of Perot's folk criticism" (Tonn and Endress 2001, 296). It seemed that Stockdale's unfocused and confusing performance caused some people to lose faith in Perot's ability to make good choices that would benefit the nation.

Unlike Stockdale, Perot excelled in his three debate performances. This was the first time since 1980 that a third-party candidate was allowed to join the presidential debates. Perot brought his folk criticism to the debates, and three out of four polls named him the winner of the first debate. He also performed well in the other two debates, and this series of debates averaged 90 million viewers for each event. It is widely believed that Perot benefitted greatly from the debate performances, and that his performances in the debates drove up the viewership of his informercials (Devlin 1997).

Perot's last infomercial in 1992 aired two days before the election, and it was titled "Chicken Feathers, Deep Voodoo, and the American Dream." It slammed Bill Clinton for his role in creating 200,000 jobs as governor of Arkansas. As Perot pointed out, many of those jobs were in the poultry industry, one noted for low wages and harsh working conditions. The chairman of the largest chicken producer in the state, Tyson Foods, contributed to Bill Clinton's presidential campaign, and the former governor and his wife took rides on the company's planes. In his distinct Perot-like delivery, this information became a warning. "If we decide to take this level of business-creating capability nationwide, we'll all be plucking chickens for a living" (Waxman 2019).

Late in October, Perot revealed that he had actually dropped out of the race earlier in the year because President George H.W. Bush's campaign was planning to smear his youngest daughter and disrupt her wedding, which took place in August 1992. He also accused the Republicans of hiring someone to wiretap his computerized stock trading company in an attempt to ruin him financially. To many, this smacked of a belief in conspiracy theories, a charge that had already been made against him in the past. Some argue that his opponents knew he had a tendency to believe in conspiracies and they endeavored to relate this story to him in hopes that his campaign would self-destruct (Ostrow and Gladstone 1992).

In an article in the Los Angeles Times in October 1992, Marlin Fitzwater, president Bush's spokesperson, called the allegation "preposterous." He said: "The stuff about his daughter is just crazy. There haven't been any dirty tricks against Ross Perot." Margaret Tutwiler, the White House communications director, said the charges were "loony" (Richter and Fritz 1992). Perot admitted he had no proof, but said he had believed the threats to be credible. He stressed that he kept the information from his daughter, but told her after the wedding, and she encouraged him to return to the race. Bush campaign aides said the FBI investigated the charges, but never found any evidence of a plot against Perot's family. The unorthodox candidate then proceeded to adopt the Patsy Cline song "Crazy" as his official campaign theme song. On the final day of the campaign, video showed Perot dancing to the song with his wife and their daughters.

It is unclear what impact the allegations had on election day. Perot failed to win any states, but did finish second in both Maine and Utah. He finished third in the national contest, behind Clinton (the winner) and then-President Bush. He received just under 19 percent of the popular vote, which was the most won by a non-major party candidate since Theodore Roosevelt in 1912.

Perot's impact on the election has been a source of debate for many years, as some argue that he might have pulled enough votes away to cost then-president Bush the re-election. Others argue that isn't correct, because an analysis of election-day votes shows that Perot pulled votes from both Bush and Clinton. In general, Perot seemed to resonate with voters who were tired of gridlock and slickly packaged politicians and who were looking for a more authentic candidate. The straight-talking Texan shunned any political packaging and went around the mainstream news outlets to speak directly to Americans. His presence in the election seemed to impact the tenor of the election, with both the Republican and Democratic candidates pursuing more issue-oriented campaigns than usual. "The recession aroused the electorate to demand change, but it was the eccentric billionaire who managed to both increase and channel that arousal in ways that changed the expectations and behaviors of voters and the campaign behavior of candidates" (Buchanan 1995, 307).

Perot was one of the first candidates to use electronic town halls, and he was one of the few third-party candidates to participate in presidential debates. But he was unable to secure a consistent and loyal voting base. ". . . even among voters who ranked Perot first both before and after the election, one out of eight reports voting for one of the major party candidates" (Abramson, et al. 1995, 363). Paul A. Beck argues that robust social network support never materialized for Perot. "To take the unconventional step of voting for a third-party candidate, it is important for voters to have others in their immediate social environment who share their third-party proclivities" (Beck 2002, 329). When potential voters look around and don't find support for a third-party candidate in their own social networks, then those voters might decide that voting for the third-party candidate would be a wasted vote. Whether voters were turned off by Perot's leaving the election and returning, did not see him as a good fit for the presidency, or felt that voting for an independent candidate would be a wasted vote, he was unable to turn his initial popular support into success on election day.

Following his loss in 1992, he focused his attention on defeating NAFTA and continued to work with his United We Stand group. In 1995, he formed the Reform Party, which gave him a platform for the 1996 presidential election.

PEROT'S CAMPAIGN ISSUES

The presidential campaign of 1996 came after mid-term elections that saw Republicans sweep control of both houses of Congress for the first time in 40 years. Republicans had popularized their "Contract with America," which echoed many of Ross Perot's 1992 campaign issues, such as a balanced budget amendment and line-item veto, welfare reform, tax cuts for families, and a pledge to roll back government regulations and create jobs. The 10-point program was signed by more than three hundred Republican candidates who said that if they broke the contract, they should be voted out of office.

President Bill Clinton was running for re-election, and Sen. Bob Dole was the eventual Republican nominee. Into this mix strode Ross Perot, the nominee for the Reform Party, who saw himself building on the momentum he achieved four years earlier. Only that momentum no longer seemed to exist.

The Republicans had already capitalized on the anger and frustration that was uncovered by the Perot campaign in 1992. They used it to sweep Republicans into office during the midterm elections in 1994 by pushing the "Contract with America." Perot raised the same issues, but found voters less interested in them, especially since the economy seemed to be healthy and more people were working. For a populist message such as Perot's to succeed, there must be a receptive audience. During periods of relative calm, when there is no perceived crisis, "there is no demand for populism, even if a populist leader *supplies* it" (Knott 2020, 17). Therefore, Perot could talk about his issues and warn Americans about the nation's crisis, but voters weren't as interested anymore.

He bought time on television and once again talked directly to Americans about what needed to be done to fix the problems. The messages in the 1996 campaign were programmed differently, with a "commercial-within-a-commercial" format. It was akin to beginning the informercial with a political advertisement. Other stand-alone advertising spots were used within the body of the infomercial to break up the long message. Perot's infomercial graphics had been upgraded, with one of them featuring states of the union flying in together to form pieces of a puzzle that fit together. On this United States map, there were twelve national issues that he was addressing through a discussion of the country's economy and the lack of high-paying jobs. "We cannot afford to have our best young minds sitting on the sideline," he intones. "We must create good jobs for them now" (Perot 1996). He goes on to explain that, even if a nation has a strong job and tax base, it cannot move forward without a "strong, moral, ethical base." In this particular ad, he is joined by his vice-presidential running mate, Dr. Pat Choate, an American economist and policy analyst. They sit at a round table and discuss issues such as U.S. trade deals and deficits, complete with bar charts and graphs. However, the format and the candidate seemed to have lost their uniqueness. "With his base not being a priority, having half the media budget of last time, and most important, having been excluded from the debates, Perot achieved but 8 percent of the vote" (Devlin 1997, 1078–1079).

Those who paid attention to Perot in this election were different from those who supported him four years earlier. "Perot supporters are 'less well-off and slightly less-educated,'" declared Perot's former pollster. "They have a more blue-collar feel, less of a suburban feel. Some suburban voters looked at him and decided he wasn't presidential" (Feldman 1996). The reason for that, many said, was because he left the race four years earlier, only to return several weeks later. They didn't see his actions as presidential, which prompted them to look elsewhere for a candidate to support. In the 2016 race, some of these Perot supporters probably saw a similar candidate in Donald J. Trump, who garnered support among lesser-educated Americans, and particularly among men in that group.

Perot had also made enemies of some of his early 1992 supporters. Many of the early organizers found themselves removed from campaigns and campaign outlets and replaced with paid workers or other volunteers. Some of them sued Perot, and several of them said they found that Perot's way of running his campaign was built around those he knew and trusted and found loyal. "God help us if this bird ever became President because he'd rule like a dictator," said one deposed county coordinator (Human Events 1996).

It was also more difficult for Perot to draw the attention of the media than it had been four years earlier. The media never warmed to his populism, and even in the 1992 campaign he often found himself painted as a caricature in newspapers and magazines. "Perot is the closest American approximation of fascism ever to have a real shot at the Oval Office," was a warning issued by the New Republic (Frank 2019).

Perot was also shut out of the debates, a format in which he did well in 1992. In fact, many thought he won the first debate that year. But in 1996, he could only watch as President Clinton and Sen. Dole debated the issues on television. Public opinion polls predicted that he would only receive 5 percent of the vote, and the Commission on Presidential Debates voted unanimously to exclude him from the debates because he had no possibility of winning the election.

Perot's messages seemed to get lost during the campaign, as President Clinton and Sen. Dole moved forward with little acknowledgement that he was in the race. He had minimal impact on the national conversation, and the Reform Party was disappointed with its first nominee's run for president. In the end, Perot finished with 8 percent of the vote, less than half of what he garnered four years before.

TRACING PEROT'S LEGACY

In the end, Perot may have had a lasting impact on American politics in two different ways. First, the issues that he raised in his 1992 presidential race resonated with enough of the public that Republican Newt Gingrich decided to borrow them. The Contract with America was largely built around Perot's ideas, and this "contract" is considered to have been influential in sweeping Republicans into both the House and Senate during the midterm elections of 1994.

Stone and Rapoport (2001) argue that Perot had a lasting impact on Republican elections until at least 2000. "Our general claim is that Perot activists and voters responded to the Republican bid by shifting their support disproportionately to GOP candidates" (53). In particular, they argue that without the support of those who joined the Perot movement in 1992, the shift to a Republican majority in the House of Representatives in 1994 would have been unlikely. In 2000, they theorize that "the likelihood that Bob Dole in 1996 or George W. Bush in 2000 would carry a non-southern state increased dramatically as the state's 1992 vote for Perot increased" (55). In other words, Perot supporters were still expressing a preference for Republican candidates eight years after his first presidential campaign.

A second way he influenced politics is that Perot was the first candidate to realize that technology had moved in the direction of allowing candidates to go around mainstream media and directly address the American public. While his videos may now appear a bit cheesy and lecturing, at the time Americans seemed fascinated with the idea of having a candidate speak directly to them about what he saw were serious concerns for the nation. Many of them seemed to make an emotional connection with Perot, even though his infomercials were more like boardroom presentations, rather than pulling heartstrings. However, some of his shorter advertisements contained an emotional appeal, and "emotional cues can take the voter to a place that facts alone may not always reach" (Lau and Rovner 2009, 291). As technology has continued to evolve, we have seen candidates using the Internet to rally support, raise money, and place messages on social media aimed at particular demographic groups. In many ways, Perot laid the foundation for that path.

Another part of his legacy was discussed in an earlier chapter, but does bear some repeating. Watching Perot from the sidelines was Donald J. Trump, who would later use some of Perot's approaches and become a political figure that, in many ways, resembled Ross Perot. Several political pundits have noted the similarities between the two men, while also admitting their differences. There is little doubt that Trump was taking notes when Perot was campaigning, and that he adopted some of Perot's rhetoric—including the push to remove career politicians from Washington, a focus on the nation's economy, and a declared hatred for NAFTA—in his outsider presidential campaign. They each pursued a populist approach, both in discourse and in performance, with each man identifying "the elites" and "the establishment" as dishonoring the average American and endangering the nation. Ross Perot has been described as "the father of Trump," and called "a secular prophet who in his time anticipated and personified the disruptive currents of the present" (Harris 2019). If that sounds familiar, it is because Trump also rode that current of dissatisfaction in his 2016 race.

Political scientist Larry Sabato said "elements of style link Trump, Perot and Buchanan" (Sabato 2016). Both Perot and Trump were brash and blunt, although Trump dished out insults often, while Perot had a more folksy delivery. Trump also adopted a similar strategy as Perot by going around the mainstream media and using a more direct way to send his messages to Americans. While social media did not exist when Perot was campaigning, his television infomercials were the forerunners of Trump's Tweets and Facebook posts.

Perot will also be remembered for establishing the Reform Party, which is still a functioning third party and named Rocky De La Fuente, a businessman from California, as its presidential nominee in 2020.

While Perot was unsuccessful in his presidential campaigns, he did have a lasting impact on politics in the United States that is still rippling through the nation.

REFERENCES

Abramson, Paul R., John H. Aldrich, Phil Paolino and David W. Rohde. 1995. Third-Party and Independent Candidates in American Politics: Wallace, Anderson, and Perot. *Political Science Quarterly* 110, no. 3 (Autumn): 349–367.

Barker, David and Kathleen Knight. 2000. Political Talk Radio and Public Opinion. *Public Opinion Quarterly* 64, no. 2 (August): 149–170.

Beck, Paul A. Encouraging Political Defection: The Role of Personal Discussion Networks in Partisan Desertions to the Opposition Party and Perot Votes in 1992. *Political Behavior* 24, no. 4 (December): 309–337.

Buchanan, Bruce. 1995. A Tale of Two Campaigns or Why '92's Voters Forced a Presidential Campaign Better than '88's and How It Could Happen Again. *Political Psychology* 16, no. 2 (June): 297–319.

Burke, Kenneth. 1937. *Attitudes Toward History*. Berkeley: University of California Press.

Casullo, Maria Esperanza. 2020. Populism and Myth. In *The Populist Manifesto*, edited by Emmy Eklundh and Andy Knott, 25–38. London: Rowman & Littlefield.

Dalton, Russell J., Paul A. Beck and Robert Huckfelt. 1998. Partisan Cues and the Media: Information Flows in the 1992 Presidential Election. *American Political Science Review* 92, no. 1 (March): 111–126.

Devlin, Patrick L. 1997. Contrasts in Presidential Campaign Commercials of 1996. *American Behavioral Scientist* 40, no. 8 (August): 1058–1084.

Feldman, Linda. 1996. "Perot's Back, but Support Has Shifted Since '92 Run." *Christian Science Monitor*. July 15, 1996. https://www.csmonitor.com/1996/0715/071596.us.us.5.html.

Frank, T. A. 2019. "What Ross Perot Got Right About America." *Vanity Fair*. July 9, 2019. https://www.vanityfair.com/news/2019/07/what-ross-perot-got-right-about-america.

Gold, Howard J. 1995. Third Party Voting in Presidential Elections: A Study of Perot, Anderson, and Wallace. *Political Research Quarterly* 48, no. 4 (December): 751–773.

Harris, John F. 2019. "Ross Perot—The Father of Trump." *Politico*. July 9, 2019. https://www.politico.com/story/2019/07/09/ross-perot-the-father-of-trump-1404720.

Human Events. 1996. "The Unraveling of Ross Perot?" April 26, 1996. Academic Search Complete.

Knott, Andy. 2020. Populism: The Politics of a Definition. In *The Populist Manifesto*, edited by Emmy Eklundh and Andy Knott, 9–23. London: Rowman & Littlefield.

Kurtz, Howard. 1996. *Hot Air: All Talk All The Time*. New York: Times Books.

Lau, Richard R. and Ivy Brown Rovner. 2009. Negative Campaigning. *Annual Review of Political Science* 12: 285–306.

Levine, Kenneth J. 2001. Election 2000, the Presidential Debates, and Nader. *American Behavioral Scientist* 44, no. 12 (August): 2219–2231.

Livengood, Mark R. 1997. Pitching Politics for the People: An Analysis of the Metaphoric Speech of H. Ross Perot. *Western Folklore* 56, no. 3–4 (Summer-Autumn 1997): 259–265.

Mele, Nicco, Ron Rapoport, and Walt Stone. 2019. "Ross Perot Was the Original Viral Candidate." *The Washington Post*. July 11, 2019. https://www.washingtonpost.com

Mudde, Cas. 2004. The Popular Zeitgeist. *Government & Opposition* 39, (3): 541–563.

Neuman, W. Russel, Marion R. Just and Ann N. Crigler. 1992. *Common Knowledge: News and the Construction of Political Meaning*. Chicago: University of Chicago Press.

Ostrow, Ronald J. and Mark Gladstone. 1992. FBI Wrestles With Tale by Perot 'Informer': Intrigue: Agency Director Tries to Settle Matter of a Failed Sting, 'Dirty Tricks' and a Man of Many Stories. *Los Angeles Times*. Oct. 27, 1992. https://www.latimes.com/archives/la-xpm-1992-10-27-mn-792-story.html.

Perot, Ross. 1992. *United We Stand: How We Can Take Back our Country*. Westport, CT.: Hyperion.

Perot, Ross. 1996. Ross Perot Campaign Video from 1996 Presidential Campaign. https://www.youtube.com/watch?v=QTJJliNNw7k.

Richter, Paul and Sara Fritz. 1992. "Perot Charges Plot Forced Him Out; 'Loony,' GOP Says: Campaign: He accuses Bush Camp of Plan to Smear Daughter and Disrupt Her Wedding, and Says He Quit Race to Protect Her. Texan Offers No Proof for Allegations." *Los Angeles Times*. Oct. 26, 1992. https://www.latimes.com/archives/la-xpm-1992-10-26-mn-761-story.html.

Sabato, Larry and Kyle Kondik. 2015. "Three's Company: Who Will Join the Democrat and Republican on 2016's Presidential Ballot?" Sabato's Crystal Ball. UVA Center for Politics. Dec. 3, 2015. http://centerforpolitics.org/crystalball/articles/threes-company/.

Sabato, Larry. 2016. "Is Donald Trump the New Ross Perot? Or the Next Pat Buchanan?" Sabato's Crystal Ball, UVA Center for Politics. July 16, 2015. https://centerforpolitics.org/crystalball/articles/is-donald-trump-the-new-ross-perot-or-the-next-pat-buchanan/.

Stone, Walter J. and Ronald B. Rapoport. 2001. It's Perot Stupid! The Legacy of the 1992 Perot Movement in the Major-Party System 1994-2000. *PS: Political Science and Politics* 34, no. 1 (March): 49–58.

Ton, Mari Boor and Valerie Endress. 2001. Looking Under the Hood and Tinkering with Voter Cynicism: Ross Perot and "Perspective by Incongruity." *Rhetoric & Public Affairs* 4, no. 2 (Summer): 281–308.

USA Today. 2012. "Perot's Economic Stance Resonates 20 Years Later." Oct. 1, 2012. https://www.usatoday.com/story/news/nation/2012/10/01/perot-20-years-later/1603897/.

Wall Street Journal. 1996. Text of Perot's Speech. Aug. 19, 1996.

Waxman, Olivia. 2019. "How Ross Perot Changed Political Campaigns." *Time*. July 2, 2019. https://time.com/5622818/ross-perot-dead-legacy/.

Chapter 8

Ralph Nader

CRUSADER AND POSSIBLE DEMOCRATIC SPOILER

People either love or hate Ralph Nader. Few seem to exist in the middle, although even some of his detractors will admit to a certain admiration of his many battles and victories over the years.

After the 2000 presidential election, the number of haters grew, as many felt that his presence in the race stole the election from former vice president Al Gore, thereby handing victory to George W. Bush. James Carville, a Democratic strategist and master of spin, spoke for many when he said, "I will not speak his name. I'm going to shun him. And any good Democrat, any good progressive, ought to do the same thing" (Corn 2000).

How did Nader come to be the poster child for Democratic Party hate? It's a complicated tale of accomplishment and advocacy, of hubris and being a folk hero. It's also the unusual case in which a popular outsider candidate may have been the spoiler in a presidential election.

Ralph Nader burst onto the American scene in 1965 when he published "Unsafe at Any Speed," which was an indictment of the automobile industry in the United States. He specifically condemned the Corvair, a General Motors vehicle manufactured from 1960–1969, for design flaws that could make the driver lose control (Time Magazine 1969). Nader first found out about possible design flaws in the vehicle from a letter that he received from a General Motors auto worker. He then began to research the vehicle and used it in his first book as an example of an auto industry compromise between engineering and styling that posed significant danger to the public. He cited grim statistics about the overall safety of American automobiles and campaigned for federal car-safety standards. Nader found himself on the cover of "Time" magazine, and he was given many opportunities to talk about his concerns. GM pulled the Corvair from production in 1969.

This proved to be the first of many battles that Nader would fight with American corporations and government. The son of Lebanese immigrants, Nader received an undergraduate degree from Princeton University's Woodrow Wilson School of Public and International Affairs in 1955. He then attained a law degree from Harvard in 1958. Always one to notice potential dangers to people or the environment, as a student he tried unsuccessfully to get Princeton to stop spraying DDT on its campus trees after he noticed several dead birds (Hamilton 2014). The pesticide was later banned by the federal government. While at Harvard, he reportedly grew bored and spent time traveling around the country for a closer look at Native American and migrant worker issues. He graduated from Harvard Law School with honors.

NADER'S DISCOURSE

A TIME Magazine article from 1969 labeled Nader "the self-appointed and unpaid guardian of the interests of 204 million U.S. consumers . . ." (Rothman 2015). After the success of his first book, he established summer research programs for college students in which they would investigate federal programs in Washington, D.C. These student interns and staff members became known as "Nader's Raiders," and they worked to prepare reports that were then used to spark legislative change (Time Magazine 1969). These young people were instrumental in establishing the modern consumer activist movement and creating a shift in corporate responsibility that resulted in federal regulations and standards.

Over the years, Nader's crusading has led to changes in various areas including the automobile industry, the food industry, the coal mine industry and in establishing rights for consumers. In 1971 he established a watchdog group called Public Citizen to investigate and lobby on consumer rights issues. He was a public face of the anti-nuclear power movement, and of several other environmental laws, including the Clean Water Act and the Whistleblower Protection Act.

While few doubted his resolve to protect the rights of Americans, not many initially saw him as someone who might take his influence and turn it into a political campaign. He was first mentioned as a possible presidential candidate in 1972, although he pushed aside the notion. It wasn't until 1996 when he was nominated by the Green Party as its presidential candidate that he began to gather a group of supporters to help catapult him in a national election. In some states he was on the ballot as an independent, while in others he was running as the Green Party nominee. He and his running mate, Winona LaDuke, were on the ballot in twenty-two states. They finished fourth in the popular vote, behind Ross Perot, the Reform Party candidate, and just ahead of Harry Browne, the Libertarian candidate. Nader refused to raise or spend more than $5,000 on his campaign, although other groups raised money and spent it on his behalf. He rarely did serious campaigning, and seemed to be mostly in favor of allowing the Green Party to increase voter numbers to allow future ballot access. He and his running mate garnered 71 percent of the popular vote. Nader did well for an outsider presidential candidate who really didn't spend much time campaigning, but traded well on his reputation as an honest, hard-working activist.

Nader's political stands were left of center and usually framed with a populist appeal that criticized corporate power and the influence that corporations enjoyed in the nation's capitol and in the Republican and Democratic parties. His discourse sought to engage individual political participation and urged Americans to push for solutions to address the inequalities that he said were impacting multiple generations in the United States.

Nader has spent most of his adult life trying to limit the power of corporations and elites, and his discourse was that of a crusading populist.

> Nader's entire career has been devoted to exposing the mechanisms by which a corporate elite gains power over public and private assets at the expense of voters, consumers, workers and shareholders, and to devising methods for counteracting elite power through citizen's organizations. Nader's practical and conceptual mastery on that tactical level is unparalleled in U.S. politics in the last three decades. (Lachmann 2002, 709)

In his activism and campaigns, Nader argued against globalism, which he said ultimately benefits international corporations that don't maintain any allegiance to a local community, thereby leaving workers and consumers—and governments—more vulnerable (Ahmad 1999). He said that globalism ultimately enhances the power of large corporations at a considerable cost to society. This attention to elites and the power system that is in place is common in populist discourse. "The specific elites targeted by populist claims can vary, from elected politicians and business leaders to intellectuals, but they are invariably portrayed as having betrayed the public trust" (Bonikowski and Gidron 2016, 1596). For Nader, who has been called the nation's leading consumer advocate, corporations have always been a favorite target, as can be seen in his initial criticism of General Motors in the 1960s and more recent criticism of Microsoft and other big technology companies. He often frames comments about corporations as a betrayal of trust, such as this comment about what he calls the "greed" of companies buying back their own stock: "When they buy the stock back, when it's near its high, is a sign of unimaginative or incompetent or avaricious management" (Cheng, 2017). His campaigns offered those who shared similar concerns about the distribution of power in American society a candidate with a proven track record of provoking change, thereby increasing his authenticity.

DISCOURSE AIMED AT CREATING
A VIABLE THIRD PARTY

In the 2000 election, he was formally nominated by the Green Party at its convention in Denver. Once again, Winona LaDuke, an Ojibwe activist from Minnesota, was the vice presidential candidate for the party. Nader seemed to have a more clear idea what he wanted to accomplish in this presidential race. He said that he hoped his presidential run in 2000 would "create a political force which can contribute to the development of what has been an underdeveloped civic culture" (Tikkun 2000). He also said that he hoped to engage young voters and create a third party that was a viable alternative to the Republican and Democratic parties. Nader argued that centrist Republicans and Democrats were effectively the same, and that a progressive third party was necessary to push political discourse in a different direction. He characterized the choice between George W. Bush and Al Gore as a "Tweedle Dee, Tweedle Dum" vote.

Nader's claim that there was no difference between the parties was not a new one. George Wallace's trademark comment that there wasn't "a dime's worth of difference" between the two parties (Wallace 1971) was used often in his presidential speeches, and other candidates have expressed similar thoughts over the years. "Wallace's message was designed to tap a sentiment that is often at the core of third party success: that the traditional parties are not receptive to voters' preferences" (Gold 1995, 752). While Wallace's comment was taken as a bit of populist oversimplification and swagger, the claim created some controversy in Nader's 2000 presidential race. "A more specific way of expressing Nader's statement might be to say that there is no difference between the parties in terms of the end product: the policies that the administration enacts or fails to enact" (Whitmore 2008, 556). Whether this was Nader's attempt to siphon supporters from Republicans and Democrats, or if it was a way to illustrate to voters that he represented something different, he spent the campaign trying to distinguish himself, his platform, and his party from the two major American parties.

In his acceptance speech in June 2000, Nader cast his presidential run in the light of historic American quests such as the revolution of 1776, the women's suffrage movement, and the consumer protection initiatives of the twentieth century (in which he played a large role). It was time, he said, that Americans fight to take back democracy from Big Business:

> This campaign is about strengthening our Republic with 'liberty and justice for all' so that freedom is defined as participation in power: power to solve our problems and diminish our injustices that cause such pain and stultify so many Americans and their children. It is good to have such dreams, my mother would

tell us, but she added a challenge. She taught us that determination puts your dream on wheels. Together we reviewed the problems and have understood that inequalities are getting worse. Together we can change the course of events as our forebears did. (Nader 2000)

Clear populist overtones are present in his acceptance speech, in which he promotes the traditional American values of hope and change (later successfully used by then-candidate Barack Obama), aligned with the belief that individuals have a role in that change. He urges voters to support him in his quest to solve the problems facing Americans, thereby creating a definite division between "the people" and "the elites," who are characterized as having betrayed the public trust.

Unlike his campaign in 1996, Nader seemed to take this presidential race seriously.

During the campaign he pushed for many of the same issues that he had been addressing for years: campaign finance reform, environmental justice, the reigning in of corporate America, and universal health care. During campaign stops, he pulled on his activist background when railing about free trade and corporate power in the United States and how the U.S. should withdraw from the World Trade Organization because it "puts commercialism over everything—over health, safety, nonmaterial values, everything" (Tikkun, 2000). Nader's views on corporations and their power in the United States were already well known and could be traced back to his initial consumer efforts against the automobile industry. In his book, "The Big Boys" in 1986, he stated "The philosophy guiding our political institutions is that when times are tough, we should leave the wealthy and powerful alone, or succor them with fruits from the public treasury. For only they can lead the country out of the valley of economic despair to the hilltops of recovery" (Nader and Taylor 1986, 506). He argued that the nation was lurching toward a corporate statism that could only be countered by a growing civic activism and the efforts of a progressive party that would combat the efforts of corporate globalization. Nader's rhetoric was that of an outside candidate and populist who was attempting to persuade voters to change the structure of the existing political system in which two parties control and exercise power.

However, his particular rhetoric seemed to stem from the hope that Americans would begin to think and consider the state of the nation, rather than lean on a set of beliefs for guidance. "There is nothing wrong with beliefs, but it would be better to have them preceded by thought and followed by action" (Nader 2000), he argued. He categorized the Green Party as a way for Americans to "grow a new political start, a green plant pushing up between the two fossil parties" (Nader 2000).

NADER'S CAMPAIGN TACTICS

Many have looked at Nader's 2000 presidential campaign and wondered if his intent was to draw votes from the mainstream candidates or to actually work at building a viable third party. While many Democrats still blame Nader for Gore's narrow loss, others say that his personal campaign appearances and speeches don't show a pattern of trying to disrupt the Democratic vote. The travel costs of campaigning in person are quite expensive, which is why some researchers view it as a good indicator of underlying campaign strategy. Research by Barry Burden indicates that in the 2000 race, Nader's in-person appearances seemed to be focused on heavily populated Democratic-voting states, or what Burden calls a vote-maximization strategy to help Nader gain more than 5 percent of the popular vote. The appearances were not responsive to the closeness of the race, but seemed maximized to gain the most Green Party votes possible. For Nader, that 5 percent was important to the future growth of the Green Party because it is the threshold established by the Federal Election Commission for a third party to qualify for public financing in the next election cycle. "Nader was a spoiler in 2000, but it was an unintentional by-product of a razor-close presidential campaign, not the result of a purposeful effect to throw the election" (Burden 2006, 873).

However, Democrats seemed to have viewed Nader's 2000 run as a threat, especially as it became apparent that former vice president Al Gore wasn't polling as well as expected. "Indeed, throughout most of the summer of 2000, Gore and his supporters worked hard to deny Nader a national forum. They were aided in this effort by the national media, which largely ignored him" (Barrett, 2001, 350). Most outsider and third-party candidates struggle to gain media coverage, and it was no different for Nader, despite the fact that he was nationally known. The media coverage he did receive often repeated the assertion that it was unlikely he would win, but would instead prove to be a spoiler in the race.

While he did not attain the 5 percent goal, Nader did get 2.7 percent of the popular vote. Third-party candidates taken all together earned less than 4 percent of the votes cast in that election, which illustrates how many more votes Nader received than his closest third-party rival, Pat Buchanan, who earned only 0.4 percent of the vote.

During the campaign, Nader dressed in his usual blue suit—his campaign uniform—and traveled mostly in coach on commercial airlines. He projected the image of an everyman, although he was one of the best-known third-party candidates. His campaign lacked the funds of the major parties, and he even occasionally slept in the homes of supporters to save money. While it may have helped campaign finances, it was also part of a populist performance, as

Nader appeared more like those he was addressing, furthering the idea that he shared their values.

In a demonstration of the power of the existing two-party system that he railed against, Nader and all third-party candidates were barred from the presidential debates in 2000 because of a new rule by the Commission on Presidential Debates stating that third-party candidates had to reach at least 15 percent in pre-debate polls in order to be included. This effectively kept all third parties from participating in the debates. Since the Commission took over running the debates in 1988, the only third-party candidate to be included in the national presidential debates was Ross Perot in 1992. Third-party debates were held in September and October, but Nader declined to participate in those debates. His running mate also declined to take part in the vice presidential debate that was held.

In the past, presidential debates were highly watched events, with the 1992 presidential debates averaging 90 million viewers per debate, making them the most widely watched political event in history (Fouhy 1992). Being included in a national debate can be a great boost for a presidential candidate, as Yawn, et al. (1998) found that viewing a debate can impact a voter's assessment of a candidate and potentially cause changes in voting. By measuring viewer responses to a Republican primary debate in 1996, they demonstrated changes in potential voters' assessments of candidate viability, electability, and found that debate performance affected vote preference. Scholars theorize that debates allow the public to learn more about candidates, which can positively or negatively benefit a particular candidate.

Nader attempted to attend the first presidential debate on October 3, 2000, as a spectator, but was blocked by a representative of the Commission on Presidential Debates and three police officers. Nader was apparently given a ticket to the debate by a student at the University of Massachusetts in Boston—where the debate was happening—and stated that he wanted to watch, not to disrupt the proceedings. Taking no chances, officials turned him away at the door, and Nader left the campus. This happened hours after he had filed suit against the commission because he was excluded from the debate.

Nader filed a complaint against the Commission on Presidential Debates with the Federal Election Commission, arguing that the Commission was violating federal election laws because it was accepting corporate contributions. The FEC disagreed, and the U.S. District Court in Washington D.C. decided not to overrule the FEC finding. Several other challenges to the Commission's rules regarding third parties have been filed since 2000, but the organization has continued its control over the presidential debates and limited them to inclusion of only Democratic and Republican presidential nominees.

Nader would probably have conceded that he was unlikely to win the presidential race, but he was sincere in trying to wrestle control of at least part of the national political conversation from the two major parties. He was virtually ignored by national media, except for an occasional interview, and most state polling organizations didn't even include his name when questioning voters about their preferences. His budget was small, which is one of the major qualifiers for coverage by mainstream media, and he couldn't afford much advertising. But he traveled to several states in an effort to get out his message.

He tended to poll as well as Patrick Buchanan in the early months, even though Buchanan was better funded. In a Gallup Poll taken in April 2000 and again in June 2000, likely voters were asked "As of today, do you lean toward Gore, the Democrat, Bush, the Republican, Buchanan, the Reform Party candidate, or Nader, the Green Party candidate?" (Gallup Poll 2000). Nader's numbers increased from 2 percent to 6 percent from April to June, while Buchanan's fell from 4 percent to 2 percent. At that point, Nader was only on the ballot in fourteen states, but was pursuing state-by-state petition drives to allow him ballot access in several others. Buchanan was on about twenty-five state ballots at that time. Given that numbers for third-party candidates rarely go above 1 percent in the actual vote, this was a strong showing for Nader at this early point in the campaign. Nader was eventually able to be on the ballot in forty-three states.

Most political commentators generally overlook third-party candidates during a presidential race, only giving coverage when they make provocative statements or drop out of the race. As the campaign progressed and Nader's numbers continued to hold him in third place, and as thoughts turned toward a close national vote, commentators began to wonder if Nader might take away some Democratic votes and sway the election for the Republicans. A CNN/Time poll conducted in October 2000 showed Nader pulling 4 percent of likely voters (Holland 2000). While that paled in comparison to the 45 percent for Gore and the 47 percent for Bush, it was becoming clear that many Americans saw Nader as an attractive and viable presidential candidate, perhaps enough to draw votes from both of the major candidates.

As the general election drew near, Nader made the decision to campaign in states where Gore and Bush were polling very close to each other. The Democratic Party grew concerned as Nader's numbers in swing states grew to between 5 and 8 percent of the vote, and an all-out pushback against Nader was organized that featured actor Robert Redford, the Rev. Jesse Jackson, the cast members of the television show "The West Wing," and singer Melissa Ethridge. As a result, Nader's numbers in the the closing days of the election began to move lower. At least one scholar argues that this was accomplished by painting Nader as a "spoiler," a narrative that is still believed by many to be true (Harold 2001).

Many saw Nader's campaign as an attempt to throw the election to George W. Bush, and they blamed him for the Democratic loss. "Everybody knew that Nader's appeal was being made to 'the left,' and Nader was concentrating his campaign now on sucking foolish leftish voters away from Gore" (Zuesse 2013). Critics charged that Nader received help from Republicans, including individual campaign donations, which caused detractors to call him a Republican mole, a vengeful man, or even a Communist. In October, Slate published an article in its Ballot Box section outlining what was seen as Nader's motivation and strategy, and openly calling him a Leninist.

> For some time now, Nader has made it perfectly clear that his campaign isn't about trying to pull the Democrats back to the left. Rather, his strategy is the Leninist one of 'heightening the contradictions.' It's not just that Nader is willing to take a chance of being personally responsible for electing Bush. It's that he's actively trying to elect Bush because he thinks that social conditions in America need to get worse before they can [get] better. (Slate 2000)

On election night, the nation went to sleep without knowing who would be president. That lasted for a month, as the votes in Florida were recounted, until the 5–4 Supreme Court vote that ended the recount. Bush was then declared the winner.

Nader received about 2.7 million votes in the election. In some states, such as Iowa, his percentage was high enough to allow the Green Party automatic ballot access in the next election. Most importantly, Nader won many votes in highly contested states such as Florida, where he received about 95,000 votes. In the end, Gore lost that state by 537 votes, leading to much anger and frustration from Democrats, who felt losing that state alone might have kept Gore from being president.

After the outcome of the election, the attacks on Nader only became louder and more fierce. Then-Delaware Sen. Joe Biden was one of the loudest critics. "He cost him the election," Biden said. "Whatever mistakes Gore made, we wouldn't even be talking about it if Nader hadn't run. God spare me the purists" (Lopez 2000). The scapegoating of third-party candidates and those who vote for them was not a new tactic (Neville-Shepard 2019), but the vitriol aimed at Nader was stronger than usual.

For his part, Nader dismissed his critics, who he called "well-intentioned cowards" (Lopez 2000). Exit polls showed that Gore lost more Democratic votes to Bush than to Nader, who as an outsider candidate also drew votes from Independents and Republicans. Nader did not seem surprised by the criticism, which he blamed on a system in which candidates for both major parties are controlled by corporations and their donations.

There are others who dispute the Democratic reasoning that Nader cost them the 2000 presidential election. Anthony Fisher published a rebuke of such Democratic claims in 2016 in Reason magazine, which is a Libertarian publication. Fisher argued that Gore should be the one blamed for the 2000 loss, and that ultimately the two major parties feel entitled to votes and will always blame third parties as spoilers when they can. Kenski, Aylor, and Kenski (2002) state that Gore "was unable to maintain the lead he had opened and made campaign errors that allowed the personality and character factor to shift again to Bush's advantage" (259).

Plotke (2001) points out that from 1980–2000, "every presidential election has seen a serious insurgent campaign from within or outside the two main parties" (343). The nation has become increasingly politically polarized, making it harder for effective third-party campaigns, but certainly Donald Trump's 2016 campaign stands as an example of a successful outsider campaign within a main party. Some scholars believe that Nader was able to push Gore further to the left than was expected so as to counter Nader's threat (Magee 2003). "The pro-Nader left was one of Gore's burdens in 2000. This was not only a matter of key votes in tough contests. Gore was required to argue with Nader and his advocates" (Plotke 2001, 343). Being forced to engage Nader and fend off his campaign attacks may have had the effect of pushing Gore out of the more centrist position he hoped to maintain during the campaign.

A more scientific look at the voting in the 2000 election indicates that, yes, Nader probably did cost Gore the state of Florida, but that any number of third-party candidates could have had the same effect, simply because the vote was so incredibly close. Michael C. Herron and Jeffrey B. Lewis analyzed the performance of third-party candidates in the 2000 presidential election and found that third-party voters were "surprisingly close to being partisan centrists." After analyzing three million individual Florida ballots, they found that 40 percent of Nader voters in Florida would have voted for Bush in an election without Nader's candidacy. The other 60 percent would have gone to Gore. In addition to Nader drawing enough votes to swing the state from Gore, so did the Socialist Worker's Party candidate, who received 562 votes, as well as the Worker's World Party candidate, who received 1,804 votes in Florida (Herron and Lewis 2007).

In his concession speech in 2000, Nader was typically defiant, and he never acknowledged defeat. Instead, he outlined the reasons that the campaign had been a success and urged his supporters to continue the fight.

While he thanked supporters for keeping his campaign energized and for turning out to make a difference in a close race, his focus was on portraying his campaign as victorious in light of the barriers that the faced in reaching voters.

More importantly, he urged his supporters to continue resisting the two-party system by participating in the grassroots movement they built for the campaign. (Neville-Shepard 2014, 225)

As Neville-Shepard points out, the rhetoric of third-party candidates is different from that of more mainstream candidates, and concession speeches often look for ways to claim victory, despite the loss at the ballot box. While Nader framed his defeat as an ultimate victory for the Green Party, the most important part of that victory—reaching the 5 percent vote goal to ensure public campaign financing—was not realized.

In the end, Nader's attempt to create a viable alternative to the major parties failed. As for whether he played the role of "spoiler," Simmons and Simmons (2006) related, "The race was quite close and turned on thousands of small and unrelated factors" (230). The loss was difficult for Nader and for the Green Party. Not only was he unable to reach the 5 percent vote threshold, but he received much negative news media attention after the election that boomeranged back onto the Green Party.

REVILED OUTSIDER CANDIDATE

In his subsequent presidential campaigns, Nader seemed to have lost the support he initially gained in 2000. Nader chose to run again in 2004, but was not welcomed by the Green Party, so he ran as an independent candidate. He was also not welcomed by the Democratic Party, which challenged his ballot petitions in several states around the nation. In some states, a number of his voter petitions were ruled invalid, and in others the barrier to ballot access as an independent candidate was actually lower if he ran as a candidate for a new political party. Nader chose to establish the Populist Party and run on that party label in many states. (Nader's Populist Party was not the same as the one that ran white nationalist David Duke for president in 1984. That party existed between 1984 and 1996.) Nader was on the ballot in roughly thirty-seven states, some as an independent, some as a Populist Party candidate. He finished third in the contest again, but with far fewer votes than in the 2000 race. In 2004, he only received .38 percent of the total vote, a far cry from about 3 percent of the total vote just four years earlier.

He ran again in 2008, as the presidential candidate for the Peace and Freedom Party. He and his running mate were on the ballot in forty-five states, and they finished third in the election, with .56 percent of the total vote. While this was higher than his total in 2004, it was still less than he collected in 2000.

Nader continued to generate controversy in his 2008 campaign, as he made comments regarding Barack Obama's political support from corporate donations and large law firms. Some of his remarks were seen as racist, especially this one made to Fox News after the election ended: "Obama has to choose between being 'Uncle Sam' for the people of this country, or Uncle Tom for the giant corporations" (Essence 2009).

This proved to be Nader's last presidential race, although he retained an interest in third-party politics. In 2012 he was a moderator for a debate for third-party candidates.

NADER'S ISSUES

In all of his political campaigns, Nader stressed similar issues, and most of them revolved around populist concerns about how power is distributed in the nation. Ever the activist, Nader campaigned to take democracy back from large corporations, which he saw as having consolidated their hold on both the Republican and Democratic parties. Many of his most pointed comments were aimed at the two major parties, and some of his most controversial statements involved those saying there was effectively no difference between the two parties. While this was in the context of promoting the Green Party, Nader has consistently criticized both parties for pandering to large corporations and political donors.

He urged Americans to change the unequal power distribution in the country—a distribution that he saw as favoring big business, defense contractors, and those with access to political power. As in all of his public campaigns and books, Nader saw change as coming in the form of active civic participation and changing the civic culture.

In addition, he campaigned for universal health care, a recognition of the damage to the environment by organizations and governments, changes in the American prison system, and he rebuked the power of commercialism.

Overall, Nader campaigned to pull the political conversation in the nation to the left, along with the political parties and voters. This was part of his strategy, as he was looking to create a viable third party and draw part of that support from traditional Democratic voters. "Andrew Sullivan, a senior editor at The New Republic, suggests that the shift to the left that became evident in some of Gore's speeches as he sought to take account of the Nader challenge lost the Democrats crucial support among important sections of the voting public" (Ashbee, 2001).

Nader urged civic activism, argued for campaign finance reform, and challenged those listening to his messages to rouse themselves and cause change in the American political system. As a populist candidate, he positioned himself as the person who could lead the nation in righting the wrongs that had been inflicted on Americans by the establishment in both the Democratic and Republican parties.

TARNISHED LEGACY?

Some feel that Nader, one of the most successful outsider presidential candidates, leaves a somewhat tarnished legacy, primarily because of the controversy surrounding the 2000 presidential election. While he might have had no control over how close the outcome would be in the national race, some feel that his unrepentant attitude about the outcome hurt his future election chances and, in the short term, also negatively impacted the Green Party.

The inability of third parties to participate in presidential debates is often mentioned as a way to keep political control within the two major U.S. parties. While Nader is not the first—or last—third party candidate to be locked out of the debates, some might wonder if this serves to limit the effectiveness of third-party campaigns. The exposure that comes from participating in debates might have been crucial for Nader, who already had a national reputation and a national organization. However, the Commission of Presidential Debates ruled that he did not meet the criteria for participation, one part of which is that there must be indicators of national enthusiasm or concern on behalf of a candidate. Nader had many supporters, but the commission apparently felt that he did not poll well enough to appear competitive in the election. "Had the commission visited college campuses throughout the United States, they may have found indications of national enthusiasm" (Levine 2001, 2228). In the end, the enthusiasm for Nader and his campaign's competitiveness were, ironically, blamed for Gore's loss.

Nader's legacy as a crusader paved the way for another Green Party candidate, Jill Stein, whose history of activism was different, but also provocative and mobilizing for the party. Ross Perot, one of the most successful third-party candidates, also shared some of Nader's frustrations about debates, although he was allowed to participate in the 1992 debates. Nader and Perot both challenged the status quo Republicans and Democrats, but in different ways.

As a populist crusader, Ralph Nader leaves a legacy far beyond that of most activists. He was the driving force behind many laws and industry standards that are now in place in the nation, and he never stopped his criticism of corporate involvement in politics and continued to call for a vibrant third party to provide balance in American politics. This is how most Americans knew him before he entered politics, and it will probably be his most lasting legacy— except for those who still view him with hatred for the circumstances of the

2000 presidential election. Nader was able to translate much of the attention he gained from his crusading activities into being an effective third-party political candidate who consistently was outside the mainstream on most issues, but always seemed genuine in his pursuit of a country with more power for individuals and less for corporations.

REFERENCES

Ahmad, Khabir. 1999. World Bank Predicts Developments for Next Century. *The Lancet* 354 (9183): 1005. https://doi.org/10.1016/S0140-6736(99)00166-X.

Ashbee, Edward. 2001. The Also-Rans: Nader, Buchanan and the 2000 US Presidential Election. *Political Quarterly* 72, no. 2 (April–June): 159–169.

Barrett, Patrick. 2001. Strategic Lessons of the 2000 Presidential Election: A Pro-Nader Perspective. *Constellations* 8, (3): 348–363.

Bonikowski, Bart and Noam Gidron. 2016. The Populist style in American Politics: Presidential Campaign Discourse, 1952-1996. *Social Forces* 94, no. 4 (June):1593–1621. https://doi.org/10.1093/sf/sov120.

Burden, Barry. 2006. A Tale of Two Campaigns: Ralph Nader's Strategy in the 2004 Presidential Election. *PS: Political Science and Politics* 39, no.4: 871–874. https://www.jstor.org/stable/20451834.

Cheng, Evelyn. 2017. Ralph Nader Blasts Corporations for Stock Buybacks He Calls 'Unimaginative' and Greedy. CNBC. Oct. 9, 2017. https://www.cnbc.com/2017/10/09/ralph-nader-blasts-corporations-for-unimaginative-stock-buy-backs.html.

Corn, David. 2000. Nader: Is there life after crucifixion? *The Nation*, Nov. 16, 2000. https://www.thenation.com/article/archive/nader-there-life-after-crucifixion/.

Essence. 2009. Ralph Nader: Obama an Uncle Sam or Uncle Tom? *Essence.com*. Dec. 16, 2009. https://www.essence.com/news/ralph-nader-obama-an-uncle-sam-or-uncle/.

Fisher, Anthony. 2016. No, Ralph Nader Did Not Hand the 2000 Presidential Election to George W. Bush. *Reason,* Aug. 3, 2016. https://reason.com/2016/08/03/ralph-nader-did-not-hand-2000-election/.

Fouhy, Edward. 1992. The Debates: A Winning Miniseries. *American Journalism Review* (December): 27–29.

Gallup Poll. 2000. The 2000 Presidential Election—A Mid-Year Gallup Report. June 22, 2000. https://news.gallup.com/poll/9898/2000-presidential-election-midyear-gallup-report.aspx.

Gold, Howard J. 1995. Third Party Voting in Presidential Elections: A Study of Perot, Anderson, and Wallace. *Political Research Quarterly* 48, no. 4 (December): 751–773.

Hamilton, Neil A. 2014. Ralph Nader. In *American Social Leaders and Activists* 281–282. New York: Infobase Publishing.

Harold, Christine L. 2001. The Green Virus: Purity and Contamination in Ralph Nader's 2000 Presidential Campaign. *Rhetoric and Public Affairs* 4, no. 4 (Winter): 581–603. https://www.jstor.org/stable/41940262.

Herron, Michael and Jeffrey Lewis. 2007. Did Ralph Nader Spoil Al Gore's Presidential Bid? A Ballot-Level Study of Green and Reform Party Voters in the 2000 Presidential Election. *Quarterly Journal of Political Science* 2, no. 3 (August): 205–226. https://doi.org/10.1561/100.00005039.

Holland, Keating. 2000. Poll: Presidential Race a Dead Heat. *CNN.com.* Oct. 6, 2000. https://www.cnn.com/2000/ALLPOLITICS/stories/10/06/cnn.poll/index.html.

Kenski, Henry C., Brooks Aylor, and Kate Kenski. 2002. Explaining the Vote in a Divided Country: The Presidential Election of 2000. In *The 2000 Presidential Campaign, A Communication Perspective*, edited by Robert E. Denton Jr., 225-263. Westport, CT.: Praeger.

Lachmann, Richard. 2002. The Political Sociology of Nader and Chomsky. *Sociological Forum* 17, no. 4 (December): 707–716.

Levine, Kenneth J. 2001. Election 2000, and the Presidential Debates, and Nader. *American Behavioral Scientist* 44, no. 12 (August): 2219–2231.

Lopez, Steve. 2000. No Apologies. *TIME*, Nov.12, 2000. http://content.time.com/time/magazine/article/0,9171,87827-1,00.html.

Magee, Christopher S.P. 2003. Third-Party Candidates and the 2000 Presidential Election. *Social Science Quarterly* 82, no. 3 (September): 574–595.

Nader, Ralph and William Taylor. 1986. *The Big Boys: Power and Position in American Business.* New York: Pantheon.

Nader, Ralph. 2000. Acceptance Statement of Ralph Nader For the Association of Green Parties Nomination for President of the United States. http://www.4president. org/speeches/nader2000acceptance.htm.

Neville-Shepard, Ryan. 2014. Triumph in Defeat: The Genre of Third Party Presidential Concessions. *Communication Quarterly* 62, no. 2 (April): 214–232.

Neville-Shepard, Ryan. 2019. Containing the Third-Party Voter in the 2016 U.S. Presidential Election. *Journal of Communication Inquiry* 49, no. 3 (January): 272–292

Plotke, David. 2008. Who Lost Tennessee? On the 2000 Presidential Election. *Constellations* 8, no. 3 (June): 339–347. https://doi.org/10.1111/1467-8675.00242.

Rothman, Lily. 2015. This Book Has Kept American Drivers Safe for 50 Years. *TIME*, Nov. 30, 2015. https://time.com/4124987/50-years-/.

Simmons, Solon J. and James R. Simmons. 2006. If It Weren't for Those?*&*@!* Nader Voters We Wouldn't Be in This Mess: The Social Determinants of the Nader Vote and the Constraints on Political Choice. *New Political Science* 28, no. 2 (June): 229–244.

Slate. 2000. Ralph the Leninist. Oct. 31, 2000. https://slate.com/news-and-politics/2000/11/ralph-the-leninist.html.

Tikkun. 2000. A Conversation with Ralph Nader. *Tikkun Magazine.* July/August 2000. https://www.questia.com/read/1P3-56589530/a-conversation-with-ralph-nader.

TIME Magazine. 1969. The U.S.'s Toughest Customer. Dec. 12, 1969. http://content. time.com/time/subscriber/article/0,33009,840502,00.html.

Wallace, George C. 1971. Speech delivered in Nashville, Tenn. Speech obtained from the Alabama Department of Archives and History in Montgomery on Feb. 25, 2003.

Whitmore, Andy. 2008. Schism on the Left: The Motivations and Impact of Ralph Nader's Candidacy. *The Political Quarterly* 79, no. 4 (October-December): 556–559.

Yawn, Mike, Kevin Ellsworth, Bob Beatty and Kim Fridkin Kahn. 1998. How a Presidential Primary Debate Changed Attitudes of Audience Members. *Political Behavior* 20, no. 2 (June): 155–181.

Zuesse, Eric. 2013. Ralph Nader Was Indispensable to the Republican Party. *HuffPost.* Nov. 11, 2013. https://www.huffpost.com/entry/ralph-nader-was-indispens_b_4235065.

Chapter 9

Jill Stein

GREEN PARTY CANDIDATE, DEMOCRATIC SCAPEGOAT

Dr. Jill Stein has been a presidential candidate twice, both times for the Green Party. A doctor who practiced internal medicine for twenty-five years, she became known as an environmental activist before seeking public office, but that's probably not what she will best be remembered for.

Instead, she will probably best be remembered as one of the people blamed by Democrats for causing Hillary Clinton's 2016 loss to Donald Trump. In the general election vote that year, she garnered more votes in several swing states than Hillary Clinton's margin of defeat. For instance, in Michigan, Stein pulled 51,000 votes, while Clinton lost to Donald Trump by less than 11,000 votes in that state. It was similar in Wisconsin and Pennsylvania, leading some Democrats to say she stole votes from Clinton and helped put Trump in the White House. This was ironic, given that in 2000 Ralph Nader, another Green Party candidate, was accused of spoiling the election for former vice president Al Gore.

Stein has also been accused by several people, including Hillary Clinton, of cozying up to Russian President Vladimir Putin, and a video surfaced of her attending a 2015 gala in Moscow and sitting at the same table as Putin. Clinton's campaign officials argued that Russians propped up Stein's campaign in order to help Trump win the election.

While it all reads like a modern-day spy plot, Stein has dismissed the charges and says that there wasn't that much difference between Trump and Clinton. "There are differences between Clinton and Trump, no doubt, but they're not different enough to save your life, to save your job, to save the planet," she says. "We deserve more than two lethal choices" (Schreckinger 2017).

The Green Party has been in existence in the United States since 1984, and the first national Green politics conference was held in 1987. It focused on educating those in attendance on Green ideas and those being addressed by other, similar movements around the country. In 1992 there were Green candidates in several states, and, as noted in a previous chapter, in 1996 Ralph Nader ran as the Green Party's first presidential nominee, although it was a campaign of limited scope and size. He was also the party's nominee in the 2000 presidential race, in which he garnered 2.9 million votes. In 2001 the organization, which is a federation of state political parties, changed its name to the Green Party of the United States and was recognized by the Federal Election Commission as a national committee. By 2012, it was the fourth-largest political party in the United States.

STEIN'S CAMPAIGN DISCOURSE

Stein faced the challenge of introducing the nation to her beliefs and ideas, as she was unknown to most voters when she ran for president. Unlike Ralph Nader, she did not have a national reputation that had been cultivated over the course of several years. She campaigned across the nation in both 2012 and 2016 using populist appeals to pull together an alliance of individuals with concerns about the nation's economic, environmental, and political sustainability.

Laclau (2005) identifies two main types of political logics—those that work to continue the existing institutional form and those that work to oppose the existing order. Populism obviously falls into the latter category, with its emphasis on creating a movement that stands in opposition to the current political elites. As Jager and Borriello (2020) point out, "enemy formation is therefore a crucial feature of every populist movement" (53). Unlike many in the past who saw populism as a recurring, but usually brief, attempt to correct or change the political system, more scholars now see populism as a frequent way of doing politics, especially for those who find themselves on the outside fringes of politics (Mudde 2004). "In elections, incumbents wield the advantage of past electoral successes and demonstrable experience in positions of political power, as well as the ability to set the terms of the public debate about their accomplishments. To counteract these advantages, challengers must 'articulate an alternative vision of the field and their position in it'" (Bonikowski and Gidron 2016, 1596). For third-party candidates, it's not just the incumbents who hold the advantage in an election—it is both of the major parties that wish to exclude any outside candidates from serious consideration. This is why Neville-Shepard (2019a) argues that outside candidates develop a style of rhetoric that can "act as 'genre-busters,' purposefully violating expectations of a class of discourse in order to achieve the complicated goals of fringe political leaders" (87). Because of her distance from the mainstream, and because of the monumental challenges faced by all third-party candidates, Stein worked to re-frame the position of the major party candidates as enemies and show herself and the Green Party as a legitimate alternative.

In her acceptance speech at the Green Party convention in 2012, she used dramatic language to outline concerns about voting for either of the established parties. "Every vote they receive is an endorsement of the deadly trajectory we're on for the American people and the planet. It's time to change that plunge into catastrophe. That change starts with voting for real change" (Stein 2012). This comment was one of many that positioned both the Democratic and Republican parties as the same—a claim made also by Nader in his 2000 presidential campaign. By grouping those parties together, she was using a strategy of polarization that utilizes exaggeration as a way to legitimize her candidacy. "While all political candidates use polarization in some form, third party candidates use it as their main strategy in an attempt to exacerbate frustration with the two-party system and to justify the cause of outsiders" (Neville-Shepard 2019a, 95). By painting the major parties as enemies—neither of which would work to fix the nation's problems—Stein differentiated herself and the Green Party and presented their issues and platform as the true way to bring about change.

One way Stein illustrated her points was by often using narratives of individuals and their struggles or successes. This is a common technique used by populists to achieve a commonality or identification with their audiences while also reminding them that they offer a type of redemption from the wrongs that have been suffered (Casullo 2020). Many of those employing populist rhetoric use stories to evoke images of the past when things were better and to illustrate the "degenerate present" (Tas 2020), and Stein often did this by painting mental images of average Americans who had no hope until a Green Party idea changed their lives. In her acceptance speech in 2012, Stein used the example of "Ricardo" and how he had been failed by the American education system.

> But he found a training program in energy efficiency and solar hot water installation offered by a remarkable green energy cooperative called Coop Power in Western Mass. Ricardo was then hired by a small green energy business where he became crew leader within one year. And while doing all that, this high school dropout held back 3 times in 9th grade entered a GED program and graduated even before his own high school class received their diplomas. (Stein 2012)

This is a common form of populist discourse, as it promotes the rhetorical position that something is wrong, but that it can be changed by giving "the people" the ability and resources to make those changes.

Stein's outsider rhetoric contains many references to giving voters more choices and protection against globalization, which she said was hurting working people. The issue of globalization has proven to be fertile ground for recent U.S. outsider candidates. Ralph Nader, Ross Perot, and Donald Trump all railed against various aspects of globalism. Mudde (2018) points out that mainstream politicians try to present globalism as both dangerous and positive at the same time, which only weakens their political positions. President George H.W. Bush proclaimed a new world order and promoted the virtues of free trade, but then Americans began to see their jobs shifting to other nearby nations. The realities of industrial loss became apparent in many large U.S. urban areas where workers lost jobs and felt ignored, and this eventually led many to support Donald Trump in 2016 (Montgomery 2017; Carnes and Lupu 2020). Stein campaigned on the idea that neither the Democratic nor the Republican parties could solve the nation's problems because those parties don't listen to the voices of Americans or share their concerns.

She advocated for the Green New Deal (Green Party Website), a proposal that she said would focus on the formation of renewable energy jobs and would eventually end unemployment and poverty. She supported maintaining a smaller military and the recalling of American troops stationed abroad. Most of her issues revolved around the transition to a more sustainable infrastructure, a movement toward sustainable organic agriculture, and raising taxes on wealthy Americans. Her messages contain many populist elements, but all centered primarily within issues related to environmental concerns and corporate elites.

She was critical of the current voting system and advocated for "rank choice voting" in the United States. In a rank-choice voting system, a voter would rank candidates based on his or her preference. A first choice would be chosen, as well as a second and third choice, if possible. If the first choice loses, then the person's vote is automatically re-assigned to the second choice. This, she felt, would benefit third parties and other outside candidates who were running for office and might facilitate a move away from a primarily two-party system. The concept is not widely known in the United States, so Stein took every opportunity to explain it to potential voters.

As a third-party candidate, Stein worked hard to articulate her positions and appeals to the American public. Because she was using populist discourse, it was important that her messages resonate with enough of "the people" to create a movement, or at least spark enough grassroots support to push her campaign forward. As Knott (2020b) states, "any attempt to appeal to the people against the establishment requires a receptive audience" (116). Without a demand for a supply of populism, the candidate cannot generate enough support to create and sustain a movement. "Populist politicians can articulate their logic repeatedly, but it only grips—populism only becomes a broader phenomenon—when there is an audience willing to receive it" (Knott, 2020a, 118). Stein was unable to generate enough support for the Green Party ideas to create a movement, although she was able to push the

Democratic Party a bit to the left. As will be discussed later, some aspects of the Green New Deal have been discussed and promoted during President Joe Biden's first term.

Stein asked for recounts in several states following the 2016 general election and called into question the integrity of electronic voting machines. She raised $7.3 million—more than her presidential campaign brought in—to pay for a recount of votes in Michigan, Wisconsin, and Pennsylvania. In Wisconsin, the only state to complete the recount before a federal judge stopped the process, a recount of the votes led to an increase of about one hundred votes for Trump and a validation of the state's results.

STEIN'S CAMPAIGN TACTICS

Stein has a history of taking unpopular stands. She has been arrested several times during protests, including in 2012, when she was the Green Party presidential nominee, after trying to enter a presidential debate to which she had not been invited. In 2017, she was charged with criminal trespass and mischief after spray painting the words "I approve this message" on a bulldozer during a Dakota Access Pipeline protest. She has protested against environmental concerns in the United States since 1998, and also in places such as South Korea, where she called for the U.S. to stop deployment of an advanced missile defense system in that country.

Stein's years as a physician and instructor of medicine at Harvard Medical School seemed to lead her into political protest. She said that she became concerned about the link between an individual's health and the quality of his or her environment. She protested against coal-burning plants in Massachusetts and co-authored reports in that state expressing concern over environmental threats to child development and healthy aging.

Because it is difficult for third-party candidates to gain media exposure, Stein leveraged her history of activism to garner attention during her presidential campaigns. Neville-Shepard (2019a) argues this is part of the genre-busting that outside candidates must do as a "way of gaining, and even keeping, media attention" (92). For instance, a newspaper story in the Boston Globe recounts how she and her supporters were looking for the best location to protest and get arrested in Hempstead, New York, the site of Hofstra University and a 2016 presidential debate that locked out all third party candidates. "The Stein protesters on Monday eventually sat down en masse in a public street, as close as they could get, given all the police roadblocks, to Hofstra University, where Clinton and Trump were preparing to debate. Their demand was that the Commission on Presidential Debates assign Stein a podium at the debate, and they intended to be taken away in handcuffs to make the point" (Arsenault 2016). They were eventually escorted from the site, assuring Stein that she would have a few seconds of coverage in the news that day, even if she wasn't on the debate stage. "Since media coverage of third party candidates typically ranges from ignoring them completely to to emphasizing their odd distinctiveness, genre-busting functions to give reporters what they want by being as distinct as possible" (Neville-Shepard 2019a, 92). Stein will likely not be the only third-party candidate to be arrested during a campaign, but she excelled at using activism to gain media attention during the election.

Stein and her running mate were also arrested in August 2012 during a sit-in at a Philadelphia bank where they and others were protesting foreclosures that were taking place in the city. Two months later, she was again arrested and charged with criminal trespass for trying to deliver food and other supplies to those protesting the XL pipeline. Once again, this afforded the campaign with national media coverage and a chance to get its candidates and messages in front of the public.

Stein also pursued media interviews, even with foreign news outlets, in an effort to introduce her messages to potential voters. Because she was given such a small chance of winning, most mainstream media outlets weren't interested in speaking with her or her campaign. In an attempt to counter this, the Green Party maintained a web site where links to interviews were posted, and the campaign made use of multiple videos and some advertisements.

Further use of online media included extensive messaging on Twitter, where she led third-party candidates in the number of tweets sent out during the 2012 campaign (Christensen 2013). In her tweets, Stein linked the Green Party to larger social movements such as Occupy Wall Street and often used the presidential debates (in which she was not allowed to participate) as a platform for messages on corporate corruption, environmental issues, and how the mainstream political parties were not working for average Americans.

STEIN'S CAMPAIGN ISSUES

Stein's slogan for her first campaign for president was "A New Green Deal for America." In securing the Green Party nomination, one of the individuals she had to defeat was Roseanne Barr, the comedienne and TV sitcom star, who advocated for drug legalization and ending the Electoral College system. Stein's plan for the Green New Deal seemed popular within the party, and she became the nominee in July, 2012 at the party's convention in Baltimore. When she became the nominee, she gave up her medical practice.

The Green New Deal is described by the Green Party as similar to Roosevelt's New Deal, which helped the nation emerge from the Great

Depression, combined with a solution for the climate change crisis. The proposal promised the creation of 20 million jobs by "transitioning to 100% clean renewable energy by 2030, and investing in public transit, sustainable (regenerative) agriculture, conservation and restoration of critical infrastructure, including ecosystems." (Green Party website, n.d.) It also promoted energy democracy and listed energy as a human right. In addition, it called for the cessation of what it called destructive environmental energy practices such as fracking, offshore drilling, natural gas pipelines, and uranium mines. It called for phasing out fossil fuel power plants, nuclear power, and imposing a greenhouse tax on corporations or organizations. The proposal also included an Economic Bill of Rights which guaranteed citizens full employment and full wages for those whose current energy jobs would be terminated and would need new employment.

Stein's campaign did not accept any PAC contributions, but focused on donations from individuals. The campaign raised $893,636, with $44,000 of that coming from the candidate herself. She was the second Green Party candidate to qualify for Federal Matching Funds, which added more than $260,000 to her campaign budget. Ralph Nader was the first to receive matching funds. (OpenSecrets, n.d.) The Green Party was on ballots in thirty-seven states, which covered about 85 percent of the nation's voters.

No third-party candidates were invited to participate in the debates between President Barack Obama and Republican challenger Mitt Romney in 2012. Because they felt that being on the ballot in so many states should qualify them for participation, Stein and her running mate, Cheri Honkala, tried to enter the debate at Hofstra University. They were stopped as they attempted to enter the debate site and eventually arrested. "We're here to stand ground for the American people, who have been systematically locked out of these debates for decades by the Commission on Presidential Debates," Stein said to the police officers who were trying to get them to leave. After they were arrested and removed from the debate site, Stein said both candidates spent eight hours handcuffed to a chair (Democracy Now! 2012). As noted earlier, Stein protested outside the same university four years later when she was again excluded from the debate.

It was no surprise when she lost in the general election, but the Green Party did gain momentum and fielded candidates down the ballot in several states. In a interview on National Public Radio in July 2012, Stein reminded listeners of the role third parties have played in American history. "We've made progress socially and economically, abolishing slavery, establishing women's right to vote, establishing the right to unionize, to have a 40-hour work week, Social Security. It all actually came through independent parties. They are not spoiling it. They are actually creating it." She also pointed out that even if she didn't win, that would not mean that progress had not happened. "You don't have to win the office in order to win the day, by driving real solutions forward. So we've got to start. We've got a long way to go, and the longer we wait, the more we are accelerating in the wrong direction" (Martin 2012).

Some researchers state that third parties have often created more impact on American elections than simply drawing votes away from the two major parties. Lee (2012) argues that "third parties are an integral component of the two-party system, and one should not take their apparent lack of electoral success as an indication of their irrelevance" (138). Third parties, he argues, are often not seen as successful because major parties take preemptive actions that will help prevent them from being successful. In other words, the established parties might take actions such as shifting their positions on particular issues to have greater appeal to their more liberal or conservative voters. This happened when Ralph Nader presented a threat to the more liberal wing of the Democratic Party in the 2000 presidential race. To counter, Al Gore, shifted some of his positions to the left. Whether those policy shifts made during the course of a campaign will remain after an election is over can vary, depending on how important it is for the major party to maintain the support of that group of voters. Collet (1996) points out that "the public shows more antipathy toward the 'system' itself—the two parties together in an abstract sense— rather than the Republicans and Democrats in general. Their support for a third party seems to be rooted in a desire for more choices at the poll rather than any deep-seated desire to replace, or do away with, the existing choices" (436). Americans now have at least two viable third parties—the Libertarian Party and the Green Party—but fewer of them now describe themselves as *not* belonging to or leaning toward one of the two major parties. In 2019, only 7 percent of Americans did not express a partisan leaning (Laloggia, 2019), which leaves precious few voters for third-party candidates.

In the general election, Stein received 469,501 votes, or .36 percent of the popular vote. She received at least 1 percent of the votes in Maine, Oregon, and Alaska. This was more votes than each of the previous two Green Party presidential nominees had garnered.

Stein essentially ran on the same issues during her 2016 presidential race, in which she was again the Green Party nominee. She accepted the nomination at a convention that featured a live video address from Julian Assange, the embattled activist and founder of WikiLeaks. While he praised political movements such as the Green Party, he fell short of endorsing the party or Jill Stein. After winning the nomination, she again fought a battle for mainstream media exposure, which is always difficult for third-party candidates. A study looking at all NBC, CBS, and ABC campaign stories from January 1, 2016 to August 31, 2016 found only .03 percent of the coverage was spent discussing third-party candidates or ideas (French 2016). Because of this, third-party candidates must use every means possible to spread their messages.

By August 2016, Stein purchased television advertising, actually outspending Donald Trump early in the campaign. Trump put a larger portion of his money into social media messages, while Hillary Clinton used traditional TV ads for much of her campaign messaging. Stein again promoted the Green New Deal as a way to solve both the United State's economic and environmental problems. In a campaign video for her 2016 campaign titled "Jill Stein on the Economy: We Need a New Green Deal," she said the Green Party had really become a party of democracy and justice. "You cannot create environmental justice unless you have economic justice," she says in the ad. "We need a world and an America that works for all of us and that puts people, planet and peace over profit" (Stein 2016a).

Stein railed against TARP, the Troubled Asset Relief Program that was originally established by President George W. Bush and continued by President Barack Obama. The program authorized $475 billion to stabilize the U.S. economic system, stimulate economic growth, and help to avoid foreclosures following the 2007–2009 economic downturn. In classic populist rhetoric, Stein argued that the federal government was willing to bail out Wall Street firms and big businesses, but did not address economic problems the crisis brought to average Americans, many of whom lost their jobs and homes and who were saddled with student loan debt. "We [the Green Party] will bail out Millennials and others in student debt," she said in her ad "Jill Stein: Cancel Student Debt." She called Millennials the "generation held hostage in debt" and said the solution was in the ideas put forth by the Green Party, not by the Republican or Democratic candidates. "We can create an America - and a world - that works for all of us. The power to do that is not just in our hopes, it's not just in our dreams. Right here and now, it's in our hands" (Stein 2016b). Those populists who are on the margins of the political spectrum, or the fringe, will pose challenges to the main parties from outside the political establishment (Palonen 2020). In Stein's case, she characterized the actions taken by the mainstream parties as favoring those with money and connections, thus leaving "the people" with little recourse to right these wrongs.

She said that she was the only candidate "not controlled by predatory banks" in an interview with BBC News, and she declared that voters were not being given much a choice with either Trump or Clinton. In a classic populist appeal, she said that the Green Party offered a "political voice of, by, and for the people" (BBC 2016).

As has become common, no third-party candidates were invited to presidential debates, because a candidate must have at least 15 percent support to receive an invitation, and most third-party candidates cannot meet that threshold. After being escorted from the site of a presidential debate in 2016, she then went to another location to "join" the debate via Twitter.

As the campaign progressed, Stein continued to try to rally her supporters and gain new ones, but her messages became increasingly drowned out by the particularly nasty campaign between Donald Trump and Hillary Clinton. She and her running mate, Ajamu Baraka, were on the ballot in most states, and they were write-in candidates in at least three states. In the general election, she garnered 1.45 million votes, which was more than three previous three Green Party campaigns combined. She won her most votes in California, taking 1.96 percent of the votes, and she tallied more than 2 percent in Hawaii, Oregon, and Vermont.

POST 2016 ELECTION CAMPAIGN

On Nov. 8, 2016, the presidential campaign ended, but the controversy did not. Democrats who were unhappy that Clinton had lost began to blame Stein and Libertarian candidate Gary Johnson for siphoning votes away from Clinton. They also wanted to know if Russian hackers had interfered with the voting, especially in swing states in which Trump did well in electronic voting. Because Clinton won the popular vote, many of those in the media and in the election community began to call for a recount of votes in some states.

Stein agreed to take leadership on the push for a recount, and she raised more money for this project than she did for her own presidential campaign. The money was to pay for recounts in Michigan, Wisconsin, and Pennsylvania. A completed recount in Wisconsin validated the original vote total, but recounts in the other states were blocked by a federal judge.

Although it appeared that votes in Wisconsin had not been tampered with, the controversy surrounding the election did not abate. As the U.S. Congress began an investigation in to Russia's possible role in trying to influence the presidential election, it came to light that Russia had launched a social media blitz in support of Stein just before the election. It seemed to specifically target African Americans, according to cyber experts who examined social media from that time period (Windrem 2018).

Although Russia denied the charges, cyber experts found that Russians working under the direction of the Internet Research Agency, which is based in St. Petersburg, Russia, tweeted the phrase "Jill Stein" more than 1,000 times around the time of the election. They did not suggest that Stein was aware of the attempts to influence potential voters, but several critics charged that Stein's policies would have benefited those of Vladmir Putin, and that she had been highly critical of Clinton, who she said would be more likely to lead the U.S. into a nuclear war with Russia than Trump.

During the Congressional investigation into possible Russian interference in the 2016 election, Stein was asked to turn over materials pertaining to her contacts with members of the Russian government and media outlets, and she partially complied. However, she refused to turn over internal communications regarding her campaign's positions on Russian policy, stating that was outside the scope of the investigation. She did agree to provide the committee with documentation stating her proposed Russia policies (Bowden 2018).

In October 2019, Hillary Clinton made comments during a podcast implying that Tulsi Gabbard, a current Democratic candidate for president, and Jill Stein were both favored by the Russian government. Of Stein, she said "Yeah, she's a Russian asset. I mean, totally" (Smerconish 2019).

Stein and Gabbard both fired back at Clinton, and in a CNN interview Stein called the comments a "completely unhinged conspiracy theory for which there is absolutely no basis in fact." She called it "wild and insulting," and suggested that Clinton was still stinging from her defeat to Donald Trump (Smerconish 2019). Stein also again took the opportunity to push for rank choice voting for national elections.

In the United States, a particularly close presidential election seems to provide the need for a scapegoat. Third parties often bear the brunt of the anger and frustration of the losing party, and often particular candidates are targeted for scrutiny. Neville-Shepard argues this is part of the rhetorical containment of third-party voters. In the aftermath of the 2016 race, "critics drew heavily on historical anecdotes to paint third-party supporters as infiltrators who were responsible for flipping elections; in other words, they were voters with a history of possessing too much influence and tipping elections based on the whims of a recalcitrant minority" (Neville-Shepard 2019b, 10). The close margin of the 2016 race evoked memories of the close 2000 race, causing political figures and media commentators to recall Ralph Nader and his impact on Al Gore's presidential chances. As Neville-Shepard points out, deflecting anger at third party candidates often masks the weaknesses of the major party's losing candidate.

STEIN CAMPAIGN LEGACY

Jill Stein is the second most successful Green Party presidential candidate, behind only Ralph Nader, who collected 2.9 million votes in 2000 and was blamed for costing Al Gore the election that year. It is ironic that both Stein and Nader were said to have cost Democratic candidates a victory in two different, but tight, election years. Stein received the second-highest number of votes for a female in a presidential general election when she won 1.5 million votes in 2016. Hillary Clinton has the highest vote count for any female, receiving almost 66 million votes in that same year.

One of Stein's legacies will be the emergence of the Green Party as a viable third party. In the past, the Greens have seen their number of votes decline when they had lesser-known candidates as the nominee. But with the candidacy of Jill Stein, especially in 2016, the party itself seemed to gain more attention and support. This is quite an achievement, given the low amount of media coverage allotted to third-party candidates and the smaller amount of money that is usually raised by those nominees. Her reliance on populist rhetoric, couched in terms of the Green Party, and Stein herself, as working to free "the people" from the tyranny of the political establishment and big corporations, resonated with many voters. It is worth noting that the other successful Green Party presidential candidate, Ralph Nader, is also known for his populist rhetoric and crusading activities.

Stein used activist tactics to gain the attention of mainstream media, which was a departure from previous Green Party candidates, but seemed quite authentic for her. Authenticity is important in politics, and especially for those candidates employing populist discourse, and Stein brought her already established activist background into her presidential campaigns. This was helpful when she needed to attract media attention through a style "disruptive of communicative norms in specific politically mediated settings" (Ekstrom, Patrona and Thornborrow 2018, 10). Stein was not averse to taking controversial stands that sometimes led to her either being arrested or fined. While that may not seem to be the best type of media coverage, such events did often land her in the mainstream media and thus she became a part of the national discussion. This will be noticed by future candidates, who will no doubt try similar tactics to attract public attention to their ideas and platforms.

Stein's decision to use the New Green Deal as the basis for her campaigns was wise, as it was offered as a solution to two different issues in the nation and provided an opportunity to pull in new party supporters. It also attracted the attention of many progressives within the Democratic Party. Some see the New Green Deal as important in the future of U.S. liberal politics. "From our vantage point, a new politics incorporating climate change while at the same time targeting wider groups and identities looks like the most likely bet to break through the current political impasse and its ongoing crisis" (Knott 2020c, 121). In March 2021, President Joe Biden released his "American Jobs Plan," a new infrastructure proposal for the nation. Critics quickly labeled it the Green New Deal, while members of Congress who support the Green New Deal said that it did not contain enough of the environmental and social justice plan that had been promoted by Jill Stein and other legislators. In April 2021, the THRIVE Act, promoted by the Green New Deal Network (green-newdealnetwork.org), was presented as a bill in the House of Representatives. This Act was based on principles in the Green New Deal, and it was backed by several grassroots groups and unions who would like to see it be the basis for infrastructure changes and recovery in the nation.

Stein was definitely a candidate from outside the mainstream, employing the rhetoric and the posturing of a populist candidate who was attempting to discredit the main parties while presenting ideas that might be new and different to many voters. Her discourse, tactics, and issues will have an impact on politics in the coming years. While she did not run for president in 2020, it is unknown if she will try again in the future. If so, it is likely that she will employ similar tactics and stands on issues, as this seems to be an ideological quest for her as much as it is a political one.

As can be seen from the third-party candidates profiled here, there has been a demonstrated quick adoption of new communication technologies among outsider candidates, and they are always on the lookout for ways to go around mainstream media and take their messages straight to the public. From Perot's television infomercials to Nader and Stein's online and social media messaging, it can be seen that third-party candidates must be resourceful in their communication methods. They also employ a discourse that is different from that of mainstream candidates, and that is often paired with a display of activism to both energize their grassroots supporters and grab mainstream media headlines. These techniques are not unique to third-party candidates, but, as will be seen, they have also influenced other fringe candidates who are looking for creative ways to deliver messages to their prospective voters. The renegade candidates who will be discussed next have also embraced some of these same tactics, as well as online resources such as social media.

REFERENCES

Arsenault, Mark. 2016. "Jill Stein Takes Aim in a Burn-Down-the-Establishment Campaign." *Boston Globe.* Oct. 4, 2016. https://www.bostonglobe.com/metro/2016/10/04/protests-principles-and-missing-foot-joint/hKOy3lOSst704HE-iSnqiDI/story.html.

BBC. 2016. "Jill Stein: I Am the Only Candidate That Is Not Controlled by Predatory Banks." BBC Global News. Aug. 12, 2016. https://www.youtube.com/watch?v=neLugGw1xGc.

Bonikowski, Bart and Noam Gidron. 2016. The Populist style in American Politics: Presidential Campaign Discourse, 1952-1996. *Social Forces,* 94, no. 4 (June):1593–1621. https://doi.org/10.1093/sf/sov120.

Bowden, John. 2018. "Jill Stein Campaign Declines Doc Requests In Senate Russia Probe." The Hill. March 28, 2018. https://thehill.com/homenews/campaign/385342-jill-stein-campaign-declines-some-requests-for-docs-in-senate-russia.

Carnes, Nicholas and Noam Lupu. 2020. The White Working Class and the 2016 Election. *Perspectives on Politics* 19, no. 1 (May): 1–18. https://doi.org/10.1017/S1537592720001267.

Casullo, Maria Esperanza. 2020. Populism and Myth. In *The Populist Manifesto*, edited by Emmy Eklundh and Andy Knott, 25–38. London: Rowman & Littlefield.

Christensen, Christian. 2013. Wave-Riding and Hashtag-Jumping. Twitter, Minority, Third Parties and the 2012 U.S. Elections. *Information, Communication & Society* 16, no. 5 (April): 646–666.

Collet, Christian. 1996. The Polls—Trends: Third Parties and the Two-Party System. *Public Opinion Quarterly* 60, no. 3 (Fall): 432–449.

Democracy Now! 2012. "Green Party Candidates Arrested for Trying to Enter Debate." Oct. 17. 2012. https://www.democracynow.org/2012/10/17/headlines.

Ekstrom, Mats, Marianna Patrona and Joanna Thornborrow. 2018. Right-Wing Populism and the Dynamics of Style: A Discourse-Analytic Perspective on Mediated Political Performances. *Palgrave Communication*, 4 (83). https://doi.org/10.1057/s41599-018-0132-6.

French, Sally. 2016. "Third Party Candidates Get Media Coverage—In the Form of A John Oliver Beating." MarketWatch. Oct. 17, 2016. https://www.marketwatch.com/story/third-party-candidates-get-media-coverage-in-the-form-of-a-john-oliver-takedown-2016-10-17.

Green Party Website. n.d. GP.org. https://www.gp.org.

Green New Deal Network. https://www.greennewdealnetwork.org. n.d.

Jager, Anton and Arthur Borriello. 2020. Making Sense of Populism. *Catalyst* 3, no. 4 (Winter): 49–81. https://catalyst-journal.com/vol3/no4/making-sense-of-populism.

Knott, Andy. 2020a. The New Moving Right Show." *Soundings: A Journal of Politics and Culture* 75 (Summer): 111–123.

Knott, Andy. 2020b. Populism: The Politics of a Definition. In *The Populist Manifesto*, edited by Emmy Eklundh and Andy Knott, 9-23. London: Rowman & Littlefield.

Knott, Andy. 2020c. A Manifesto and Populism. In *The Populist Manifesto*, edited by Emmy Eklundh and Andy Knott, 107-122. London: Rowman & Littlefield.

Laclau, Ernesto. 2005. *On Populist Reason*. London: Verso.

Laloggia, John. 2019. 6 Facts About U.S. Political Independents. Pew Research Center. May 15, 2019. https://www.pewresearch.org/fact-tank/2019/05/15/facts-about-us-political-independents/.

Lee, Daniel. 2012. Anticipating Entry: Major Party Positioning and Third Party Threat. *Political Research Quarterly* 65, no. 1 (March): 138–150.

Martin, Michael. 2012. "Candidate Wants to Green Up the White House." *NPR.org*. July 18, 2012. https://www.npr.org/2012/07/18/156976060/candidate-wants-to-green-up-the-white-house.

Montgomery, Martin. 2017. Post-truth politics? Authenticity, Populism and the Electoral Discourses of Donald Trump. *Journal of Language and Politics* 16 (4): 619–639.

Mudde, Cas. 2004. The Popular Zeitgeist. *Government and Opposition* 39 (3): 541–563. doi:10.1111/j.1477-7053.2004.00135.x.

Mudde, Cas. 2018. Studying Populism in Comparison Perspective: Reflections on the Contemporary and Future Research Agenda. *Comparative Political Studies* 51, no. 13 (November): 1667–1693.

Neville-Shepard, Ryan. 2019a. Genre-Busting, Campaign Speech Genres and the Rhetoric of Political Outsiders. In *Reading the Presidency Advances in Presidential Rhetoric*, edited by Stephen J. Heidt and Mary E. Stuckey, 86–105. New York: Peter Lang.

Neville-Shepard, Ryan. 2019b. Containing the Third-Party Voter in the 2016 U.S. Presidential Election. *Journal of Communication Inquiry* 49, no. 3 (January): 272–292.

OpenSecrets. n.d. "Candidate Summary 2012 Cycle." OpenSecrets.org. http://www.opensecrets.org/pres12/candidate.php?id=n00033776.

Palonen, Emilia. 2020. Ten Theses on Populism—and Democracy. In *The Populist Manifesto*, edited by Emmy Eklundh and Andy Knott, 55–69. London: Rowman & Littlefield.

Schreckinger, Ben. 2017. "Jill Stein Isn't Sorry." *Politico Magazine*. June 20, 2017. https://www.politico.com/magazine/story/2017/06/20/jill-stein-green-party-no-regrets-2016-215281.

Smerconish, Michael. 2019. "Stein Says Clinton Promoting 'Unhinged Conspiracy Theory.'" *CNN*. Oct. 19, 2019. https://www.youtube.com/watch?v=3oFSSWRJ2Yo.

Stein, Jill. 2012. Acceptance Speech of Jill Stein at the Green Party National Convention. Sept. 10, 2012. https://time.com/wp-content/uploads/2015/04/stein_green_party_nomination_acceptance_july_14_2012.pdf.

Stein, Jill. 2016a. "Jill Stein on the Economy: We Need a New Green Deal." Stein/Baraka 2016. https://www.youtube.com/watch?v=O5tAO2ul0Ts.

Stein, Jill. 2016b. "You are Not a Loan—Cancel Student Debt." Stein/Baraka 2016. https://www.youtube.com/watch?v=qYBXVaNHTaI.

Tas, Hakki. 2020. The Chronopolitics of National Populism. *Identities*: https://www.tandfonline.com/doi/full/10.1080/1070289X.2020.1735160.

Windrem, Robert. 2018. "Russians Launched Pro-Jill Stein Social Media Blitz to Help Trump Win Election, Reports Say." *NBCnews.com*. Dec. 22, 2018. https://www.nbcnews.com/politics/national-security/russians-launched-pro-jill-stein-social-media-blitz-help-trump-n951166.

PART IV

Renegade Candidates

Chapter 10

George C. Wallace

DISRUPTIVE, DISORDERLY, AND DISCORDANT RENEGADE CANDIDATE

Historians and biographers have struggled for many years to forge a coherent picture of the real George C. Wallace. Was he simply a populist who had an uncanny sense of which way the political winds were blowing in the country? Was he a lucky opportunist with a large dose of raw charisma? Or, was he, as history professor and biographer Dan T. Carter claims, "one of the great transitional figures in American politics"? (Carter 1991, 44).

Wallace was elected as governor of Alabama four times—1962, 1970, 1974, and 1982. He ran for president in 1964 as a Democrat, in 1968 as an independent candidate and in 1972 and 1976 as a Democratic candidate. It was during the 1972 race that he survived an assassination attempt that left him in a wheelchair for the rest of his life. Wallace's rhetoric—fiery, populist, and racist—is most often identified with opposition to desegregation and his rhetoric against the federal courts. The stands that Wallace took on racial issues contributed to the beatings and deaths of several Civil Rights activists and volunteers and left behind a legacy of pain and suffering in the South.

WALLACE AS A DEMOCRATIC RENEGADE

Political party affiliation did not seem as important to Wallace as taking personal advantage of a political situation. Always a Democrat, perhaps because that was the majority party in Alabama at the time, Wallace refused to join the Dixiecrats in their walkout from the Democratic Party in 1948. Wallace negotiated a fine line between participating in the segregationist political party and not placing himself in danger of retribution from the Democratic Party. While it is unclear if he sympathized with the Dixiecrats, it seems that Wallace had the political savvy to see that the upstart party was doomed to fail. As Dan Carter wrote in his seminal biography of Wallace: "The young man from Barbour County was a segregationist in 1948, but he wasn't a stupid segregationist" (1995, 88).

Later, though, after he had an established political base and reputation, Wallace delighted in tweaking the national Democratic Party and in pushing the boundaries of race and hatred. In doing so, he became an example of the rebellious Southern Democrats and a renegade within his own party. Not even when the National Guard was federalized by President John F. Kennedy in 1963 to block Wallace's stand in the schoolhouse door did he relent. Instead, he saw this as providing him with a introduction to the nation and setting him on the path to run for president.

Wallace was a consummate populist, and he carefully cultivated his audience by positioning himself as the spokesperson for "the people" who were basically good, decent, and moral folks whose way of life was being threatened by immoral elites, as is common in populist discourse (Mudde and Kaltwasser 2017). As Zweirs points out, Wallace's messages "combined race and class issues in a gendered discourse that defended traditionalism and white privilege" (2019). Wallace took extremely conservative stands on current issues such as race, political protests, and crime in the United States. The federal government's increasing intervention in racial issues in the South made that issue "exceedingly salient, especially in the states with the largest black populations and in those sections of both subregions where blacks constituted substantial percentages of the population" (Black and Black 2002, 148). While other parts of the nation were having protests against the Vietnam War, politicians in the Deep South were not only dealing with traditional racial politics, but were also immersed in them to a large degree, simply because of having been raised in a segregated culture. Wallace was able to craft political messages that appealed to those who felt the federal government was working to destroy their way of life and endanger their livelihoods.

WALLACE'S PRESIDENTIAL CAMPAIGN DISCOURSE

Wallace was a complicated figure who seemed to thrive on the accumulation of power and the adrenaline of campaigning. His 1968 presidential campaign, in particular, featured rhetoric aimed at U.S. citizens who felt alienated from their government. In this election, he segued from geographical politics—primarily involving racism and forced integration—into a spokesperson for mainly white Americans looking for solutions to the war in Vietnam, the counter-culture revolution, their feelings of diminished power, and concerns that they had been disenfranchised by their elected officials. He ran as a candidate for the American Independent Party, although most people still associated him with the Democratic Party. His slogan was "Stand Up for America," and he worked to portray himself as a candidate different from the others in the race.

To effectively set himself apart from the other candidates in the race, Wallace needed to accomplish at least two things: (1) He needed potential voters to see the two main parties as essentially the same, so that he could paint himself as the only alternative to improve the situation and (2) He needed to be seen as authentic, as someone who understood what was happening because he had experienced it. Because he was centering his appeals on a particular segment of the population that shared similar values and concerns, there was somewhat limited heterogeneity, meaning that his speeches and discourse could remain quite consistent during the campaign (Bonikowski and Gidron 2016). He tapped into the anger and alienation that many white Americans felt at the time, and distrust of the government became a foundational issue in his campaign (Gold 1995).

Typical of his rhetoric was this comment heard on the campaign trail: "You can take all the Democratic candidates for President and all the Republican candidates for President. Put them in a sack and shake them up. Take the first one that falls out, grab him by the nape of the neck, and put him right back in the sack. Because there is not a dime's worth of difference in any of them" (Wallace 1971). That comment might sound familiar, as it has been used by many populist candidates over the years. Wallace's allusion might be more colorful, but it is no less populist than comments by later presidential candidates such as Ralph Nader and Jill Stein who stressed there was no difference between Democratic and Republican candidates.

Wallace positioned himself as an outsider candidate running against the political establishment mainly through his rhetoric, which was divisive, hostile, populist, and sometimes crude. "George Wallace was the first politician to sense and then exploit the changes that Americans came to know by many names: white backlash, the silent majority, the alienated voters, but—beyond a generalized hostility toward the federal government—he had little to offer in terms of policies or solutions" (Carter 1996, 12). However, his rhetoric was combative and exhibited a resentment toward the affluent, the liberal elite, and the federal government, all of which were seen as threats by his supporters. While he might not have had many solutions, he excelled at emotional discourse that could whip his supporters into a frenzy during his speeches.

Comparisons have been made of Wallace and President Donald Trump, who also often used combative and controversial rhetoric to separate himself and his supporters from the political status quo. According to most biographers, Wallace decided early on to pursue an image that would gain favor with those who favored segregation, mainly because he lost his first race for governor in the Democratic primary to John Patterson, an avowed racist. Until that point, Wallace was known as the leading liberal in the Alabama legislature. Once his image as a fighter for segregation was established, Wallace, as an outside candidate, then used event staging and different rhetorical approaches to solidify his support among white voters who felt disenfranchised by the government and both political parties. "Third-party candidates, as quintessential outsiders, approach the fixed situations of campaign speech genres with an aim to create controversy, embracing authenticity over traditional markers of legitimacy" (Neville-Shepard 2019, 96). In the 1968 race, Wallace was technically running as a third-party candidate, but few really seemed to separate him from the Democratic Party, which he returned to in the 1972 race. In his discourse, Wallace said controversial things, made outlandish statements, and he would often intentionally provoke members of the audience while giving speeches. He seemed to thrive on the energy of those events, and he stayed on the attack during his campaign stops.

The issue of performance is key for populist discourse, as an audience must find a candidate authentic and his or her rhetoric emotionally appealing before it is accepted. For that reason, "populism only becomes a broader phenomenon when there is an audience willing to receive it" (Knott 2020a, 118). The "bad manners" displayed by Wallace in his speeches—calling people names, provoking members of the audience, and speaking in a disjointed style—are typical elements of a populist political style (Ekstrom, Patrona and Thornborrow 2018; Moffitt and Tormey 2014).

Wallace consistently positioned himself as a man who was willing to speak out on behalf of "the people" against perceived injustices by the federal government, but it was usually done in the name of freedom. Freedom was often mentioned in his speeches, including "freedom of choice," "individual freedom," and "a system of freedom." Wallace often made references to the degree of control being asserted by the federal government—which he positioned as the opposite of freedom. This theme was consistently carried through Wallace's speeches, with him always being positioned as someone who shared the same cultural references and history (even if it was American history and not just the South), and who gave voice to the disenfranchised who were unhappy with the current situation. "On flickering television screens and in giant political rallies, in speeches as much religious exorcism as political argument, he offered frightened and insecure millions a chance to strike back—if only rhetorically—at the enemy" (Carter 1996, 9). Wallace's populist discourse found a home with members of the white working class (a group that would also later support Donald Trump), as well as those who wanted an end to the Vietnam War.

Populist rhetoric is seen as confrontational: an uprising of "the people" against those in power who have somehow betrayed them. While "the people" can be a loose association of various groups and individuals who share common values, the concept of an enemy varies, depending on the where and when a populist movement is taking place. This requires that an enemy be identified and articulated to an audience (Jager and Borriello 2020) in a way that energizes "the people" and sparks the birth of a movement by pulling back the curtain to reveal a festering crisis in society. This is what Wallace accomplished.

CAMPAIGN TACTICS

One of the most well-known moments in Wallace's life was him standing in the door at the University of Alabama to prevent the enrollment of black students. But what most people did not know is how Wallace and his aides staged that moment. What is now known as the "Stand in the Schoolhouse Door" at the University of Alabama took place on June 11, 1963. In this event, which catapulted Wallace into the national spotlight, Wallace kept a campaign pledge that he would stand in a schoolhouse door to block integration of Alabama public schools. Wallace stood in the doorway of Foster Auditorium at the University of Alabama and read a proclamation as he attempted to block two black students, Vivian Malone and James Hood, from registering at the school. After President John F. Kennedy federalized the Alabama National Guard and ordered its units to the university campus, Wallace stepped aside. The students were later allowed inside the building.

While some saw this as simply the actions of a fringe political actor who would soon be forgotten, others saw the rise of a political hero. After the event, Wallace received thousands of messages, with most of them supportive of his actions and comments. "Over half came from outside the South, and 95 percent supported him. George Wallace, the national political figure, was born" (Carter 1996, 8).

Of course, the debate still rages over whether or not Wallace was truly in favor of segregation, or if he sensed that the political winds were blowing in that direction. It is interesting that two journalists who regularly covered Wallace both expressed the opinion that Wallace was not racist.

Veteran Alabama newspaper reporter Frank Bruer covered events in the state for forty-two years and knew Wallace.

> I personally do not think that George Wallace was that much of a racist. I sense it was the thing to do politically, because there was a strong amount of sentiment at that time. . . . But, from my personal contacts with him, I never heard him talk about 'the niggers and the whatever.' I never heard anything like that, and I think it was a purely political thing. (Bruer 2003)

Robert (Bob) Ingram, another Alabama journalist, agreed, and added that Wallace's campaigning fervor may have boxed him in on occasion, including when he pledged to block integration.

I was there the night he made the opening speech, when he said, 'I'll do anything to preserve segregation. I'll even stand in the door.' He didn't really mean
at that time that he was gonna literally stand in the door. It was just a figure of
speech . . . but we of the press, we jumped on it when he said stand in the door
and, after about a month and people liked it, he said, 'By God, I will stand in
the door. (Ingram 2003)

Many accounts of what happened that day have surfaced. It is known that
more than four hundred reporters were on hand for the event. According to
one source, the crowd of reporters was so thick that it was hard for the university president and trustees to see what was taking place (Clark 1995). The
event was designed so that the confrontation would be between Wallace and
the federal authorities. The confrontation occurred before Malone and Hood
even arrived at the building. That scripting better fit the image that Wallace
had been developing for himself. "Thus, it was possible to sustain Wallace's
fiction that he was challenging the constitutional validity of a federal order,
not blocking the integration of the university" (Carter 1995, 148). During
the standoff, Wallace gave a 15-minute speech in which he denounced the
federal government's intrusion into the University of Alabama's business,
and labeled it "an illegal and unwarranted action by the central government" (Clark 1995, 226). His followers who supported segregation, however,
probably interpreted the event as a stand against integration. It was populist
performance of the highest order, and it catapulted Wallace into the national
conscience.

Ingram was one of only two reporters granted a private interview with
Wallace before the event. "Oh, it was orchestrated from day one. Everybody
knew how it was gonna end before it started. But, that was an exceedingly
smart [move]. It made George Wallace the one man above all who represented opposition to integration. Defiance of the federal courts. He became a
national, and even international, figure all because of that little circus on the
campus of the university" (Ingram 2003).

That one media event garnered Wallace the kind of media coverage that
some politicians only dream about. He was on the cover of national magazines, he was invited to debates and talk shows, and his name recognition
grew all over the country, which help to lay a foundation for his future presidential campaigns.

Bill Jones, press secretary for Wallace during that period, said he personally picked out a door at Foster Auditorium that that would allow the best
media access to the event. That orchestration led to one of Wallace's most
defining moments, and launched him on a path that he thought could lead to
the White House.

However, Wallace found that the rhetoric that put him in the governor's mansion in Alabama and on the cover of national magazines wasn't going to increase his appeal in other parts of the country that he needed to win in order to become president. So, in the 1968 race, Wallace veered slightly from the issues of segregation and instead embraced an "Us vs Them" rhetoric that revolved around topics such as "law and order" and taking the nation back from what he called the "anarchists" who wore sandals and needed haircuts. "The stand gave him the opportunity to reframe his segregationist message into an all-American defense of constitutional values" (Zwiers 2019, 4). This was a populist approach that worked better in the rest of the nation, as he identified a large swath of Americans who were concerned about what they saw as a growing liberalism in the country.

Wallace began his political career when "stumping" was the primary method of campaigning. Modern elections have moved away from this type of one-on-one, look people in the eyes-type of campaigning. However, Wallace seemed to thrive on the constant traveling and speechmaking. The act of talking about politics, expressing his views, and trying to win people to his beliefs seems to have been a source of excitement for Wallace. In fact, those who knew Wallace said he did the same thing when he was around friends and family. "He was on the stump even in private. He'd dominate conversations," (Ingram 2003). Wallace seems to have gotten an incredible amount of pleasure from speaking to crowds—especially when he felt that things had gone well. Another Southern populist, Huey Long, also seemed to derive much pleasure from speaking in front of crowds and inundating them with emotionally charged discourse that stoked resentment toward "the elites." It is worth noting that Donald Trump seemed to also derive pleasure and self-edification from these types of events.

Charlie Snider, one of Wallace's aides, said in a personal conversation (2003) that in private, the governor had mood changes like everyone else. But a really good political rally would cause Wallace to be in a great mood. For Wallace, life seemed to be about running for office, and speaking to crowds was one of the exciting parts. Dan Carter recounts an experience that Hunter S. Thompson had at a Wallace rally in 1972, when Thompson said that five minutes into the speech, the air was already electric. Halfway through, "the audience of Polish Americans was on its feet, cheering every line, laughing, shouting, exhilarated by the furious energy of Wallace's snarling attacks on hippies, civil rights agitators, welfare recipients, atheists, beatniks, anti-war protestors, communists and street thugs" (Carter 1996, 9–10). Wallace had the ability to whip a crowd into a frenzy and then hold it through his discourse. He seemed to realize this was one of his strengths, and he used his ability to work a crowd to his advantage during his presidential campaigns.

Wallace paid to air television commercials in 1968, 1972, and 1976, but the spots were poorly produced and he appeared stilted and awkward in them. "He really came across much better [in person]. He got in and could fire them up much better than he could in these canned TV performances" (Bruer 2003) For instance, in one titled "Busing," (Wallace 1972) Wallace is only seen in snippets apparently taken from a debate or speech, as he is standing behind a podium. Most of the ad is composed of film images with a voiceover by someone else setting up a "response" from Wallace in which he always begins with "as president." Wallace outlines a brief response to the issues of the busing of schoolchildren, protest violence, and the "giveaways" of American money to anti-American countries. The ad ends with the voiceover intoning that Wallace has "the courage to stand up for Americans." It was easy to see that television was not Wallace's natural campaign medium, but by airing ads in contested states, he reminded voters of his presence in the race. In 1972 some Democratic state parties paid to air anti-Wallace ads the weekend before primaries in an effort to block him from taking votes away from Sen. George McGovern and Sen. Hubert Humphrey (Flint 1972). They were right to be concerned, as Wallace won the Democratic presidential primary in Michigan and also in Maryland on the same day, and McGovern came in second. However, Wallace was in the hospital after being shot five times the previous day while campaigning in Maryland, which effectively ended his campaign.

WALLACE'S ISSUES

Wallace was often described as a populist, but in the 1960s, as today, that term had several different meanings. It is probably most often intended as a political insult, but those who study the term describe a populist candidate as one who stands in opposition to an enemy (either real or manufactured) that is often exemplified by the political system and is blamed for a variety of ills in society.

The rhetoric of a populist is usually versatile, and it always stands in opposition (Knott 2020a; Mudde 2004). For instance, a populist will be anti-intellectual or anti-capitalist, rather than speaking in favor of a particular idea. This is because speaking against an issue or person is generally more fiery and crowd pleasing than the opposite. Populists speak against the political establishment, but they don't usually provide solutions to the problems or provide alternatives. Wallace often reminded crowds that Congress had failed "the people" by allowing forced "busing, foreign aid, higher taxes" and failing to take steps to insure "law and order." The promise, sometimes spoken and sometimes implied, was that Wallace could single-handedly fix these situations, but he never really provided any details about how that might happen (Carter 1996). In his 1964, 1968, and 1972 campaigns, his most common issues were his opposition to the Civil Rights Act and Civil Rights agitators, comments about United States Supreme Court justices, government bureaucrats, liberal educators, and forced school busing. In 1972, his opposition to racial busing was his signature issue, and this pushed the other candidates to also discuss the topic during the primary campaign.

In this way, Wallace used populist rhetoric to his advantage. He used rhetoric that exaggerated a lack of trust in the political establishment to increase his appeal among white Americans who already felt that the government or courts had abandoned or alienated them. Wallace was attempting to appeal to a wide range of groups—those opposed to civil rights, those opposed to the growth of government, those who were unhappy with the federal courts, and those who felt disenfranchised by the two major political parties. A common thread among these groups was that they were all looking for someone to be a "voice" and a "fighter" for them (Zwiers 2019).

Although much remains to be learned about how verbal behavior affects a voter's image of a political candidate, Dan Nimmo identified certain characteristics common to the development of a political candidate's image. An image is not simply the product of one dimension, trait or activity. Instead, he argued there are at least three elements working together to produce a relationship between a particular candidate and the voters' perceptions of that candidate. Candidates portray political and stylistic roles in relation to voters, and elements in the political role include (but are not limited to) a candidate's past, his or her qualifications for office, and his or her community involvement (Nimmo 1976). Stylistic roles are seen as distinctive personal qualities or traits. "Candidates formulate and project not only images of themselves and each other, but also imagine what voters think of them as office-seekers," (Nimmo 1976, 36). George Wallace was a politician who was not shy about emphasizing his personal qualities in order to win votes. Because of his past success as a Golden Gloves boxer, he promoted the image of himself as a fighter, which helped to create in the minds of his supporters the image of a politician who would stand up in the ring and fight for their interests (Bonikowski and Gidron 2016). Zweirs (2019) notes that "voters distressed by rapid social change turn to strong masculine leaders who promise a restoration of control and order," which is what Wallace promised to his supporters.

Whether he was appealing to his blood brothers and sisters in the South, to his fellow conservatives who feared the growing power of the federal government, or to members of the middle class who were feeling squeezed by economic conditions, Wallace presented this image: I am your spokesman. We are in this together, and I can change things.

Nimmo concludes that in the process of image formation, the personal traits and linked symbols projected by a candidate become associated with their stylistic roles. Voters are looking for cognitive shortcuts, and the cues and symbols used in political communication can oftentimes provide "markers" for voters awash in a sea of political advertising, sound bites, and direct mail.

For Wallace supporters, the verbal cues and symbols in his speeches reminded them that he was "like them." He understood what they were going through—that he would fight for them and change things. By using terms such as "law and order," which could mean one thing to a Southerner and something very different to someone in a state such as Pennsylvania, he could appeal to those who still saw him as an opponent of Civil Rights and those who saw him as standing up against the decay and disrespect they felt was happening in American society.

In his major presidential campaigns, Wallace chose issues that were not uniquely Southern, but that hovered on current pressure points in society. He grabbed onto a political opportunity that many other politicians had not yet seen as existing. "Issue alienation played a role as many of his supporters rejected the Democrats and Republicans on the basis of social issues" (Gold 1995, 754). Wallace was especially good at revealing what Carter called the "hollow core of the Democratic Party" (1996, 10). As a political renegade, Wallace pushed the more mainstream candidates into discussing many of his issues, but none of them could tap into the national distrust of the federal government as effectively as the feisty Alabama governor.

The Rev. Martin Luther King, Jr. considered Wallace a great threat to the South and to the country. "The civil rights leader believed that Wallace was 'perhaps the most dangerous racist in America today . . . I am not sure that he believes all the poison he preaches, but he is artful enough to convince others that he does.' He 'is smart enough so that he only gives three, maybe four speeches,' King observed to [Dan] Rather. 'He just has four, but works on them and hones them, so that they are little minor classics'" (Rieder 2013, 16).

King was correct that Wallace continually revised his speeches, improvising to try out new rhetorical strategies and always tailoring his messages for the current audience. He would rock back and forth while giving speeches and jab his fist in the air with a defiant gesture as he denounced various aspects of society, including Communists, intellectuals, men with long hair and sandals, and the U.S. Supreme Court. It was always "us" versus the federal government or establishment, and it was popular with many voters. In fact, Wallace pushed the 1968 race to the point that, had he "carried the three states in which he came in second to Nixon (North Carolina, South Carolina, and Tennessee), Nixon would have won only 270 electoral votes, and a faithless elector would have deprived him of a majority" (Abramson et al. 1995,

359). Few people realize how close Wallace came to being a true spoiler in that election.

WALLACE'S IMPACT ON POLITICAL DISCOURSE

One of Wallace's innate personal skills seem to have been an uncanny political intuition. This intuition usually served him well, as he was able to latch onto an issue long before it became apparent to other politicians. By the time others figured out that it was important, Wallace might have already been using it in his campaigns, and therefore could say that the other candidates were copying him or stealing his issues. As was mentioned earlier, many people see Wallace as the forerunner of today's conservative Republicans. As a far-right populist, Wallace seems out of place in what we now see as the 1960s and 1970s Democratic Party. However, the 1960s were a politically tumultuous time for both parties, with various constituencies reacting to the escalation of the Vietnam War, the Civil Rights movement, college campus protests, riots in large cities, and the aftermath of several assassinations, including that of a president. Wallace was able to perceive the anger and fear sweeping through many Americans and "made commonplace a new level of political incivility and intemperate rhetoric, and focused that anger on a convenient set of scapegoats" (Carter 1996, 6). Although Wallace might never have been accepted by the Republican Party, some Republican candidates have had success using issues which he popularized in the late 1960s and early 1970s.

In particular, President Ronald Reagan picked up on Wallace's themes and made them his own. In a way, Reagan's work was easier because of the spadework which had been done by Wallace. As a result, Carter asserts that it was easy for the audience to know what Ronald Reagan was talking about "when he began one of his famous discourses on welfare queens using food stamps to buy porterhouse steaks. His audience was already primed to make that connection" (Carter 1995, 349). Of course, Reagan served two terms as president of the United States and Wallace was never elected. In fact, Carter calls Wallace "the most influential loser in twentieth-century American politics" (Carter 1995, 468).

In 1968, Wallace and his running mate, Gen. Curtis LeMay, received 13.5 percent of the vote in the 1968 presidential election. Wallace won five Southern states, and he is still the last third-party candidate to win states in the Electoral College.

In 1972, Wallace, running again as a Democrat, wasn't able to finish the race after the attempt on his life left him paralyzed from the waist down. Even so, he received 3.7 million primary votes, which was the third-highest total among the Democratic contenders. In 1976, Wallace found that people were unaccepting of him in a wheelchair, and he received only 1.9 million votes during the primary.

In many ways, Wallace was a thoroughly modern candidate. He used symbols and issues in his speeches thirty years ago which are still being used by conservative politicians today. Some of Wallace's campaign workers and directors were active in Ronald Reagan's campaigns, primarily because in Reagan they saw a reflection of Wallace's conservatism. Wallace displayed a remarkable understanding of how to manipulate the media and create a public image for himself that would be appealing to some Americans today. He anticipated political trends and located the undercurrents which were invisible to political party leaders of his day.

> It's been said so many times—and it sounds ridiculous, but it's true—that he seemed to sense and identify long before anybody else did the concerns and fears of the people. The issues he was raising in the '60s, aside from race, the concern about big government, welfare, law and order and the breakdown of our society and moral values seems to have been embraced by the conservative folks of this country. Much of what they're saying today is what George Wallace was talking about long before Ronald Reagan picked up on it. (Ingram 2003)

Wallace's words, while cast in a different tone, are still being used to protest the growth of the federal government, high taxes, and inept bureaucrats.

Many people identified similarities between Donald J. Trump's rhetorical style and that of George C. Wallace during the 2016 presidential election. While similarities exist, perhaps it is mainly because both used a populist-type rhetorical style—fiery, explosive, long on criticism, but short on solutions. Even their slogans—Wallace's "Stand up for America," and Trump's "Make America Great Again," — share a degree of similarity. Peggy Sue Wallace Kennedy, daughter of the late governor and presidential candidate, pointed this out in an interview with USA Today. "Compare 'Stand Up For America' with 'Make America Great Again,'" she said. "It doesn't suggest how you're going to do that, but it makes the average American really feel great" (O'Donnell 2016).

Wallace biographer Dan T. Carter also noticed similarities between Wallace and Trump. "There are a lot of people who essentially want the world to stop and want it to stop changing," Carter said. "And when that happens, you look for a strong individual. And to me that's the big appeal and the big similarity between George Wallace and Donald Trump" (Elliott 2016).

There are those who argue that it is George Wallace who has won the Republican Party now, and not Donald Trump. Wallace's political lineage can be seen in the presidential campaigns of Pat Buchanan and in the tactics and strategies of Newt Gingrich. Trump's base shared much in common with Wallace's, including its tendency to be overwhelmingly white and middle-class. Trump used this base to win the White House and take power away from the Republican Party establishment. But will these voters stay in the Republican Party after Trump is out of office? "We also can't know whether Trump will bring the Wallace vote durably into the Republican fold or whether the movement will remain true to its roots as a political third force—anti-establishment in its credo, disruptive in its influence, an opportunistic in its partisan attachments. . . . Wallace voters have captured the Republican Party, but whether it has captured them remains to be seen" (Rauch, 2020).

Many argue that the Republican Party should have seen this coming, but chose to look the other way instead of addressing a nagging unease among White, middle-class Americans with the GOP establishment and the growing influence of alt-right ideas. "These latent white supremacist sentiments—articulated by George Wallace, cultivated by the Republicans, and ignored or disparaged by the Democrats—finally burst into the open in 2016, when the establishment of both parties was caught unawares by a phenomenon they had created: a déjà vu of the 1968 campaign, but this time, the demagogue won" (Zwiers 2019, 11).

For some conservatives in the Republican Party, Trump represents a test of whether the party will survive his embracing of the adversarial nature of the populist movement. "Trump's appeal is his contrarian stance, his 'stick it to 'em' appeal that Bryan, Roosevelt, Lindbergh, the Birchers, and, yes, even George Wallace inspired among those who know something is wrong with America, but don't know how to fix it" (Newstex Blogs, 2015). The ghost of George Wallace's populism is hovering over the Republicans in the form of Donald Trump, a fact that is not lost on political observers. "If you had to boil the history of the modern Republican Party down to a single sentence, you could do no better than this: Barry Goldwater got in a fight with Nelson Rockefeller and George Wallace won" (Rauch, 2020). It is interesting to note that there has been a gradual migration of working-class Americans to the Republican Party, and Trump inherited many of those voters.

The discourse of George C. Wallace found its way into the Republican Party and helped it to coalesce into a competitive party in the 1990s, thanks in part to Congressman Newt Gingrich. This will be discussed in more depth in a later chapter, but Gingrich adapted Wallace's style of discourse—not the ideas themselves—and combined it with the ideas of Ross Perot to fashion a rough-and-tumble, take-no-prisoners type of dialogue that catapulted the Republican Party into its first competitive era in sixty years. We find that both Gingrich and Trump emulated discourse and tactics first made popular by Wallace fifty years ago. In this way, Wallace continues to have an impact on the discourse and politics in the nation, especially among those who are Republican or lean Republican.

Wallace was a renegade candidate with actual outsider credentials and the fiery rhetoric of a populist. However, he lacked the sophisticated campaign organization and technology that other national candidates were using, as well as the types of resources that come with being the nominee for an established political party. His discourse still echoes in the national conversation and provides a glimpse into the importance of his place in American political history.

REFERENCES

Abramson, Paul R., John H. Aldrich, Phil Paolino and David W. Rohde. 1995. Third-Party and Independent Candidates in American Politics: Wallace, Anderson, and Perot. *Political Science Quarterly* 110, no. 3 (Autumn): 349–367.

Black, Earl and Merle Black. 2002. *The Rise of Southern Republicans*. Cambridge, MA: Harvard University Press.

Bonikowski, Bart and Noam Gidron. 2016. The Populist style in American Politics: Presidential Campaign Discourse, 1952-1996. *Social Forces* 94, no. 4 (June):1593–1621. https://doi.org/10.1093/sf/sov120.

Bruer, Frank. Personal conversation, April 25, 2003.

Carter, Dan T. (1991). *George Wallace, Richard Nixon, and the transformation of American politics*. Waco, TX: Markham Press Fund, Baylor University Press.

Carter, Dan. T. 1995. *The politics of rage: George Wallace, the origins of the new conservatism, and the transformation of American politics*. New York: Simon & Schuster.

Carter, Dan T. 1996. Legacy of rage: George Wallace and the Transformation of American Politics. *The Journal of Southern History* 62 (1): 3–26.

Clark, E. Culpepper. 1995. *The schoolhouse door: Segregation's last stand at the University of Alabama*. New York: Oxford University Press.

Ekstrom, Mats, Marianna Patrona and Joanna Thornborrow. 2018. Right-Wing Populism and the Dynamics of Style: A Discourse-Analytic Perspective on Mediated Political Performances. *Palgrave Communication* 4 (83). https://doi.org/10.1057/s41599-018-0132-6.

Elliott, Debbie. 2016. *Is Donald Trump a Modern-Day George Wallace?* NPR All Things Considered. April 22, 2016.

Flint, Jerry M. The 1972 Campaign. *New York Times*. May 15, 1972. https://www.nytimes.com/1972/05/15/archives/wallace-rebuked-on-tv-by-michigan-democrats.html.

Gold, Howard J. 1995. Third Party Voting in Presidential Elections: A Study of Perot, Anderson, and Wallace. *Political Research Quarterly* 48, no. 4 (December); 751–773.

Ingram, Robert. Personal conversation, May 5, 2003.

Jager, Anton and Arthur Borriello. 2020. Making Sense of Populism. *Catalyst* 3, no. 4 (Winter): 49–81. https://catalyst-journal.com/vol3/no4/making-sense-of-populism.

Knott, Andy. 2020a. The New Moving Right Show." *Soundings: A Journal of Politics and Culture* 75 (Summer): 111–123.

Moffitt, Benjamin and Simon Tormey. 2014. Rethinking Populism: Politics, Mediatisation and Political Style. *Political Studies* 62, no. 2 (June): 381–397.

Mudde, Cas. 2004. The Popular Zeitgeist. *Government & Opposition* 39 (3): 541–563. http://works.bepress.com/cas_mudde/6/.

Mudde, Cas and Rovira Kaltwasser. 2017. *Populism: A Very Short Introduction.* Oxford, UK: Oxford University Press.

Neville-Shepard, Ryan. 2019. Genre-Busting, Campaign Speech Genres and the Rhetoric of Political Outsiders. In *Reading the Presidency Advances in Presidential Rhetoric*, edited by Stephen J. Heidt and Mary E. Stuckey, 86-105. New York: Peter Lang.

Newstex Blogs. 2015. The Ghost of George Wallace. Newstex Blogs Bearing Drift (Virginia). https://advance.lexis.com/api/document?collection=news&id=urn:content Item:5GS6-2RP1-DXKX-000H-00000-00&context=1516831.

Nimmo, Dan. 1976. Political Image Makers and the Mass Media. *American Academy of Political and Social Science* 427 (1): 33–44.

O'Donnell, Jayne. 2016. George Wallace's Daughter on How Her Dad Compares to Trump. *USA Today*. Jan 17, 2016. https://www.usatoday.com/story/news/politics/onpolitics/2016/01/17/george-wallace-donald-trump/78942536/.

Rauch, Jonathan. 2020. It's George Wallace's World Now. Wallace Never Won the Presidency, but the Base He Mobilized Has Found a Home in Today's Republican Party. *The Atlantic*. April 26, 2020. https://www.theatlantic.com/ideas/archive/2020/04/george-wallace-donald-trump/607336/.

Rieder, Jonathan. 2013. *Gospel of freedom: Martin Luther King, Jr.'s Letter From a Birmingham Jail and the Struggle That Changed a Nation.* New York: Bloomsbury Press.

Snider, C. Personal conversation. April, 2, 2003.

Wallace, George. 1971. Campaign speech delivered in Nashville, Tenn. Speech obtained from the Alabama Department of Archives and History in Montgomery on Feb. 25, 2003.

Wallace, George. 1972. Busing. https://www.youtube.com/watch?v=BtiLdZcJNTg.

Zwiers, Maarten. 2019. The Whistles of George Wallace: Gender and Emotions in the 1968 Presidential Campaign. *European Journal of American Studies* 14, no. 1. https://doi.org/10.4000/ejas.14452.

Chapter 11

Patrick Buchanan

FAR-RIGHT OUTSIDER WITH D.C. CREDENTIALS

To explain the outsider status of Patrick Buchanan requires a trip back through history to 1961. Buchanan was working on a Master's degree in journalism at Columbia University when he was hired by the St. Louis Globe-Democrat, probably the closest he has ever come to being associated with the word Democrat. He went on to become the assistant editorial page editor of the very conservative newspaper in 1964, a post from which he supported the right-wing presidential campaign of Barry Goldwater.

Buchanan came of age at a time when journalism was making a transition to television from being either print or radio, and it was becoming an evening mainstay in many homes. Americans were coming to trust Walter Cronkite, especially after the CBS news coverage of President John F. Kennedy's assassination in 1963. Newspapers were still trusted and read, but television was gaining traction and importance. It was into this world that Pat Buchanan began his political and journalistic ascent. He would go on to become a TV political news host on CNN, MSNBC, and public television, as well as a syndicated columnist commenting on political topics. But first, he would be advisor to President Richard Nixon, Vice-President Spiro Agnew, President Gerald Ford, and later the White House Director of Communications for President Ronald Reagan from 1985–1987.

Buchanan entered politics during the 1960s, which was a political and cultural turning point in United States history. Several social movements peaked or began in that decade, causing social and cultural upheaval that was disorienting and frightening for many people. In the mid-to-late 1960s, there was the rise of multiculturalism, which included the peak of the Civil Rights movement, the rise of feminism, the protests against the Vietnam War, the clash of cultures on college campuses, and the Black Power movement. Those on the left of the political spectrum advocated different approaches to these movements, effectively upending the Democratic Party during that decade. Republicans saw these movements as an assault on American culture, and its discourse of rejection breathed energy into the party. "In terms of lifestyles and in many cultural spheres the protesters of the 60s seemed to have won the battle for ideas or at least the cultural battle for society was profoundly changed in its behaviors and consumption habits" (Guerlain 2013, 169). What emerged politically was a new war of good and evil, of embracing multiculturalism or rejecting it and what was seen as its attack on the traditional values and beliefs of Americans.

Buchanan believed in the traditions and morality of the nation, and he saw the societal and cultural movements of the 1960s as having harmed the country's foundation and legacy. As an advisor to Nixon, he was responsible for writing speeches and advocating presidential and campaign actions that were sometimes seen as controversial, but generally were effective. He coined the phrase "the silent majority" for Nixon during the 1968 election, and he penned a now-famous speech delivered by vice-president Spiro Agnew that blasted the mainstream media as "a small and unelected elite" that wielded great power over the American public (Alberta 2017). Even though he often criticized journalists and their cultural power, he never strayed far from the mainstream media, and it became the launching pad for his own presidential campaigns.

BUCHANAN'S DISCOURSE

Buchanan's close relationship with presidents and elected officials often makes people question his validity as an outside candidate, and for good reason. Most outsider candidates tend to be challengers looking to upset the current power structure, rather than insiders, because it is hard to position oneself as an outsider if he or she is already wielding political power. But for some, such as Pat Buchanan, their outsider status is related more to their unconventional stands on issues which put them outside the dominant political consensus of the major political parties. This is why Buchanan is listed as a renegade here, rather than as outsider. He was still a part of the Republican Party, although his discourse and rhetoric set him far to the right of the party's mainstream conservatives.

Some call him a neoconservative, which seems odd, given that Buchanan labels himself a paleoconservative and is regarded as a right-wing populist. He has taken neoconservatives to task for various sins, including leading the United States to war in Iraq. From most perspectives, Buchanan was always on the right (his biographical memoir was entitled "Right From the Beginning"), but his views wound up even to the right of President Ronald Reagan, who was seen by most as a very conservative Republican. Paleoconservatives harken back to what is often called the "Old Right" and tend to view the passage of the Civil Rights Act and changes to immigration law in the 1960s as watershed moments in American history. They trace those events to current political and cultural issues and blame what they see as the pursuit of equality—epitomized by the LGBTQ+ movement—"as a political or social project" (Gottfried 2019). One scholar describes paleoconservatives as drawing "on a particular conception of 'middle America' that is rooted in the white ethnic neighbourhoods and communities of the early twentieth century" (Ashbee, 2001). It is important to recognize that paleoconservatives are not just speaking out against what they see as a liberal assault on the nation and its values. It is a splintering of the Republican Party whose theorists "seek to mobilize 'populist' themes, but they do so within clear and highly strategic political visions, not as knee-jerk or 'know-nothing' responses to political events" (Drolet and Williams 2019, 17). They are seeking to remake the Republican Party and reclaim the ideals and values of traditional "classical conservatives." Those who identify with these ideas often view the country as being in danger because of immigration and globalization, and they see the nation as needing to take back its culture and return to its religious underpinnings.

Buchanan has often warned about such dangers, and during his presidential campaigns he approached these issues as a populist politics of protest, as a warning about how far the nation had drifted from its religious and moral underpinnings. A devout Catholic, Buchanan often lamented the demise of Christian values in America, and he did it in such a way that strong appeals were made to the white working class. "The United States is divided not only between Left and Right. What is social progress to secular America is advancing decadence to traditionalist America" (Buchanan 1988, 340). Buchanan, in fact, lectured fellow Republicans about the "culture war" in his 1992 speech at the party's national convention. In that speech, Buchanan targets the heart and soul of the nation. For him, politics "is not about the distribution of resources but is about identity, values and a commensurate difference in belief systems. On one side are righteous Americans, on the other a culture of immorality that threatens the proper religious basis of the nation" (Davis 2018). The "culture war" became a phrase that stuck with Buchanan as he tried to influence the the Republican Party to look at America's problems as morality issues, rather than economic or political challenges, and to return to what he saw as true conservatism.

Buchanan is at heart a paleoconservative populist, and he used language that evoked the struggle between ordinary people and what he characterized as the untrustworthy elites who were taking actions that would undermine the moral and cultural cohesion of the nation. He was a social conservative who saw the solutions to America's problems in her past. "We need to revive the old ideas of traditional values, individual responsibility, limited government and economic freedom, if we are to become that great force for good in the world in the 21st century that we were in the 20th" (Buchanan 1992a). As has already been noted in other chapters, for a populist rhetoric to thrive and grow, there must be a receptive audience (Knott 2020). To be successful, "this alternative must be 'populist' in the sense that it claims to speak on behalf of a Middle America portrayed as the primary victim of the dominant liberal regime, and it must mobilise their cultural resentments and further their economic interests" (Drolet and Williams 2019, 25). Buchanan used a divisive, pugilistic type of discourse to outline the dangers facing the nation, and he received more than three million votes in his 1996 campaign.

Buchanan's rhetoric, which was anti-immigration, anti-NAFTA, isolationist, and anti-foreign aid, struck a nerve among working-class Americans, many of whom felt their standard of living had not been increasing. To reach these voters who felt disenfranchised, Buchanan adopted a discourse that evoked the image and identity of being American. When he says "we must take back our cities, take back our culture, and take back our country" (1992a), there is no direct mention of race, but he uses what Davis (2018) terms a "code" that makes it clear to his supporters that he is speaking about taking back the white culture. In much the same way that George C. Wallace used terms such as "law and order" that had a dual meaning, Buchanan spoke in terms of different cultures as being a threat to the nation, not different races. The use of such a language code ultimately serves two purposes, as it "veils the racism that characterizes U.S. society, and on the other hand, it insidiously perpetuates both ethnic and racial stereotypes that devalue identities of resistance and struggle" (Bartolome and Macedo 1997, 225).

One accusation that has followed Buchanan, and often paleoconservatives in general, is that he is anti-Semitic and supportive of white nationalists. This came about because of various comments he made in his syndicated columns stating that Hitler should have been appeased, rather than opposed, and comments that seemed to imply that the Holocaust did not happen. He argued that it would have been impossible for the Jewish deaths attributed to the Treblinka death camp to have ever occurred, which garnered him the vitriol of many Jewish members of government and media, as well as the Anti-Defamation League. In 1991 William Buckley and his staff devoted an entire issue of the conservative magazine "National Review" to the exploration of anti-Semitism, and in the 40,000-word essay Buckley came to the conclusion that Buchanan was guilty of being an anti-Semite. Buchanan denied the characterization and said it was retaliation of his criticism of the United States entering into wars in the Middle East.

Comments Buchanan made in a book in 2011 caused his dismissal from MSNBC. In "Suicide of a Superpower," Buchanan lamented the demise of a majority-white America. In his syndicated column on the day of the book's launch, he wrote, "Can Western civilization survive the passing of the European peoples whose ancestors created it and their replacement by Third World immigrants?" (Buchanan 2011). He said he doubted this would be possible because new immigrants to the country were not interested in preserving the culture already established in the United States. Instead, they brought some aspects of other cultures with them and merged the two. To his way of thinking, immigration has caused the phrase "one nation under God" in the country's pledge of allegiance to become obsolete. His references to cultural differences as harming the nation have resonated with alternative right groups and white supremacist groups. "Similarly, right-wing Whites in America now echo a view of difference not as a marker for racial superiority but as a signifier for cultural containment, homogeneity and social and structural inequality" (Giroux and McLaren 1993, 6). It is interesting to note that Donald Trump was accused of welcoming alt-right groups into his voter base and, by extension, into the Republican Party fold. Once again, one can see a confluence of issues and moral concerns among Buchanan and Trump supporters.

Buchanan was never able to garner enough support to win a presidential election, but many felt that his main desire was to alter the path of the Republican Party, much as had been done by his hero Barry Goldwater, who was credited with igniting conservatism within Republican ranks. Buchanan's attempts to push the party in a more conservative direction were unsuccessful, although it can be argued that Donald Trump embraced many of Buchanan's issues.

CAMPAIGN TACTICS

Buchanan ran for president three times, in 1992 and 1996 as a Republican, and in 2000 as the Reform Party candidate. His only victories came in 1996 when he won the New Hampshire, Alaska, Louisiana, and Missouri primaries. As a candidate, he often gave stirring speeches with the theme "America First—Second, and Third" that railed against taxes, quotas in federal government programs, abortion, gay rights, foreign aid, and immigration.

Buchanan spent ten weeks in New Hampshire in 1992, running against incumbent President George H. W. Bush. He relied on his media celebrity for name recognition, and he often seemed a bit hesitant as he made his transition from being a media pundit to political candidate. His speeches and meetings across the state usually fell along these lines: "stimulate the economy by cutting taxes and regulations, slash foreign aid, and, most importantly, replace Bush with a 'real Republican'" (Stradling 2015).

As the only well-known Republican to oppose Bush in the election, Buchanan chipped away at the sitting president's support, winning 38 percent of the vote in the New Hampshire primary. Although this was the high-water mark for Buchanan in this election, it was seen as an indication the the president might be vulnerable to a solid Democratic challenge. It should probably be noted that President Bush was widely perceived as going back on a 1988 campaign promise to Americans not to raise taxes, which left him at risk of losing many Republican-leaning supporters. The country was also in the midst of a recession, and Ross Perot was mounting a stiff independent challenge to the president. It is worth noting that voting for an independent, third-party, or renegade candidate requires most voters to abandon previous party affiliations or leanings and cast votes that they are told—by major parties and the media—will be worthless. Simmons and Simmons (2006) call voting for a third party candidate an "extraordinary act" (231) that overcomes several barriers that have been put in place to favor the major parties and mainstream candidates.

It is always difficult to challenge a sitting president, especially if you are in the same political party. The challenger is often derided as not supportive of the party and can be regarded as a pariah or traitor. Buchanan made no secret of his dislike of Bush and what he saw as the fight for the soul of the Republican Party, stating: "We must not trade in our sovereignty for a cushioned seat at the head table of anybody's new world order!" (Alberta 2017). Bush, he said, embodied the wave of globalism sweeping around the world. Buchanan displayed a new nationalism, one that would appeal to those who felt left behind or ignored by new American trade deals, wars in foreign countries, and social programs that seemed to give preference to minorities. Buchanan tapped into their frustration, as populists generally do, and used his rhetoric to exploit their fears and concerns about the direction of the country. Paleoconservatives argue that the modern brand of Republican conservatives cannot successfully defeat the gathered forces of globalism and multiculturalism, and they aren't even trying very hard to do so. Instead, paleoconservatives call for a "reorientation of US and global politics" (Drolet and Williams 2019, 25), as well as a change in the values of the current party, which is not uncommon in populist discourse (Mudde 2014). This is the alternative that Buchanan presented to the nation in 1992, and he was among the first paleoconservatives to use a national platform to push for this reorientation.

Buchanan won just under three million votes in the primaries, and Bush won more than nine million. It became obvious after Super Tuesday that he had no path to the nomination, and Buchanan suspended his campaign and endorsed Bush. Buchanan's paleoconservative rhetoric nudged the Republican Party to the right, and he was invited to give the keynote address at the Republican Party convention in Houston. This is where he delivered the now-famous "culture wars" speech that pitted the Republican Party against those who favored "amoral" gay marriage, abortion, and Supreme Court justices who re-wrote the Constitution, rather than uphold it. "There is a religious war going on in our country for the soul of America. It is a cultural war, as critical to the kind of nation we will one day be as was the Cold War itself," Buchanan said in his fiery address (Buchanan 1992b). He urged Americans to take back their country and their culture. He urged the "Buchanan brigades" to unite around Bush and keep the Democrats out of the White House.

The speech was not well received by many Republicans, and it was rejected by Democrats. Molly Ivins, the liberal political columnist, remarked that she didn't care for the speech, but that "it probably sounded better in its original German" (O'Donnell 2012). Many Republicans thought the shrill tone would drive away moderates who would be necessary for the president's re-election. Others rejected the comments of someone they considered to be anti-Semitic and homophobic. While it is still talked about today, the speech did little to help unite the Republican Party, and Bush went on to lose the election. However, it introduced the party and the nation to the burgeoning "culture war" and released this phrase into the national political lexicon, where it slowly began to further divide an already fissured Republican Party.

Buchanan learned many lessons in his first presidential campaign, and when he announced his intention to run in 1996, he had transformed into a seasoned candidate. He was more animated in his speeches and more energized by his supporters. The message, though, remained the same:

> I see an America where the dream of equal justice for all and special privilege for none has become a reality. I see an America where the jobs are coming home and no longer being sent abroad. And I see an America where we become one people, one nation, one family, again. This is the kind of America I'm working for and fighting for. (Buchanan 1996a)

He advocated for a balanced budget, a line-item veto for the president, ending foreign aid, full legal protection for the unborn, reversing treaties such as NAFTA, ending quotas, and shuttering the Department of Education. He called upon voters to help him reconstitute the Supreme Court and provide constitutional protection for the United States flag.

His populist appeal seemed stronger in the 1996 campaign, as he won primaries in four states and had a strong early showing. However, Sen. Bob Dole eventually emerged as the nominee, and Buchanan suspended his campaign in March 1996.

Buchanan supporters proved to be reliable and passionate. Some of them had been Ross Perot supporters in 1992 and were looking for a candidate with similar ideas to re-energize the Republican Party. Others were encouraged by Buchanan's populist appeals and responded to his labeling them as "peasants with pitchforks" by gleefully hoisting pitchforks in photos to embrace the moniker. Buchanan was even presented with a 4-foot-tall pitchfork by some zealous supporters, which he kept encased in glass in his home afterward.

He urged supporters to keep their pitchforks sharp so they could "stick it" to politicians who didn't share their ideological beliefs.

The Buchanan Brigade marched across primary states, revving up the rhetoric as Buchanan's chances of success grew slimmer. At a rally in Tampa, Florida, he urged those in attendance to reject the burgeoning new world order. "What is developing now—and you can see it clearly if you look hard—are the embryonic institutions of a world government that has been placed over your country," he told the Christian school rally, to gasps and boos. There's going to be an explosion in this country—and there ought to be an explosion," (Baer 1996). His rallies became even more rowdy, and Buchanan, now the seasoned populist candidate, urged them on and vowed to refuse to quit fighting against Dole. He even hinted that he would create an uproar at the party's nominating convention. "Here's what we do," he told about seven hundred students and parents. "We go to San Diego. We break the doors open to this party, and we TAKE IT OVER!" (Baer 1996).

For all of his rhetoric, Buchanan and his brigade did not take over the national convention. In his address at the Texas GOP convention in June, which was punctuated by much cheering and applause from his supporters, he slammed NAFTA, illegal immigration, and what he termed the New World Order, which he saw as the United States ceding more of its authority and military to the United Nations. He said the country was facing a crossroads, and that a new Republican Party needed to emerge to confront the "struggle for the soul of our country" (Buchanan 1996b). He slammed President Bill Clinton and alluded to conspiracy theories surrounding both the president and Hillary Clinton in Arkansas, and said the mistake of placing Clinton in office in 1992 needed to be reversed in 1996. He intimated that he and his brigade would have a significant impact at the party's national convention.

After his controversial 1992 convention speech, Buchanan was not given a speaking slot at the 1996 Republican Convention in San Diego, angering both the candidate and his supporters. Instead, Buchanan issued a one-page statement endorsing Dole's nomination. Buchanan did not walk away empty-handed though, as the party platform reflected much of his ideology, and it was termed the most conservative platform in many years. Dole chose to distance himself from the platform and adopt a more moderate stance on most issues, but was unable to draw enough votes in the general election to unseat President Clinton.

Buchanan's final presidential campaign is the only one not undertaken as a Republican, although it began that way. He announced his candidacy in March 1999, but in October of that year, he publicly left the Republican Party and sought the nomination of the Reform Party. The Reform Party had been formed by in 1995 by Ross Perot, who was the party's nominee in the 1996 presidential election. The party's most notable elected official was former wrestler Jesse Ventura, who was voted governor of Minnesota on the Reform Party ticket in 1998.

Buchanan said he was leaving the Republican Party because it was not serious about changing the direction of government. In his acceptance speech for the Reform Party nomination, he laid it out in colorful terms which were re-used by President Donald Trump in 2016. "Neither beltway party—Neither beltway party's gonna to drain this political swamp because to them it's not a swamp, it's a protected wetland. It's their natural habitat," Buchanan said, reiterating that the Reform Party was the only one that would stand up for the nation's sovereignty and against multiculturalism (Buchanan 2000).

CAMPAIGN ISSUES

The issues Buchanan promoted during his presidential campaigns didn't really vary much between elections. He was always against abortion, calling it evil and an indication that the nation was heading in the wrong moral direction. In a debate with Ralph Nader on Meet the Press, Buchanan strongly condemned an at-home abortion pill. "RU-486, in my judgment, is a human pesticide. It is anti-child. It is anti-woman. It is anti-family. It basically is a drug which only a nation would accept which has embraced, I believe, the culture of death that the pope and others have condemned" (Washington Post, 2000). However, many felt that Buchanan did not give this issue as much attention in his 2000 presidential run as he had before. This was a surprise to many on the far right who felt that he represented them on this issue.

Buchanan said he would intervene in the U.S. economy to save American jobs, but was against intervention when it came to foreign policy and wars. He railed against NAFTA and globalization. He reserved some of his harshest rhetoric for social issues, which he saw as an indication that the traditional religious beliefs of the nation were being eroded. "We will preserve our heritage by passing on to our children, through locally controlled education, a love of our land, our history, our English language, and our traditional sense of right and wrong" (Buchanan 1999). Once again, Buchanan used coded discourse to imply that the white heritage needed to be preserved, as well as the English language, which he believed should be made the official national language and required of those who immigrate to the United States.

Immigration was actually one of the most consistent topics in Buchanan's columns and commentaries, as well as in his presidential campaigns. Hartnett and Ramsey examined more than thirty of Buchanan's campaign speeches, publications, and Internet postings from 1991–1996 and found that "it is fair to conclude that one of Buchanan's most consistent argument maneuvers involves renaming 'illegal' immigrants from Mexico as 'invaders' who, based on a string of both military and racial associations littered throughout his speeches, are represented as the first wave of shock troops in an 'invasion'" (1999, 98–99). He painted illegal immigration from Mexico as a crisis that should be dealt with by the construction of a fence along the United States and Mexico border. This became one of Donald Trump's signature issues in 2016, when he famously promised to build a wall and have Mexico pay for it. This is yet another example of Trump lifting an issue from Buchanan's campaigns to make his own.

It's interesting to note that Buchanan and Trump actually battled each other for the Reform Party nomination in 2000. Trump also quit the Republican Party in 1999 and joined the Reform Party. For the 2000 election, the party was on the ballot in every state, and it qualified for federal matching funds, so it was a good nomination to secure. Trump entered the race in October, just as Buchanan swapped over to the Reform Party, setting up a contest between the two. Trump was the showman, going on TV talk shows, making promises, and entertaining crowds. Buchanan was the idealist, continuing to look for help in returning the United States to its former days of glory. Trump called Buchanan a Hitler lover, and in return Buchanan said neither the party nomination nor the presidency could be bought.

However, the Reform Party was plagued by internal strife and bickering in 2000, and Trump exited the race, saying that the nominee would not have adequate support from the party because of the infighting. This left Buchanan as the frontrunner for the nomination. Once he secured it, Buchanan found himself and his supporters often disagreeing with Perot loyalists who were concerned Buchanan supporters were going to take over their party. The internal strife took a toll on Buchanan's campaign, and he failed to win any state primaries or electoral votes.

Some argue that American society had changed since Buchanan's first run for president, and that his angry, divisive messages were far less effective than before. "However, the angry distrust that characterized US politics in the early 1990s had lost much of its intensity by 2000 . . . the 2000 election represented the taming of political insurgency rather than a prelude to further upheaval or long-term realignment" (Ashbee, 2001).

But that did not stop Buchanan from attempting to push the national conversation to the right. During the campaign, Buchanan was accused of running a television ad that bordered on racist. Buchanan saw immigration as an important issue in the nation, and argued that English should be the official language in the country. The controversial ad shows a man eating spaghetti and meatballs as a TV commentator announces that an unnamed president has signed an executive order saying that English is no longer America's official language. The man chokes on a meatball upon hearing the news, goes to the phone to call 911 for help and is greeted by an emergency system asking him to "listen for your language." As he listens to a list of other languages, he falls out of sight, ostensibly dying from lack of oxygen. It aired in twenty-two states, including California and Arizona, two states with high levels of immigration. While some saw it as a statement about the importance of English being designated the official language of the nation (it currently has no official language), others said it was a blatant and racist attack on immigration.

Buchanan found himself at the center of the post-election controversy, as no clear winner emerged from the general election. Eventually there was a vote recount in the state of Florida, and it was found that Buchanan won 20 percent of his Florida votes in Palm Beach County, where some Gore voters apparently accidentally voted for Buchanan when they were confused by the butterfly ballots used in the county (Levy n.d.).

Buchanan finished fourth in the general election, and, despite spending more than $38 million during the campaign, managed to capture less than 450,000 votes, which was substantially less than he garnered in 1996.

BUCHANAN'S COMPLICATED LEGACY

Few former presidential candidates can claim to have lost so many battles, yet possibly won the political war. Buchanan failed to become elected president, but it's unclear if his real purpose in running was to win, or if it was to change the direction of the country in whatever way he could. "He never came close to winning, but each time he nagged at something, rubbed a nerve in just enough voters of a particular kind—what he called 'peasants' and we call the white working class—to send ripples of panic through the Republican party" (Tanenhaus 2017). As Knott stresses, the populist appeal to return to the way things *were* is founded on the idea that things are no longer acceptable, and that the nation should return to its former days of glory (2020). This tends to be a very popular appeal for right-wing populists such as Buchanan, who articulated a clear vision of what was wrong with the nation—and with the current Republican Party.

After the 2000 election, he identified as a political independent, although he returned to the Republican Party in 2004. He went back to working as a columnist and political analyst, and he lamented that the country was still heading in the wrong direction. In the 2000s, the degree of political partisan polarization widened, leaving less room for third-party candidates and independents. This could have been a factor in Buchanan's lackluster vote count in 2000. As noted by Gold, "although issue alienation and unpopular candidates may undermine the partisan attachments that citizens hold, third parties are still not likely to break through in an era of strong partisanship" (1995, 753). In other words, when more Americans strongly identify with mainstream political parties, there aren't as many possible independent or third-party votes available.

But in 2016, Buchanan saw many of his own ideas coming back around, courtesy of Donald J. Trump (Davis 2018, Nash 2016). The nationalist ideas, the comments about draining the swamp and changing Washington, D.C., the battle against illegal immigration, and even Trump's slogan "Make America Great Again," were all echoes from the Buchanan campaigns. "The ideas made it, but I didn't," Buchanan said (Alberta 2017). He said that he was delighted that Trump was elected president, and he was happy to see his ideas taking root within the Republican Party.

In some ways, he is the patriarch of this movement that propelled Trump into the White House. Although he hoped it would happen one day, Buchanan had to wait a long time. "When the chickens come home to roost," he predicted to The New York Times (after the 2000 loss), "this whole coalition will be there for somebody. They're going to think, 'Whatever happened to that guy back in 2000?' There's no doubt these issues can win" (Tanenhaus 2017).

The issues could win, but not with Buchanan. Instead, sixteen years later Donald Trump adopted them, stamped them with his own brand of showmanship and populist rhetoric, and rode them into the White House, minus the social conservatism of Buchanan's earlier campaigns. Perhaps Buchanan's timing was off, or, more likely, the ideas needed to be seeded into the political discussion for later campaigns. Buchanan never stopped talking about them through his syndicated columns and his television appearances. Ever the accomplished writer, he published several books after his failed campaigns, many with controversial titles or content, (including the one that got him fired from MSNBC) but all of which kept hammering at his desire to see America turn back toward the Old Right. He continued to craft messages, turning out two syndicated columns a week, and his populist rhetoric continued to flow out to the public through his online site. Even as he continued to push paleoconservative ideas and urge the nation to change course, the "culture wars" discourse continued, with conservative online sites and alt-right media seeking to grow an anti-establishment political movement (Davis 2018). As a renegade in the Republican Party, Buchanan is one of the rare presidential candidates who lived to see his brand of populism develop into a successful movement in the hands of another person.

REFERENCES

Alberta, Tim. 2017. "The Ideas Made It, But I Didn't: Pat Buchanan Won After All. But Now He Thinks It Might Be Too Late For the Nation He Was Trying to Save."

Politico. May/June 2017. https://www.politico.com/magazine/story/2017/04/22/pat-buchanan-trump-president-history-profile-215042.

Ashbee, Edward. 2001. "The Also-Rans: Nader, Buchanan and the 2000 US Presidential Election. *Political Quarterly* 72, no. 2 (April-June):159–169.

Baer, Susan. 1996. "'Bad Dog Buchanan' Grows More Fierce, More Defiant: Lacking Delegates, Republican Still Seeks Major Convention Role." *The Baltimore Sun.* March 9, 1996. https://www.baltimoresun.com/news/bs-xpm-1996-03-09-1996069073-story.html.

Bartolome, Lilia I. and Donaldo P. Macedo. 1997. Dancing With Bigotry: The Poisoning of Racial and Ethnic Identities. *Harvard Educational Review* 67, no. 2 (Summer): 222–246.

Buchanan, Pat. 1988. *"Right From the Beginning."* Boston: Little, Brown.

Buchanan, Pat. 1992a. "Pat Buchanan for President 1992 Campaign Brochure. Putting and Keeping America First." http://www.4president.org/brochures/1992/patbuchanan1992brochure.htm.

Buchanan, Pat. 1992b. 1992 Republican National Convention Speech." Aug. 17, 1992. https://buchanan.org/blog/1992-republican-national-convention-speech-148.

Buchanan, Pat. 1996a. "Pat Buchanan For President 1996 Campaign Brochure. Reclaiming the American Dream." http://www.4president.org/brochures/1996/patbuchanan1996brochure.htm.

Buchanan, Pat. 1996b. "Speech at 1996 Texas GOP Convention." June 22, 1996. https://buchanan.org/blog/speech-at-1996-texas-gop-convention-188.

Buchanan, Pat. 1999. www.GoPatGo.org/. "Issues: Education of America's Children," June 11, 1999.

Buchanan, Pat. 2000. "Reform Party Nomination Acceptance Address." Aug. 12, 2000. https://www.americanrhetoric.com/speeches/patbuchananreformpartyacceptance.htm.

Buchanan, Pat. 2011. *"A.D. 2041- End of White America?"* Oct. 18, 2011. https://buchanan.org/blog/a-d-2041-end-of-white-america-4912.

Davis, Mark. 2018. 'Culture as Inseparable from Race': Culture Wars from Pat Buchanan to Milo Yiannopoulos. *M/C Journal* 21 (5). https://doi.org/10.5204/mcj.1484.

Drolet, Jean-Francois and Michael Williams. 2019. The View From MARS: US Paleoconservatism and Ideological Challenges to the Liberal World Order. *International Journal* 74 (1): 15–31.

Giroux, Henry A. 1993. Living Dangerously: Identity Politics and the New Cultural Racism: Towards a Critical Pedagogy of Representation. *Cultural Studies* 7, no. 1 (January): 3–28.

Gold, Howard J. 1995. Third Party Voting in Presidential Elections: A Study of Perot, Anderson, and Wallace. *Political Research Quarterly* 48, no. 4 (December); 751–773.

Gottfried, Paul. 2019. "What's Paleo, and What's Not?" *Chronicles Magazine.* December 2019. https://www.chroniclesmagazine.org/2019/December/43/12/magazine/article/10847261/.

Guerlain, Pierre. The Double Matrix of the 60s: Progressive and Reactionary Legacies of the Sixties. Alizes: *Revue angliciste de La Reunion*, Faculte des Lettres et Sciences humaines (Universite de La Reunion), Side Views: 164-177. Hal-01639860.

Hartnett, Stephen and Ramsey Eric Ramsey. 1999. 'A Plain Public Road': Evaluating Arguments for Democracy in a Post-Metaphysical World. *Argumentation and Advocacy* 35 (Winter): 95–114.

Knott, Andy. 2020. A Manifesto and Populism? In *The Populist Manifesto*, edited by Emmy Eklundh and Andy Knott, 107-122. London: Rowman & Littlefield.

Levy, Michael. n.d. "United States Presidential Election of 2000." https://www.britannica.com/event/United-States-presidential-election-of-2000.

Mudde, Cas. 2014. The Popular Zeitgeist. *Government and Opposition*, 39 (4): 541–563. https://doi.org/10.1111/j.1477-7053.2004.00135.x.

Nash, George H. 2016. Populism, I: American Conservatism and the Problem of Populism. *The New Criterion* 35, no. 1 (September): 4–14.

O'Donnell, Lawrence. 2012. "From Too Extreme to Mainstream." *MSNBC.com*. Aug. 29, 2012. http://www.msnbc.com/the-last-word/too-extreme-mainstream.

Simmons, Solon J. and James R. Simmons. If It Weren't for Those?*&*@!* Nader Voters We Wouldn't Be in This Mess: The Social Determinants of the Nader Vote and the Constraints on Political Choice. *New Political Science* 28, no. 2 (June): 229–244.

Stradling, Richard. 2015. "Pat Buchanan's Awkward '92 Run." *The Boston Globe*. July 31. 2015. https://www.bostonglobe.com/news/politics/2015/07/30/pat-buchanan-awkward-run/hK4AIOSeYreYil4mcdb48O/story.html.

Tanenhaus, Sam. 2017. "When Pat Buchanan Tried to Make America Great Again." *Esquire. com*. April 5, 2017. http://www.esquire.com/news-politics/a54275/charge-of-the-right-brigade/.

Washington Post. 2000. Text: NBC's Meet the Press. Oct. 1, 2000. https://www.washingtonpost.com/wp-srv/onpolitics/elections/nbctext100100.htm.

Chapter 12

Newt Gingrich

POLITICAL LANGUAGE, HARDBALL TACTICS
TRANSFORM REPUBLICAN POLITICS

If someone is looking for where the seeds of Donald Trump's Republican Party were sown, Newt Gingrich might be a good place to start. Gingrich, born in Pennsylvania, but raised in Georgia, seemed to have his eye on power from the very beginning.

He received his doctorate in European History in 1971 from Tulane University, and by 1974 he was already running for Congress, having taken unpaid leave from his teaching job at West Georgia College to campaign. He lost in 1974 and 1976 to a twenty-year incumbent Democrat named Jack Flynt. But in 1978, Flynt decided to retire, and Gingrich won the seat. He was then re-elected five times from this district, eventually becoming House Minority Whip in 1989. In 1994, Gingrich was instrumental in drafting the "Contract with America," which was a ten-point program signed by more than three hundred Republican candidates who pledged to bring these ten policies to the House floor within the first one hundred days of a new Congress. The ten policies were based on what Republicans called the five principles that described their basic philosophy of American Civilization. Those five principles were individual liberty, economic opportunity, limited government, personal responsibility, and security at home and abroad. "Based on these principles House Republicans outlined a vision for America's future and the role of government" (Contract with America 1994, 5).

The "Contract" lifted some ideas and policies from Ross Perot's popular "United We Stand" book from two years earlier, which intoned in the introduction that "You can change our country. You can pass on the American dream to our children. You can change the world" (Perot 1992, 4). That sort of talk was still popular with voters two years later when Republicans debuted their policies in a brand new book. "The Contract with America" promises resonated with voters, and in the 1994 mid-term elections, the GOP won back control of the House for the first time since the 1950s, and it also won control of the Senate. This was the first time in 40 years that Republicans had control of both houses of Congress. Dubbed "the Republican Revolution," many called it the "Gingrich Revolution," because it made Gingrich into a household name and he was voted Speaker of the House. As Speaker, Gingrich set the Republican Party on a path that would promote partisanship at every turn with confrontational rhetoric and tactics that included angry assaults on those who opposed him or stood in the party's way.

This set the stage for his eventual presidential campaign of 2012, even though he resigned from Congress in 1998 after losing the support of his fellow Republican Party members in Congress after a disappointing election season. What propelled Gingrich seemed to be a long-sought individual quest to save the nation, and hence save Western civilization from its decline. He worked to remake the Republican Party in his own image, which was bombastic, extreme, and rebellious. The South, he foresaw, was about to go undergo a political realignment, and he wanted to be at the center of that change.

GINGRICH'S DISCOURSE

Gingrich was elected to Congress at a pivotal moment in Southern politics. The region had long been a bastion of Democratic policies and politicos, but he saw the future of the region intertwined with the Republican Party. Somewhat like George Wallace, who saw change happening in the Democratic Party and worked to influence its direction, Gingrich sensed an opportunity to push the Republican Party to the right. Ronald Reagan's election as president in 1980 helped accelerate what had been a slow, modern exodus of mainly white working class voters, as well as elected officials, from the ranks of the Democratic Party in the South.

Taesuh Cha (2015) discusses the "Southernization" of the Republican Party and its impact on "anguished White workers in the age of economic crisis" (358) and how changes in the GOP contributed to a 21st century version of American Exceptionalism. That many former Southern Democrats moved to the Republican Party is not really in question. But Gingrich did not begin the process—instead, the seeds had been sown decades before with the Dixiecrats, George C. Wallace, and Ronald Reagan (Kousser 2010). Strong (1977) asserts that the realignment of politics in the South began in 1952, when Southern states began giving electoral votes to Republican presidential nominees. He points out that the party realignment began at the presidential level and worked its way down to Congressional elections. Zelizer (2010) writes that, as Southerners (who were more conservative) moved into the GOP, the Democratic Party then moved to the left. This also meant that the Republican Party, infused with more conservative members, saw a decrease in liberal Republicans (381).

Many of those who swapped parties intoned just like Reagan had in 1962 that they didn't leave the party, but the party left them. They moved over to a GOP which was socially conservative, promoting school prayer and Second Amendment rights and standing against abortion and same-sex marriage. Those were social issue stances that already appealed to many religiously conservative Southerners, who found themselves voting for some of their already-established elected officials, but just on a different ticket. Of course, the shift wasn't just happening in the South, but also in other parts of the nation.

The importance of this shift was not lost on Gingrich, who set about exploiting a new way of communicating to the voting public and to those holding political office. By using discourse featuring name calling and character assassination, and by grandstanding for television cameras, Gingrich often found himself featured in the news media. That placed him squarely in front of the voting public. Historian Julian Zelizer (2020a) concluded that Gingrich intended to draw attention to himself through his communication strategies. Zelizer argued that, to influence the discourse, Gingrich "thought a lot about confrontation and saying things that were explosive because he believed that the more confrontational, the more outlandish you were, the more the media would cover you and the more the media would replicate what you said about your opponent—whether it was true or not true." Gingrich's discourse was raucous, confrontational, and intensely partisan, which he believed was necessary. "He argued that if the GOP ever wanted to defeat the Democrats, they needed to embrace a smashmouth style of partisanship which revolved around character assassination, violating norms and tearing down governing institutions" (Zelizer 2020b).

One thing to keep in mind about Gingrich is that he was anti-establishment, even though he was a prominent member of Congress. As Lindberg (1999) points out, this was a productive strategy for Gingrich and his acolytes, because it "united the various strains of conservatism" (9) that existed in the nation. The United States had been in an economic slump, and many middle-and lower-class Americans had yet to emerge from the recession. There was a lag in job creation, leaving many voters angry about their own economic situations and government policies which they saw as benefitting those who were already wealthy. Washington D.C., as Gingrich painted it to potential voters, was out of touch with average Americans, and simply making the government larger would not solve that problem. What was needed was true conservative reform, and Gingrich devised a new type of discourse to provide an authenticity to this rebellion against the Washington establishment. It would have been easy to slip into a populist brand of discourse, but Gingrich instead went in a different direction, one that more resembled his own personality. His discourse was brash, sweeping, usually frank (although exaggeration was often acceptable), and sought to sweep Democrats, personified as absolute evil, out of office. As Serazio (2016) points out, "'anti-establishment' attacks are thus a way of channeling revolutionary undercurrents—many derived from economic dissatisfaction—into safer ideological and political harbors" (186). Rather than the usually vague promises of populists, Gingrich was eager to make specific promises of conservative reform.

Gingrich was also known for his intellect and knowledge of issues, but eventually that was eclipsed by his renegade behavior. "In the public mind, however, the intellectual aspect of Gingrich's personality was overwhelmed by his long track record of arrogant self-promotion, angry assaults on his political adversaries, and rank hypocrisy" (Brattebo 2013, 47). This came back to haunt him when he was campaigning for president in 2012, as many remembered the rebellious and rude rhetoric displayed years earlier. "When Republican voters in Iowa expressed concern that Gingrich had 'too much baggage' to win a national election, it was like saying that Samsonite would have a hard time cramming its global inventory into a footlocker" (Brattebo, 2013, 47). Gingrich used his time as Speaker of the House to harass and goad people into doing what he wanted, and his approach to discourse still echoes in the Republican Party today. Many see Donald Trump and the party faithful he commands as the natural evolution of Gingrich's remaking of the party during the 1990s (Carter 1996).

In his 2012 presidential campaign, Gingrich softened his rhetoric a bit, but still attacked Democrats for trying to push solutions onto the American public for problems that he said didn't really exist. In his video announcing his presidential campaign, he said he wanted to clear away liberal policies and "dishonest scare tactics" used by President Barack Obama. "There are some people who don't mind if America becomes a wreck so long as they dominate the wreckage. We know better. We owe it to our children, our grandchildren, our country and ourselves to get together, look reality in the face, tell the truth, make the tough choices and get the job done. There's a much better American future ahead" (Gingrich 2012a). In this announcement, he also referred to his accomplishments as Speaker of the House, listing balancing the budget, decreasing unemployment and creating jobs for Americans.

Gingrich's ambition had never been in doubt. Strahan and Palazzolo (2004) offered up a bit of insight into the Georgia politician's plans in a comment made more than a decade before he was elected Speaker of the House: "I have an enormous personal ambition. I want to shift the entire planet" (112). One might conclude that Gingrich was not just personally ambitious, but that he truly trying to do what he thought was necessary to save the nation and Western civilization. In what they call the "Gingrich Effect," Strahan and Palazzolo note that his leadership style showed that "congressional leaders can—and sometimes do—act independently of contextual conditions and member's expectations and they sometimes succeed in shaping those conditions and expectations in a direction consistent with their own goals"

(2004, 113). However, his hubris led to a short leadership in the House of Representatives after the midterm disappointment of 1998. One must remember that the Republican Party is comprised of multiple groups, and the task of keeping a coalition together within the GOP is just as difficult as it is within the Democratic Party. Gingrich wanted to grab the attention of Americans and then educate them about what needed to be done, rather than focus on the everyday details of Congressional business, and this was part of the reason he was an ineffective leader in the House. The impact of his discourse and tactics, however, have had a lasting effect on the politics of the Republican Party and the nation. As Brattebo noted: "Lo, these many years later, the inmates are still out of the asylum, running barefoot through the temple of democracy and swinging from the statuary. It was Newt Gingrich who helped unlock the gate" (2013, 48). As a rhetorician and tactician, Gingrich was successful at molding the GOP into a new, competitive party. But when it came to his presidential campaign, he found that the discourse he had unleashed had found new roots, and his efforts were less successful than before.

CAMPAIGN TACTICS

Gingrich was especially good at verbal warfare, but it remains to be seen if he really believed many of the specific issues and policies that he championed. He took every opportunity to position Democrats as the reason for Congressional dysfunction, as well as target specific members of Congress who he said had taken advantage of incumbency for their own gain. While this rhetoric was effective in the 1994 midterms, it would later boomerang on him, as he endured his own financial and ethical scandals. Some argue that Gingrich, a student of history, should have realized that his attempt to basically burn down the government so it could be built back differently would ultimately fail.

> The strategy's fatal defect was that Gingrich, an intellectual and pragmatist on many public policy issues, did not believe the rhetoric he spouted—but his followers did. Gingrich's assumption was that, once he came to power, he would have sufficient standing to compel highly ideological Republicans to revisit their fundamental convictions about the role and scope of government. (Brattebo 2013, 57)

However, Gingrich was often unable to curb his own rebellious actions and facilitate compromise in order to pass legislation. This led to frustration among the American public, who expected more action after returning both houses of Congress to Republican control.

Gingrich loved the spotlight, and he loved taking credit for Republican victories. Douglas B. Harris argues that Speakers of the House have been becoming increasingly more public in their roles, and that Gingrich was the "most public Speaker in memory" (1998, 198). A trend toward a more public role for House speakers in the media has often made them celebrities in more modern times. "Aided by increased media attention, as well as their own activities, speakers have transformed the speakership into a public office in which the responsibilities of external leadership rival their traditional internal responsibilities" (Harris 1998, 199). Gingrich excelled at grabbing the headlines, often for the outrageous comments that he issued which seemed almost off-the-cuff, but were quite calculated for effect. Interestingly, Gingrich often strongly criticized the media while at the same time mugging for the cameras. He realized that the news media yawned when he spoke like an academic, but fawned over him when there was conflict.

> "The number one fact about the news media," he said, "is they love fights." When he gave "organized, systematic, researched, one-hour lectures did CBS rush in and ask if they could tape one of my one-hour lectures? No. But the minute Tip O'Neill attacked me, he and I got 90 seconds at the close of all three network news shows. You have to give them confrontations. When you give them confrontations, you get attention; when you get attention, you can educate." (Ioffe 2016)

While in Congress, Gingrich usually positioned himself so that his over-the-top rhetoric would grab the media's headlines, and he used this tactic during his 2012 campaign for president. He rarely failed to provide a good sound bite for the TV media, which was always looking for something sensational or controversial. Some of his better-known outrageous statements were collected by The Atlanta Journal Constitution and labeled "Newtspeak." The newspaper included this snippet: "During his final South Carolina primary debate in 2012, he started by getting a rousing ovation when he blamed the 'destructive, vicious, negative nature' of the media for making it so hard to govern. He ended the debate calling President Barack Obama 'the most dangerous president of our lifetime' who, if re-elected, would bring a 'level of radicalism' that would be 'truly frightening'" (Salzer 2017). This type of rhetoric was similar to that he had invoked while engineering the rise of the Republican Party, and his earlier efforts had helped the GOP become more reliably competitive in national politics.

Gingrich had been hailed as the architect of the Republican House and Senate takeovers in 1994 (Highton 2002), and he traded on that reputation in his 2012 campaign, often referring to his accomplishments from his time as speaker. He ran as an outsider, promoting his past, but also proclaiming that his vision was necessary to save not only the party, but the nation. He still drew crowds, and his oratory often caused them to break out in applause or cheers. Lindberg states that Gingrich has "an ideologue's sense of the connectedness of things" (1999, 10) that allowed him to relate well with an audience of like-minded voters.

But perhaps one of his most lasting accomplishments was the legacy of more conservative Republicans in the House and Senate in the years following 1994. By the time Gingrich ran for president in 2012, many of his former House colleagues had migrated to the Senate, where they added a new dimension of conservatism to the GOP. Theriault and Rohde (2011) call these and the following generations of "Gingrich Senators" because they found that "Gingrich's former colleagues are almost twice as conservative as their fellow Republicans" (1013). They attributed an increased political polarization in the Senate to the presence of these more conservative members. Brattebo (2013) credited Gingrich with drawing "idealogues" into the GOP that changed the atmosphere in Washington into one that is more divided and less willing to compromise.

By the time Donald Trump was elected president, each succeeding Republican generation in Congress seemed to have moved a bit more to the right. As an example, when Rep. Doc Hastings of Washington retired in 2014, he was one of only a remaining handful of the original Republicans elected in the 1998 sweep of Congress. In 2009, the year before the Tea Party gained seats in Congress, Hastings was ranked as the 72nd most-conservative member of the House. But just four years later, he was ranked as the 175th most-conservative member of the House (Davis 2014). In short, Trump inherited a Republican Congress that has been steadily becoming more conservative after Gingrich. This, and the bipartisan divide that exists in the country, allowed Trump to push the party further to the right while invoking language and tactics similar to those used by Gingrich.

GINGRICH'S ISSUES

Many have crowned Gingrich the king of "wedge issues," or issues that divide Americans, to contrast the Republican and Democratic parties. Social issues such as abortion, school prayer and even flag burning became important to Republican voters after Gingrich and his allies made them into hot-button issues. This was reminiscent of Pat Buchanan's social issues or "culture war" topics that had become important to many Republicans after the 1992 presidential campaign. Gingrich also had additional goals that included a balanced federal budget and cutting taxes (Strahan and Palazzolo 2004), both of which were issues that he felt could shift the national debate more in a conservative direction.

But it wasn't just the issues that were important. It was the words that were chosen to frame the issues that Gingrich felt made the difference. In fact, in 1990 he distributed a list of pollster-tested words that he recommended Republican candidates keep in mind and use during their campaigns. The memo encouraged candidates to memorize the words and make them part of their election messaging. "The 'optimistic positive governing words' included change, moral, courage, reform, freedom and common sense. Negative, contrasting words to be used on opponents included destructive, liberal, welfare, traitors, radical and corruption" (Salzer, 2017). Gingrich used these words in his own campaigns, and even in his 2012 presidential race. During that campaign, he produced advertisements that stressed positive words such as "rebuilding" America, "reviving" the economy, "regaining" the world's respect and "returning" power to the American people. One video ad uses the words "freedom," "opportunity," and "control" in a statement about returning power to the citizens of the country (Gingrich, 2012b).

He returned to his past and touted a "21st Century Contract with America," which he said would be "far deeper and far bolder" than the first one in 1994. He said it would include a balanced budget amendment and include the signing of several executive orders on his first day in office. He proposed building a fence along the southern U.S. border to control immigration, and he advocated a reduction in the size of federal government. Issues that he often used in advertisements and speeches included school choice, unemployment, and creating jobs. When referring to those still out of work from the Great Recession, he commented that, for those people, it was a depression, not just a recession. He took every opportunity to characterize President Barack Obama as overseeing a "nation in crisis," and in one ad Gingrich proclaimed he was "THE RIGHT Message," THE RIGHT Experience," "THE RIGHT Ideas," and "THE RIGHT Candidate," at "THE RIGHT time" (Gingrich, 2012c). It is obvious that he was searching for those Republicans who were more to the political right, and he used the language he had spent a lifetime cultivating to pull in votes. Gingrich spent most of his time criticizing President Obama, but also lobbed negative comments at Mitt Romney, especially as it became obvious that Romney was pulling ahead in the race for the Republican nomination.

THE 2012 ELECTION

Gingrich was a familiar name to many voters, but a new face to others. In November 2011, he was the frontrunner in the Republican primary. After surging in the polls in December, Gingrich reached into the past and pulled out some bluster to confidently predict that he would be the nominee. "I'm going to be the nominee," he said. "It's very hard not to look at the recent polls and think that the odds are very high I'm going to be the nominee" (New York Post 2011).

During the campaign, Gingrich garnered much support from those in the Tea Party movement, and he wasted no words when criticizing his fellow Republicans while campaigning in Florida: "Remember: The Republican establishment is just as much as an establishment as the Democratic establishment, and they are just as determined to stop us," (Gardner and Helderman 2012). In a throwback to the discourse he was famous for, he also used the term "stupid" several times to describe Romney voters, and he characterized the presidential campaign as one that would determine the future of the Republican Party.

But, for all his bluster, Gingrich's campaign began to stall as other Republican candidates went on the attack against him. The media began to feature stories about the controversies that had surrounded him while he was in Congress, and the race with Romney tightened. Gingrich did well in South Carolina, but began to fall behind Romney in other Southern states. As Iyengar and Simon (2000) point out, a candidate must anticipate not only the opponent's possible strategies, but also those of the "evolving behavior of the news media" (162). The media which once seemed to love Gingrich and kept him front and center in the news cycle seemed to mainly focus on his past controversies, not on his current campaign. He announced that he was suspending his campaign on May 2, taking with him a rumored $4 million in campaign debt.

He produced a thank-you video to donors, volunteers, and staff on May 1, but the following day held a news conference where, surrounded by family, he said he was still committed to the role of being an active citizen. He recited his accomplishments in Congress, and said that he has a "deep commitment on American exceptionalism and American history, and our sense that we cannot truly be Americans if we have amnesia about who we are, where we came from, and what principles have made us great." He also called President Obama "the most radical, leftist president in American history." (Gingrich 2012d)

One thing Gingrich did not do at that event was endorse Romney. He later gave a lukewarm endorsement of Romney, whom he said he favored over Obama. Normally, a concession speech for a candidate in a major party includes an endorsement of another party candidate or the nominee. However, as Neville-Shepard (2014) points out, third-party presidential concessions are structured differently and instead look for ways to reframe the campaign as having been successful. Although Gingrich was not a third-party candidate, he was a renegade candidate within the Republican Party, and in a somewhat rambling 24-minute speech (Gingrich 2012d), Gingrich outlined many of his issues and the "solutions" he had proposed, as well as talked about what he planned to do in the future. In many ways, he sought to "reframe" the election result as a type of victory for his campaign and a vindication of his conservative issues, rather than take the opportunity to try to unify and rally the party.

Gingrich finished third in the Republican primary, gathering 142 delegates to Mitt Romney's 1,489. Candidate Ron Paul collected 154 delegates, coming in second to Romney.

GINGRICH'S POLITICAL LEGACY

Some give Newt Gingrich credit for having almost single-handedly brought Republicans into consistent political competition with the Democratic Party, which had been king in the South for more than fifty years. While that may be part of an ongoing debate among political historians (Phillips-Fein 2011), it is clear that the tactics he used in accomplishing this task were destructive in the long term. By using language in a very strategic way, he mobilized both conservative and far-right conservative Republicans and shifted the balance of power within the party. "Over the course of his career, Newt Gingrich methodically whipped up the expectations of the most extreme elements of the Republican Party's base as a way to come to power" (Brattebo 2013, 66). Through attacking opponents, and Democrats in general, in ways that labeled them as destructive, radical, and anti-American, he exacerbated a natural divide that exists between the two parties and their approaches to government. He elevated the importance of party identification, often at the expense of effective governance.

And yet, perhaps more than any other candidate profiled in this text, Gingrich seems to have been motivated by a desire to transform—and save— American politics. He has been quoted as saying that he was trying to reshape not only the federal government, but also the political culture of the nation (Strahan and Palazzolo 2004). Black and Black characterize Gingrich as "a polarizing politician who thought and acted in terms of either/or dichotomies: win/lose, good/evil, allies/enemies" (2002, 232). While this allowed him to gather in a new group of conservatives for the GOP, moderates were repelled by his discourse and tactics. However, he was able to pull a new conservative element into the party, one whose progeny seems to have contributed to the nation's partisan divide over the years.

This division has now become a wide gulf that separates Republicans and their supporters from Democrats and their supporters, sometimes to the point of violence. Trump was able to appeal to the Republican Party voters as an outsider candidate using language co-opted from George Wallace, Patrick Buchanan, and Newt Gingrich. As president, he took over a party that seemed ready to follow his strong and outspoken personality. Many lay the blame for this at Gingrich's feet, and it seems he would be unlikely to deny the extent to which he changed the trajectory of the Republican Party. "The party gate-keepers of yesteryear opened the doors to all of this. In 2020, not only can the so-called 'establishment' not contain the renegades, the renegades have become the establishment" (Zelizer 2020b).

Perhaps, in the same way that Patrick Buchanan never won the White House, but saw his ideas sweep someone else into the presidency, Gingrich never won the White House, but set a course for the Republican Party that created a path for Trump's eventual victory. In many ways, Trump owes a debt of gratitude to both of these renegade candidates for allowing his style of partisan warfare and populist discourse to drive the modern Republican Party.

REFERENCES

Black, Earl and Merle Black. 2002. *The Rise of Southern Republicans*. Cambridge, MA: Harvard University Press.

Brattebo, Douglas M. 2013. You're a Mean One, Mr. Gingrich: The Inbuilt, Ruinous Incivility of Newt. *American Behavioral Scientist* 57 no.1: 46–49.

Carter, Dan T. 1996. Legacy of rage: George Wallace and the Transformation of American Politics. *The Journal of Southern History* 62 no.1: 3–26.

Cha, Taesuh. 2015. American Exceptionalism at the Crossroads: Three Responses. *Political Studies Review* 13, no. 3 (August): 351–362.

Contract With America. 1994. Republican National Committee. New York: Times Books.

Davis, Susan. 2014. Few GOP "Revolutionaries" of 1994 Remain in Congress. *USA Today*. Feb. 13, 2014. https://www.usatoday.com/story/news/politics/2014/02/13/doc-hastings-gop-retirements/5458363/.

Gardner, Amy and Rosalind S. Heldermen. 2012. Newt Gingrich Launches Furious Atttacks Against Mitt Romney in Florida Speech. *Washington Post*. January 26, 2012.

Gingrich, Newt. 2012a. Newt Gingrich Presidential Campaign Announcement. https://www.c-span.org/video/?299483-1/newt-gingrich-presidential-campaign-announcement.

Gingrich, Newt. 2012b. Rebuilding the America We Love. Newt Gingrich campaign ad. https://www.youtube.com/watch?v=B7fJnDuVkTY.

Gingrich, Newt. 2012c. Newt Gingrich: Ad for President. Jan. 5, 2012. https://www.youtube.com/watch?v=J1fEGjU3yu4.

Gingrich, Newt. 2012d. Newt Gingrich Campaign Suspension Announcement. CSPAN. May 2, 2012. https://www.c-span.org/video/?305789-1/newt-gingrich-campaign-suspension-announcement.

Harris, Douglas B. 1998. The Rise of the Public Speakership. *Political Science Quarterly* 113, no. 2: 193–213.

Highton, Benjamin. 2002. Bill Clinton, Newt Gingrich, and the 1998 House Elections. *Public Opinion Quarterly* 66, no. 1 (March): 1–17.

Ioffe, Julia. 2016. The Millenial's Guide to Newt Gingrich. *Politico Magazine.* July 14, 2016. https://www.politico.com/magazine/story/2016/07/2016-newt-gingrich-scandals-accomplishments-veepstakes-running-mate-trump-gop-republican-214050/.

Iyengar, Shanto and Adam F. Simon. 2000. New Perspectives and Evidence on Political Communication and Campaign Effects. *Annual Review of Psychology* 51 (February): 149–169.

Kousser, J. Morgan. 2010. The Immutability of Categories and the Reshaping of Southern Politics. *Annual Review of Political Science* 13: 365–383. https://doi.org/10.1146/annurev.polisci.033008.091519.

Lindberg, Tod. 1999. Gingrich Lost and Found. *Policy Review*, April 1, 1999. https://www.hoover.org/research/gingrich-lost-and-found.

Neville-Shepard, Ryan. (2014). Triumph in Defeat: The Genre of Third-Party Presidential Concessions. *Communication Quarterly* 62, no. 2 (April): 214–232.

New York Post. 2011. Gingrich Confidently Predicts 'I'll Be the Nominee.'" Dec. 2, 2011. https://nypost.com/2011/12/01/gingrich-confidently-predicts-ill-be-the-nominee/.

Perot, Ross. 1992. *United We Stand. How We can Take Back Our Country.* Hyperion: New York.

Phillips-Fein, Kim. 2011. Conservatism: A State of the Field. *The Journal of American History* 98, no. 3 (December): 723–743.

Salzer, James. 2017. The Words of Newtspeak Transformed U.S. Politics. *Atlanta Journal Constitution.* Politics. May 15, 2017. https://www.ajc.com/news/state--regional-govt--politics/the-words-newtspeak-transformed-politics/nfWIIkAqXknLToMHnsjTxI/.

Serazio, Michael. 2016. Encoding the Paranoid Style in American Politics: "Anti-Establishment' Discourse and Power in Contemporary Spin. *Critical Studies in Media Communication* 33, no. 2 (May): 181–194.

Strong, Donald S. 1977. *Issue Voting and Party Realignment.* Tuscaloosa: University of Alabama Press.

Strahan, Randall and Daniel J. Palazzolo. 2004. The Gingrich Effect. *Political Science Quarterly* 119, no. 1 (Spring): 89–114.

Theriault, Sean M. and David W. Rohde. 2011. The Gingrich Senators and Party Polarization in the U.S. Senate. *The Journal of Politics* 73, no. 4 (August): 1011–1024.

Zelizer, Julian E. 2010. Rethinking the History of American Conservatism. *Reviews in American History*, 38, no. 2 (June): 367–392.

Zelizer, Julian E. 2020a. How Newt Gingrich Shaped the Republican Party. Interview by Jeremy Hobson, wbur. July 7, 2020. https://www.wbur.org/hereandnow/2020/07/07/newt-gingrich-republican-party.

Zelizer, Julian E. 2020b. How Newt Gingrich Laid the Groundwork for Trump's Republican Party. *Time*. July 7, 2020. https://time.com/5863457/how-newt-gingrich-laid-the-groundwork-for-trumps-republican-party/.

PART V

Implications for Outsiders

Chapter 13

Trump and the 2020 Presidential Election

Populism, Pandemic, and Post-Election Violence

Donald J. Trump accomplished the improbable in 2016: He was the first true outsider to be elected president of the United States. He ran as a populist and an outsider, and he employed some of the most divisive and jarring rhetoric ever heard from a major party's presidential candidate.

In 2020, he attempted to repeat that victory, but the magic had faded enough that he lost his bid for re-election.

What happened in the four years of his presidency that led to enough loss of support to usher Joe Biden into the White House? This chapter will take a quick look at Trump's 2020 presidential campaign and examine how his discourse, campaign tactics, and issues compared to his 2016 race. It will also provide a brief overview of his contentious years as president and consider how his loss might impact presidential elections in the future.

THE 2020 CAMPAIGN

There was never any doubt that Trump would be running for re-election in 2020, as he actually filed the paperwork for his 2020 campaign on his inauguration day in 2017. He held his first rally less than a month later, and he continued to hold large rallies throughout his presidency. It seemed that Trump fed off these large rallies, basking in the afterglow in a way reminiscent of George Wallace. Those who were close to him at the White House said that Trump often watched replays of his rallies and debates, not unlike a football coach might watch his team's game performance. "Only, instead of looking for areas where things went wrong or places to improve, Trump 'luxuriates in the moments he believes are evidence of his brilliance' (Levin 2018). The craving for a feeling of being loved by a crowd would come back to haunt him during his 2020 campaign. Casullo (2020) notes that a populist candidate will construct a narrative which indicates that he or she entered politics because of outrage over how the elite were treating "the people." This allows "him or her to become not just a representative of some objective 'interest groups' but a true redeemer," (30) which is how Trump wanted to be seen.

Trump loves being the center of attention, and during his presidency he was rarely out of the public spotlight. He sent out more than 26,000 tweets while he was president, many of them quite disparaging of his enemies, while others purported to announce new initiatives or policies (sometimes catching his staff by surprise). His discourse continued the partisan divides that had been established before his presidency, but he sharpened the edges with his outspoken nature and messages that were unlike any president before him. While many Republicans supported Trump, only a small number of Democrats expressed confidence in his ability to lead the nation. According to the Pew Research Center, Trump's overall approval rating never got above 50 percent, and it fell to 29 percent in his final weeks of office (Dimock and Gramlich 2021). Those who supported him often did it with great depth, emotion, and even religious fervor, as some Christians expressed the belief that Trump had been chosen by God to be president. Those who did not support him were just as vocal, although in the opposite ways.

> To conservatives in the "Never Trump" movement who have vowed never to vote for him under any circumstances, Trump is an ignoramus and carnival barker at best, and a bullying proto-fascist at worst. To many on the other side of the Great Divide, it is not Trump but an allegedly corrupt and intransigent conservative establishment that is the threat, and they are attacking it savagely. The ideological tug of war has become personal, and arguments that turn personal are rarely easy to resolve. (Nash 2016)

According to Pew's research, Americans began to shun talking about politics with those whom they knew felt differently about the president than themselves, with many of them citing the stress and frustration of such conversations (Dimock and Gramlich 2021). Part of the frustration may have been that the United States has become so politically divided between Democrats and Republicans that it is as if there is "Team Blue" and "Team Red," and voters cheer them on as fans. Street observed that "it does appear that Trump elicits a form of adoration that closely resembles the behaviour of fans" (2019). Not unlike fans of professional football or basketball teams, there is a lot of trash talking back and forth between fans of the two political "teams," and very little dialogue capable of persuading one to swap sides.

Trump's particular brand of celebrity populism has served him well in politics. Populist leaders can become known more for their media performance than even for their political ideas and issues (Moffit 2016). As Schäfer-Wünsche and Kloeckner note, "Trump's anti-intellectualism and peddling of conspiracy theories has long served for him to cultivate a mediated fan community deeply distrustful of the elite he has always been a part of " (2016). They argue that Trump emerged as a candidate viewed as "authentic" in his 2016 campaign, and that his celebrity status guaranteed that he would generate attendance at events, giving them greater impact. As Street points out, "the art of politics becomes the art of performance, the art of being a celebrity" (2019). In this regard, Trump injected a new dynamic—the citizens as fans—into his 2016 campaign, the intervening four years as president, and in the 2020 election.

In his 2016 victory, Trump was able to attract some Democratic voters who saw in him a voice for their feelings of disenfranchisement. As a right-wing populist, Trump's discourse identified the elites as having ruined the present, but he vowed that he could return the nation to greatness, hence his "Make America Great Again" slogan. It is common for populists to appeal to "the way things were" in contrast to the present (Knott 2020,110). This message hit home for many Americans who felt that they were being economically squeezed and politically forgotten. One of the more striking divides between Trump supporters and those who opposed him was the large number of rural votes that he received in both 2016 and 2020. His support remained strong in farming and rural areas, while large metropolitan and coastal areas tended to lean more Democratic. Those in rural communities have been hard hit in recent years by a loss of jobs and economic opportunities. This left many feeling that their concerns were not being heard and their values were not appreciated by "the elites." It is worth noting that this pattern was also found in the Agrarian Movement in the 1890s and early 1900s in the United States, and similar feelings of resentment also resulted in a populist candidate running for president (Gerteis and Goolsby 2005).

It is interesting that the political magazine National Review wrote an article in May 2011 envisioning what form a Trump presidential administration might take. Author Rob Long refers to Trump as "an unembarrassable self-love machine. A relentless name-stamper. A roaring glutton for credit and praise. In other words, Donald J. Trump possesses, along with his resorts and his chocolates, everything it takes to be president of the United States" (2011). Only five years later, Trump was elected to the presidency, and those characteristics were on full display, and they began to further divide a nation that already had serious cleavages.

As Trump's 2020 presidential campaign moved into full swing, his rallies and rhetoric reflected his version of the state of the nation's affairs, as well as a reiteration of his outsider status. It became obvious as the campaign continued that Trump was running as both an incumbent and an outsider, which is an unlikely combination. As president, one should automatically be seen as the ultimate insider. However, Trump continued to position himself as an outsider even during his presidency. At an Ohio rally in 2020, he painted Joe Biden as the career politician and ultimate insider, but himself as the outsider who was still working to root out career politicians. "You elected an outsider as president who is finally putting America first" (Provance 2020). He went on to paint Biden as a forty-seven-year career politician who he said had used his public office for the benefit of himself and his family.

But for Trump, painting himself as both an incumbent and an outsider was necessary to hold onto the coalition of voters who put him in office in 2016. Unfortunately for Trump, that coalition had already begun to develop cracks.

TRUMP DISCOURSE IN 2020 CAMPAIGN

In the 2016 presidential campaign, Trump held many rallies, and thousands of supporters would cheer and chant as he delivered his speeches. These speeches were usually marked by belligerent comments about his opponents, enemies (or perceived enemies), and he was prone to veer off planned remarks to repeat and emphasize certain phrases. It became a type of personalized speech pattern for him, unlike any of the other candidates. Trump's style of speaking and the content of those speeches both violated political norms (Theye and Melling 2018). He threw the (mostly) unwritten rules about presidential discourse out the window and intentionally broke the rules, and he did not appear concerned about political correctness. Neville-Shepard (2019) argues that outsider candidates often adopt a style of rhetoric that violates norms because they are looking to gain media coverage and get their messages in front of potential voters. This might have been expected during his campaign as an outsider in 2016, but Trump never transitioned to a more accepted type of discourse even after he was elected.

He utilized the same type message delivery in his 2020 rallies, continuing his tendency to speak in short, punchy sentences and repeat selected phrases. This type of rhetoric was categorized by Martin Montgomery as a combination of Aristotle's "pathos" and "ethos" combined with Habermas's "sincerity" to produce what he termed "authenticity."

> It is as if Trump's exaggerated and inappropriate claims about himself carried a strong appeal for his core constituency on the grounds that they come across as

an authentic form of self-expression: Trump speaks how he feels and says what he means. (2017, 637)

This produced short sound bites for news organizations, which usually had at least one camera crew in attendance. As in 2016, Trump simultaneously fed off the energy created during the events and created more passion in the crowd through his verbal messaging style. He coined a nickname for Joe Biden in the 2020 campaign, calling him "Sleepy Joe." Here are some typical comments that were delivered in a campaign rally in Reading, Pennsylvania, on Oct. 31: "Sleepy Joe Biden is a diehard globalist who spent the last 47 years outsourcing your jobs, opening your borders, and sacrificing American blood and treasure in endless foreign wars in countries that most of you have never even heard of before" (Trump 2020a). During most of his fall rallies, he also played clips of verbal gaffes by Biden during the campaign in order to drive home Trump's contention that Biden's mind couldn't be trusted: "He's gonzo. We all know it. They just don't want to say it," (2020a) he told the crowd, with the implication being that Biden had suffered some type of mental deterioration.

Trump's tendency to repeat certain words, to almost create a distinct speaking rhythm, continued. In this speech on November 1, 2020, in Macomb County, Michigan, Trump is more than an hour into his speech when he asks the crowd to go out and vote for him on election day.

But you have to go out and vote on November 3rd. We must finish the job. Drain the swamp. The swamp is deeper, and stronger, and more vicious than ever, but we've done a hell of a job, and they cannot believe that we're in this position. We're now leading. Look, we're leading in Florida. We're leading in Georgia. We're leading. (Trump 2020b)

He not only repeats words, but seems to move between short, punchy sentences and longer ones with more emotional punch. The repetition often flows into the next sentence, as when he repeats "we're leading" and adds in a couple of states, but then returns to the repeated phrase "we're leading." This pattern was familiar to those who attended his rallies or watched his campaign speeches. He was often interrupted by chants of "USA, USA," or "Four more years!" prompting him to smile and thank the crowd, which only spurred them on to additional chants. There was a rhetorical rhythm that was achieved in some of his speeches, with a give and take between the president and his audiences.

Trump's choice of adjectives used to describe his opponents and enemies in 2016 included: "foreign, special, radical, illegal, bad, corrupt, congressional, criminal, terrible, massive and disastrous" (Cinar, Stokes, and Uribe 2020).

These words contain clues to Trump's positioning of "the people" versus "the elites." That positioning continued in his 2020 campaign, with words such as corrupt, vicious, radical, not a smart person, and dummy-and-a-half being used in speeches to refer to Joe Biden.

Once again, Trump seemed to tap into a reservoir of anger and tried to build onto his base by identifying common enemies, including Joe Biden, Nancy Pelosi, RINOs, and other prominent Democrats, who he positioned as waiting in the wings to destroy America. This type of populist rhetoric worked well with his base supporters, many of whom echoed his comments in their own social media messages. Trump also spent much time denouncing "fake news" and the news media in general, as well as pollsters, cancel culture, and what he called censorship by big tech, which apparently were references to social media platforms enforcing rules about political postings. His tweets were simple, often relying on name calling or labels to convey emotion. But that was intentional, argue Theye and Melling, who say "the simplicity of the constructions gives the appearance that they are Trump's words and they have not been screened by any focus groups or consultants" (2018, 326). This fed directly into his perception as being "authentic," because it seemed that his staff would never have allowed such messages to be sent out to the public. Through his anti-establishment messaging, Trump was able to position himself authentic, but paint those in "the establishment" as inauthentic and untrustworthy because they were controlled by lobbyists and special interests (Serazio 2016).

In 2020, Trump made numerous references to sending him back to the White House to "finish the job." In most of his speeches, he referred to being elected as an outsider and "working hard for you." He consistently positioned Joe Biden as a career politician, and he used an unpolished, populist rhetorical style to connect with his audiences. "Appearing to be close to 'ordinary' people and taking up their concerns against a powerful, privileged and distant elite is another of the characteristics of populist style that has been identified in much political communication research" (Ekstrom, Patrona and Thornborrow 2018). Trump consistently portrayed himself as standing up for the Americans who were "smart" like him and "understood" what was going on. "People get it. People are smart. The backlash against this censorship is driving more and more people to support our campaign" (Trump 2020b). In this way, he established a link between himself and the "smart" people—his supporters—who could see through the attempts by the elites to silence them or censor their comments. Even though his supporters realized that he wasn't really like them—after all, he said he was a billionaire—they still rallied to him as someone who could fight for them in Washington to make their voices heard. Similar to supporters of George Wallace or Patrick Buchanan, Trump's base saw him as a charismatic outsider who could give voice to their grievances about being overlooked, taken for granted, and disrespected. They established a bond with him, primarily through his populist discourse and performance.

As Knott (2020) noted, attempts to motivate the public against the establishment depend on having a receptive audience, or else the messages gain no traction. Trump seemed to feel that his political legitimacy came more from perceived mass opinion—the love shown to him in large rallies—than from the ballot box, which was a belief that would cause upheaval after he lost the 2020 election.

TRUMP CAMPAIGN TACTICS IN 2020

The coalition that came together to put Trump into the White House in 2016 lost some supporters during his four years in office. Perhaps it was more of his personality than his political issues that caused some people to look for change in 2020. During his four years in office, he fulfilled some campaign promises, but the focus during the entire time was on Donald J. Trump the personality, not on being president. While many admitted early on that he was in many ways flawed, they still believed in him and what he said. "In Donald Trump many of those "below" have found a voice for their despair and outrage at what they consider to be the cluelessness and condescension of their "betters" (Nash 2016). When Trump berated the media, or when he mocked Rep. Nancy Pelosi, his true believers loved him all the more. However, while many still felt that he was the voice representing them, others grew tired of his temperament. Trump was what some scholars called the "disruptor-in-chief" (Cinar, Stokes and Uribe 2020) because of his reliance on bombastic proclamations, a discounting of evidence, demonization of enemies, and his propensity to use social media to propel his "good versus evil" discourse. In short, he was unlike any president the United States has ever seen. In an article in The Atlantic, Cas Mudde referred to Trump's behavior and lack of political skills. "The amateurism of Trump is absolutely unique. I honestly have never seen anything like that in an established democracy" (Friedman 2017).

In considering Trump's tactics in the 2020 campaign, a distinction will be made regarding his strategy and political maneuvering before the general election and after Biden was declared the winner of the general election.

BEFORE THE GENERAL ELECTION

Trump's tactics in 2019 and early 2020 were reminiscent of his political campaign in 2016. He remained in almost constant motion, speaking at large rallies, sending out Twitter messages, and using the populist rhetoric that has already been discussed. He continued to berate the Democrats, and he punctuated rallies with comments about how hard he had been working for them. As it became clear that Joe Biden would be the Democratic nominee, he pursued a game of what some might call psychological warfare involving the manipulation of information and the distortion of what was real and what was not. In doing so, he reduced the confidence many Americans had in the country's basic institutions.

This seemed to grow exponentially when COVID-19 became a national issue. Not only did he continue to blame China for the virus, he also became belligerent toward Democratic governors who opted to close cities and enforce quarantines. He participated in Coronavirus Task Force news conferences, often providing misleading or potentially harmful information, rather than relying on the nation's health experts to relay updates to the American people. At one of these news conferences on April 4, it is twenty-eight minutes into the news conference before Trump allows FDA director Dr. Stephen Hahn and Dr. Anthony Fauci, director of the U.S. National Institute of Allergy and Infectious Diseases, to speak regarding updates about the virus. This is a trend that continued, as Trump would begin the news conferences and talk about his own efforts to "aggressively" work to end the pandemic and get the country open again. He focused many comments on opening up the nation for business. This comment from the April 4 news conference is typical:

> My administration is working very aggressively to pioneer new medical countermeasures to treat and prevent infection working on a lot of things. We must utilize our nation's scientific brilliance to vanquish the virus. We have to vanquish the virus as quickly as we can because we have a lot of things happening in this country and we have a great future, but we have to get back to work. (Trump 2020c)

At every chance, Trump made sure to highlight his own contributions in the race to find a cure for the pandemic, but his comments were generally seen as self-serving and not reliant on trusted scientific principles. His campaign continued to hold rallies in the fall, despite the pandemic and possible COVID-19 transmission. The campaign also did not require individuals to wear masks, perhaps because Trump himself rarely wore one.

In October 2020, Trump and his wife, Melania, were diagnosed with COVID-19. His son, Barron, was also diagnosed with the virus. Several members of Trump's staff also were diagnosed about the same time. While Melania Trump remained in seclusion at the White House, her husband was taken to Walter Reed National Military Medical Center, where he was treated for the virus. Although talk of his illness was downplayed, the president was treated with a variety of drugs and monoclonal antibodies. During his stay at the hospital, Trump demanded to go "a short, last-minute ride to wave to his supporters" who were outside (Jackson and Subramanian 2020). Concerns were raised about the wisdom of such a ride, as it placed him in contact with Secret Service and hospital personnel, when guidelines called for those diagnosed with the virus to self isolate. This brought questions to the forefront about his judgment and perceived lack of concern for others as he took a spin around the block and waved to supporters outside the hospital.

Even after his own brush with the virus, Trump continued to hold rallies in which the crowd was not required to wear masks. During his last few days of the presidential campaign, he made numerous stops to hold rallies and give speeches. He almost never wore a mask, and at almost every stop his stump speech involved touting how great the American economy was prior to the pandemic. This comment is typical, coming at twenty-eight minutes into the speech: "And then all of a sudden we got hit with the China Plague. And now we're back to the drawing boards and next year is going to be one of the greatest economic years and all of that" (Trump 2020d). The typical wording at his rallies was to call COVID-19 "the China virus" or the "China plague." Although the virus was first identified in Wuhan, China, the exact cause of the virus was still being investigated. But Trump continued to link China to the virus, contributing to conspiracy theories that China made the virus in one of its labs. Many Americans believed this theory, and Trump did nothing to dispute this origin story. As noted by Richard Hofstadter in his seminal 1964 article and 1965 book, the paranoid style of politics is not new, but the current version has found conspiracies in new places: "Their predecessors had discovered conspiracies; the modern radical right finds conspiracy to be betrayal from on high" (1964). It might be noted that Hofstadter wrote these words about supporters of Barry Goldwater, but more recent historical articles are less judgmental about the conservative movement he ignited. But, to place it in context, when Hofstadter wrote these words, the Internet and social media did not exist to perpetuate and spread the conspiracy theories. However, these mass media outlets were indispensable for Trump and his supporters who used social media to disseminate messages blaming China for having produced the virus.

This was not the only conspiracy theory that Trump promoted during the election. He consistently repeated that the Democrats would try to steal the election, and, as it became clear that many states would be using a large number of mail-in ballots to avoid crowds on election day, he began to speak against the reliability of mail-in ballots. He intimated that it would be easy for his enemies to interfere with them, and his comments prompted large numbers of Republicans to vote in person, rather than mailing in a completed ballot. He also repeated lies touted by QAnon that the number of COVID-19 deaths was exaggerated, and that it was safer to be in public than the medical experts were saying. In his speech at the Republican National Convention in Charlotte, N.C., in August, Trump said that individually requested absentee ballots would be a good alternative for those who needed to use them, but he otherwise urged people to go out and vote because it would be safe. But a reliance on mail-in ballots, he said, was not safe.

> But this is big stuff. This is stealing millions of votes. And it's going to be very hard. Now we're in courts all over the country. And hopefully, we have judges that are going to give it a fair call because if they give it a fair call, we're going to win this election. The only way they can take this election away from us is if this is a rigged election. (Trump 2020e)

In this way, Trump continued to place the idea of a "stolen election" in front of the American public, and in doing so, he planted the seeds for post-election violence.

AFTER THE GENERAL ELECTION

It was not until January 7, 2021, that Trump said for the first time that he would not serve a second term, but he never congratulated president-elect Joe Biden. This admission came after weeks of attempting to overturn the results of the November election, both in federal courts and in the court of public opinion. It also came after pro-Trump supporters stormed the U.S. Capitol, where Congress was working to certify the results of the Electoral College.

Ever since the general election, Trump had insisted that there had been vote fraud in multiple states, with him alleging that Dominion Voting Systems, which operates much of the country's voting machinery, had deleted millions of votes for him and increased the votes for Biden. Several of his surrogates went on television news shows and repeated the allegations, which were never proven (Kennedy and Chappell 2021). The security director for Dominion was forced into hiding because of death threats from Trump supporters. In another unsubstantiated claim, Trump said that Republican poll watchers were not allowed to monitor votes in cities in key states. Despite the lack of evidence for thse claims, Trump continued to promote them through his own social media accounts and through other members of his family and campaign staff.

Some scholars argue that populist leaders have the capability to harm the institutions in the nations in which they are operating, simply because they cast the battle in terms of morality and "good" versus "evil," which can lead to a loss of political libery (Urbaniti 2013). This can be seen in

Trump's desperate attempts to hold onto the presidency. Cas Mudde explains it this way:

> You can't compromise in a moral struggle. If the pure compromises with the corrupt, the pure is corrupted . . . You're not dealing with an opponent. An opponent has legitimacy. Often in the populist mind and rhetoric, it is an enemy. And you don't make deals with enemies, and you don't bend to illegitimate pressure. (Friedman 2017)

In other words, for Trump's supporters, Biden and the Democrats were enemies, and they were being painted as having stolen the election from Trump. As Trump's team filed lawsuit after lawsuit, and as the conspiracy theories about the election continued and gained traction, especially among QAnon believers, the agitation among Trump's supporters continued to grow. This eventually led to the events on January 6, 2021, in which a mob of Trump supporters overran Capitol Police and entered the Capitol building, forcing the hasty evacuation of members of Congress who were working to certify the Electoral College results. Many of the supporters came directly from a Trump "Save America Rally" at a park near the White House. Trump addressed his supporters for more than an hour, insisting that the election had been stolen from him. Near the end of his speech, Trump urged supporters to walk to the Capitol: "We fight like hell, and if you don't fight like hell, you're not going to have a country anymore," Trump said. "So we are going to walk down Pennsylvania Avenue—I love Pennsylvania Avenue—and we are going to the Capitol" (Petras et al. 2021). Soon after this, his supporters began fighting against Capitol Police, eventually gaining access to the building. Rioters were eventually photographed on the Senate floor, in Rep. Nancy Pelosi's office, and in trying to force their way into the House Chamber. Five people died, including one U.S. Capitol police officer.

Trump was ultimately impeached—for the second time—for his role in inciting violence against the government of the United States. While he survived the impeachment vote in the Senate, he becomes the first president to be impeached twice, with the second impeachment hearings coming after he left the White House.

Trump's populist campaign tactics and rhetoric can be partially blamed for the assault on the Capitol. After telling his supporters over and over during the election that he could only lose if the election were stolen, he primed his supporters to be angry and look for an outlet for their anger and frustration. He had also welcomed the support of those on the far right, although that door had already been opened by Patrick Buchanan and Newt Gingrich (Davis 2018). Nash used this description: "Joining the Trumpist effort to reconfigure the Republican Party on nationalist-populist lines is an array of aggressive dissenters called the 'alternative right' or 'alt-right,' many of whom openly espouse white nationalism and white identity politics and denounce their conservative opponents in the most vituperative terms" (2016). While many Trump supporters quietly seethed about the "stolen election" at home, others were drawn the the idea of a rally in Washington on the day that Congress would be certifying the Electoral College votes. Trump's comments at the rally were enough to push this array of alt-right groups, QAnon conspiracy theorists, white supremacists, and a variety of other state and national groups into action.

TRUMP'S CAMPAIGN ISSUES IN 2020

The issues Trump talked about in 2016 were often on display again in his 2020 campaign: jobs, the economy, immigration, the Supreme Court, and "fake news." However, some of these were given a new spin, based on what Trump had done in those areas. For instance, his appointment of three U.S. Supreme Court justices was a point he usually made in speeches. This was an important issue to evangelical conservatives, who are hoping those appointments will help overturn the nation's current laws allowing abortion.

Trump often mentioned the number of jobs that had been created and the healthy economy that existed before COVID-19. He used this as a segue into discussing how Biden would "lock down" the nation and trigger an economic disaster.

In the spring and summer of 2020, Trump threatened to use the power of the federal government and federal troops against those protesting the death of George Floyd during an arrest by Minneapolis police. As protests against racial discrimination continued across the nation, Trump heavily criticized decisions by mayors and governors who were attempting to manage the protests. On June 1, 2020, Trump finished a speech in the Rose Garden and then headed down the street to St. John's Episcopal Church, which had been damaged in a recent protest. National Guard members were initially said to have pushed aside a peaceful protest to make way for the president, who posed for photos outside the church while holding a Bible. He then walked back to the White House. Criticism of his action was swift, especially when it came to light that peaceful protesters had been gassed, struck by projectiles, or injured as they attempted to run from police and National Guard members, as well as federal agents (Allen, Clark, and Shabad 2020). An inspector general's report released in 2021 found that U.S. Park Police had already begun clearing the area for a contractor to install fencing before Trump made the decision to visit the church, although it did acknowledge problems with how the event was handled (Montanaro 2021).

But the issue that became of overriding importance to Americans was the pandemic. A growing number of Americans were dying, and there was a burgeoning divide between those who were willing to wear masks and social distance and those who were not. In this area, Trump displayed a lack of sustained leadership. His insistence on recommending untested, and often unorthodox, possible cures for COVID-19 became fodder for late-night comedians and newspaper cartoonists. They also became a concern when he suggested nonsensical alternatives, such as when he said injecting cleaning disinfectants might kill the virus. Trump's inability to stand back and allow the medical officials to give advice and steer the discussions became a serious issue which was indicative of his desire to be in the spotlight and take credit for progress that was being made. When he discussed the pandemic in his speeches, he touted his own recovery from the virus and continued to promise vaccines that would allow a swift economic recovery under his policies:

> But the vaccine is going to make it quicker. It's coming in a matter of weeks, it's going to be distributed immediately. We're going to start with the seniors, but it's going to go very, very quickly, very, very quickly. It's going to be really fantastic. It's going to be, I think you'll see something that's going to be absolutely amazing. (Trump 2020b)

Medical officials never really endorsed Trump's rosy predictions about the availability of a vaccine, although it was true that progress was being made faster than in any previous vaccine development. But Trump never flagged in his excitement about the availability of vaccines, which he said were coming quickly.

Trump also took credit for a soaring stock market, the renegotiation of NAFTA, the establishment of the U.S. Space Force, and working to force China to have better trade policies with the United States.

TRUMP'S POLITICAL IMPACT ON FUTURE ELECTIONS

There is no doubt that Trump tapped into a vein of resentment among rural and working class Americans against the establishment elites. These blue collar, less educated, and lower-income citizens were looking for someone to voice their grievances, and Donald J. Trump became their spokesman. Many are still true believers, and they hold out hope that he will return to the White House.

Most of Trump's supporters are Republican, although saying all of them favor the GOP is painting with too broad a brush. However, he retains a significant amount of support, and he is still able to raise large sums of money.

This concerns those who would prefer not to see Trump run for president again. While he has not been clear about his future political intentions, he was invited to speak at CPAC in March 2021, where he gave his first speech since returning to private life. In that speech, he said that he would not form a third party, and that he would remain active in Republican politics. This seems to be an indication that he could campaign for certain candidates in the next few years, possibly helping to shape a new Republican Party.

This seems to have been part of his intent from the beginning—burn much of it down to build it back up in his image. And this is what concerns the Republican establishment, many of whom are having increasing trouble seeing where they fit into the Republican Party's future.

Many conservative Republicans have at least two major concerns: A divided and conflicted Republican Party and a Trump populist message that still resonates with almost half of Americans. While the media fixated on Biden winning 80 million votes, less attention was paid to the fact that Trump won more than 74 million. That means that he potentially has control over the future of the Republican Party. While many elected Republicans seem to be trying to mend fences with him, others continue to call out his misleading comments, brash behavior, and reliance on falsehoods. This has led to a divided Republican Party at a time when it should be gearing up for midterm elections. Historically speaking, the party out of the White House does well in midterm contests, but without a unified party, that would seem difficult, as campaigns take large amounts of money and support.

Which brings them back to Trump. Not only does he retain the support of many party loyalists, he also is still capable of raising large sums of cash. The party literally cannot afford to ostracize him, as it needs his base of voters and the cash he might be able to pull in for candidates.

In the same way that Newt Gingrich sought to change the future of the Republican Party—and did—Trump is attempting to remake the party in his own image. While he owes a debt of gratitude to Gingrich, he has co-opted the party in a way that Gingrich enjoyed only in his dreams.

What is the future of the Republican Party? It is important to remember that political parties often go through transition, and that they are made up of groups of people with sometimes conflicting ideas about what should be done. "American conservatism, then, remains at heart a coalition. Like all coalitions, it contains within itself the potential for splintering—and never more so than right now" (Nash 2016). The Republican Party stands on a precipice, contemplating its future. Whatever that might be, Donald J. Trump will have changed its trajectory, and what it will look like is anyone's guess.

REFERENCES

Allen, Jonathan, Dartunarro Clark and Rebecca Shabad. Police, National Guard Clash with Protestors Before Trump Photo Op. *NBC News.* June 1, 2020. https://www.nbcnews.com/politics/politics-news/after-night-significant-damage-d-c-mayor-bowser-imposes-earlier-n1221126.

Casullo, Maria Esperanza. Populism and Myth. In *The Populist Manifesto*, edited by Emmy Eklundh and Andy Knott, 25-38. London: Rowman & Littlefield.

Cinar, Ipek, Susan Stokes and Andres Uribe. 2020. Presidential Rhetoric and Populism. *Presidential Studies Quarterly* 50 (2): 240–263.

Davis, Mark. 2018. 'Culture as Inseparable from Race': Culture Wars from Pat Buchanan to Milo Yiannopoulos. *M/C Journal* 21 (5). https://doi.org/10.5204/mcj.1484.

Dimock, Michael and John Gramlich. 2021. How America Changed During Donald Trump's Presidency. Pew Research Center, January 29, 2021. https://www.pewresearch.org/2021/01/29/how-america-changed-during-donald-trumps-presidency/.

Ekstrom, Mats, Marianna Patrona and Joanna Thornborrow. 2018. Right-Wing Populism and the Dynamics of Style: A Discourse-Analytic Perspective on Mediated Political Performances. *Palgrave Communication* 4, no. 83. https://doi.org/10.1057/s41599-018-0132-6.

Friedman, Uri. 2017. What Is a Populist? And is Donald Trump One? *The Atlantic*, February 27, 2017. https://www.theatlantic.com/international/archive/2017/02/what-is-populist-trump/516525/.

Gerteis, Joseph and Alyssa Goolsby. 2005. Nationalism in America: The Case of the Populist Movement. *Theory and Society* 34, no. 2 (April): 197–225.

Hofstadter, Richard. 1964. The Paranoid Style in American Politics. *Harper's Magazine*, November 1964. https://harpers.org/archive/1964/11/the-paranoid-style-in-american-politics/.

Jackson, David and Courtney Subramanian. 2020. 'Interesting Journey': Donald Trump Drives By Supporters Outside Walter Reed, Claims Progress in Another Video. *USA Today*, Oct. 5, 2020. https://www.usatoday.com/story/news/politics/2020/10/04/great-reports-donald-trump-cuts-another-video-claims-progress/3617839001/.

Kennedy, Merrit and Bill Chappell. Dominion Voting Systems Files $1.6 Billion Defamation Lawsuit Against Fox News. *NPR*, March 26, 2021. https://www.npr.org/2021/03/26/981515184/dominion-voting-systems-files-1-6-billion-defamation-lawsuit-against-fox-news.

Knott, Andy. 2020. A Manifesto and Populism? In *The Populist Manifesto*, edited by Emmy Eklundh and Andy Knott, 107-122. London: Rowman & Littlefield.

Levin, Bess. 2018. Trump Loves Watching Replays of His Own Rallies, Cooing Over His Performances. *Vanity Fair*, Aug. 6, 2018. https://www.vanityfair.com/news/2018/08/trump-loves-watching-his-own-rallies-debates-tivo.

Long, Rob. 2011. President Me: Imagining a Trump Administration. *National Review*. May 2, 2011, 27–28.

Moffit, B. Tormey. 2016. *The Global Rise of Populism: Performance, Political Style, and Representation*. Stanford, CA: Stanford University Press.

Montanaro, Domenico. 2021. Watchdog Report Says Police Did Not Clear Protestors to Make Way for Trump Photo-Op. *NPR*, June 9, 2021. https://www.npr.org/2021/06/09/1004832399/watchdog-report-says-police-did-not-clear-protesters-to-make-way-for-trump-last-.

Montgomery, Martin. 2017. Post-truth politics? Authenticity, Populism and the Electoral Discourses of Donald Trump. *Journal of Language and Politics* 16 (4): 619–639.

Nash, George H. 2016. Populism, I: American Conservatism and the Problem of Populism. *The New Criterion* 35, no. 1 (September): 4–14.

Neville-Shepard, Ryan. 2019. Genre-Busting, Campaign Speech Genres and the Rhetoric of Political Outsiders. In *Reading the Presidency Advances in Presidential Rhetoric*, edited by Stephen J. Heidt and Mary E. Stuckey, 86–105. New York: Peter Lang.

Petras, George, Janet Loehrke, Ramon Padilla, Javier Zarracina, and Jennifer Borresen. 2021. Timeline: How the Storming of the U.S. Capitol Unfolded on Jan. 6. *USA Today*, Jan. 6, 2021. https://www.usatoday.com/in-depth/news/2021/01/06/dc-protests-capitol-riot-trump-supporters-electoral-college-stolen-election/6568305002/.

Provance, Jim. 2020. At Ohio Rally, Trump Seeks to Cast Himself as the Outsider, Attacks Biden as "career politician." *Pittsburgh Post-Gazette*, October 24, 2020. https://www.post-gazette.com/news/politics-nation/2020/10/24/Donald-Trump-rally-Circleville-Ohio-Columbus-Joe-Biden-campaign-2020/stories/202010250169.

Schäfer-Wünsche, Elisabeth and Christian Kloeckner. 2016. Politics of Celebrity: The Case of Donald Trump. Lecture Series: The Road to the White House, North American Studies Program, University of Bonn, July 19, 2016.

Serazio, Michael. 2016. Encoding the Paranoid Style in American Politics: "Anti-Establishment' Discourse and Power in Contemporary Spin. *Critical Studies in Media Communication*, 33, no. 2 (May): 181–194.

Street, John. 2019. What is Donald Trump? Forms of 'Celebrity' in Celebrity Politics. *Political Studies Review* 17, no. 1: 3–13. https://journals.sagepub.com/doi/full/10.1177/1478929918772995.

Theye, Kirsten and Steven Melling. 2018. Total Losers and Bad Hombres: The Political Incorrectness and Perceived Authenticity of Donald J. Trump. *Southern Communication Journal* 83, no. 5 (November-December): 322–337.

Trump, Donald J. 2020a. Donald Trump Rally Speech Transcript, Reading, PA October 31. Rev, Nov. 1, 2020. https://www.rev.com/blog/transcripts/donald-trump-rally-speech-transcript-reading-pa-october-31.

Trump, Donald J. 2020b. Donald Trump Rally Speech Transcript, Macomb County, MI Nov. 1. Rev, Nov. 1, 2020. https://www.rev.com/blog/transcripts/donald-trump-rally-speech-transcript-macomb-county-mi-november-1.

Trump, Donald J. 2020c. Donald Trump Coronavirus Task Force Transcript April 4. Rev, April 4, 2020. https://www.rev.com/blog/transcripts/donald-trump-coronavirus-task-force-transcript-april-4.

Trump, Donald J. 2020d. Donald Trump Rally Speech Transcript Rome, Georgia November 1. Rev, Nov. 1, 2020. https://www.rev.com/blog/transcripts/donald-trump-rally-speech-transcript-rome-georgia-november-1.

Trump, Donald J. 2020e. Speech: Donald Trump Addresses the Republican National Convention in Charlotte, August 24, 2020. Factbase, Aug. 24, 2020. https://factba.se/transcript/donald-trump-speech-republican-national-convention-charlotte-august-24-2020.

Urbaniti, Nadia. 2013. The Populist Phenomenon. *Raison Politiques* 51, (3): 137–154.

.Chapter 14

The Future of Outsider Presidential Candidates

This book has looked at the presidential campaigns of ten different candidates. Each one was distinct, and each one took a slightly different route in pursuit of the White House. Some of them knew they would not be elected, but they were forging a path for their ideas, political party, race, or gender. Most seemed motivated by a desire to change the nation and, in the process, help their fellow citizens.

As a rhetorical history, this text has attempted to show how previous candidates often launched an idea, popularized a new rhetorical approach, cleared a path, or even adopted a new technology that influenced a presidential campaign in the future. As such, it follows the path of those who have studied the analysis of history in terms of rhetoric and its impact on the collective memory, but examines it in light of current research, thought, technology, and concepts (Murphy 2015). The story of how those candidates influenced the rhetoric and tactics of later fringe campaigns brings us to this time and place in the nation's history. As Bruce Gronbeck noted, "Key to narrativization is the casting of a context that frames the historical enterprise generally and seemingly identifies and organizes a series of past events so they can be narrativized, that is, bound together into a story" (1995). The narrative recounted in this book provides a way of better understanding this point in time and our arrival at this moment in the nation's political history.

It is worth repeating that the narrative presented here shows how candidates from both the left and right of the political spectrum have influenced recent political campaigns. For instance, Shirley Chisholm and the Rev. Jesse Jackson forged a lasting impact on the Democratic Party, as did Ralph Nader and Jill Stein. These candidates have pushed the Democratic Party to the left, and they introduced issues and tactics that are being embraced by current members of the party. On the other end of the political spectrum, a number of candidates profiled here have pushed the Republican Party to the right, including George Wallace (ironic, given that he was a Democrat), Patrick Buchanan, Newt Gingrich, and Donald J. Trump. Ross Perot and Ron Paul have influenced both parties through their adoption of new technologies that allow candidates to send messages directly to voters, and those technologies are having a lasting—and complicated—impact on today's elections.

The United States has reached a juncture in which there are deep political divisions that have led to gridlock within its legislative bodies and discord in its culture. Some of those cleavages have developed over time, many as a result of the rhetoric and and issues that have been already been discussed. The technology that many idealistically thought could help save it—the Internet—has actually contributed to these divisions, and it seems unlikely that it will eventually lead to a reversal of the current polarization. Several scholarly studies have been published that attempt to find the causes for this polarization (Serazio 2016, Nash 2016, Shermer 2018, Guerlain 2019) and, while they all have slightly different approaches to answering the question, most seem to indicate that Americans have become more divided and have a deep distrust of the other political party.

This partisan identification has been increasing for several years, according to the Pew Research Center, which has been tracking political trends for several decades. Since 2012, Pew has found an increasing number of Americans who say the conflicts between Republicans and Democrats are stronger than conflicts between different socio-economic groups or different races. In 2019, Pew found that 55 percent of Republicans said that Democrats were "more immoral," when compared to other Americans. The percentage of Democrats who said the same of Republicans was 47 percent. Just three years earlier, those respective numbers were 47 and 35 percent (Pew Research Center 2019).

Political shifts have been happening in the United States for several decades, but they seemed to pick up speed after the election of President Ronald Reagan. As noted in earlier chapters, the South began to shift politically in the 1960s, giving an opportunity to populist George Wallace (Black and Black 2002). In the 1990s, Newt Gingrich sensed that many Southern Democrats were shifting alliances, and he used abrasive political tactics to bring the Republican Party into legitimate contention for power and pushed it in a very conservative direction (Strahan and Palazzollo 2004). In 2016, Donald Trump capitalized on these shifts that had been happening and rode them into the White House.

By fixating on Trump and his allegedly unique appeal to the working class, observers have missed larger trends that predate Trump, that have nothing to do with his unique campaign and presidency, and that will likely continue long after he leaves office. The relationship between education, income, race, and presidential voting is evolving. (Carnes and Lupu 2020)

What happened in 2016 was simply a manifestation of the changes that had been taking place for a number of years and that have left steep political cleavages in the nation. A recurring theme in this book has been the regular emergence of vestiges of populist rhetoric and narratives among outsider candidates. Populism is not prevalent in only one party, but can be seen in candidates from both established parties as well as in third party and independent candidates. While a populist approach may partially be a way of distinguishing and separating one candidate from a group, it also reflects a rather constant tension in the nation between different groups, especially those with less education and lower incomes and those who are better educated and have higher incomes. Many years ago, the sociologist Seymour Martin Lipset noted the importance of education levels in people's gravitation toward authoritarianism. "Both inferior education and low occupational position are highly intercorrelated, both are part of the complex making up low-status, and are associated with a lack of tolerance" (1959). Lipset argued that lower-class people are "isolated from the activities, controversies, and organization of democratic society" (1959) which makes them less likely to understand the complex nature of United States' politics. Although we now live in a society with much information (and misinformation) available to every potential voter, few people actively research candidates and issues before voting. Instead of educating themselves about the political processes in the nation, many less-educated and lower-income individuals look for a spokesperson who "understands" their grievances, anger, and frustration (Bonikowski and Gidron 2016).

That often leads them to support a populist candidate—such as Donald Trump—who they see as having the ability "fix" whatever they feel needs to be changed. This is not to say that less-educated people cannot understand the political processes and situations in the nation, but that they are often so busy with working and taking care of families that they don't have enough time or energy to devote themselves to self-education about the current state of government. They experience their own economic and social frustrations and have a nagging feeling that no one cares about them.

One outgrowth of Americans' current assessment of the state of the nation and its political division seems to be the desire for change. Every political candidate runs on the idea of change, but the American public appears to be looking for deep, institutional-level change. For many, that was the allure of a Donald Trump presidency—someone who wasn't a politician, who wasn't being handled by political professionals, and who seemed authentic (Theye and Melling 2018). Many saw him as the person who would have the gumption to stand up to career politicians and get rid of business-as-usual in Washington, D.C. For those with less education and lower incomes, he became a surrogate spokesperson. But he leaves a complicated legacy, especially after his loss in 2020.

One thing to remember is that the United States has a history of political division. Politics in the United States. have always been rough and tumble, and the nation even went through a Civil War that came about because of political polarization. There have been many periods of division and civil unrest, including the 1960s, that saw disruption from burgeoning social movements. But most often in those times, the political disruption was mainly within parties, not necessarily between them. A Gallup Poll in October 2019 found that 47 percent of Americans identified themselves as Democrat or Democrat-leaning independents, while 42 percent identified as Republican or Republican-leaning. This leaves only 11 percent not identifying with either of the major parties. In 2015, just before the 2016 presidential race, the respective numbers were 45 percent Democrat and 43 percent Republican (Jones 2019).

It is important to understand the current political identification landscape, because a quick glance at the numbers indicates that an outsider candidate would probably need to come from one of the two main parties to have a chance of success. This is what happened in 2016 when Trump was elected. Mainstream Republicans were less than thrilled with the prospect of having Trump as president, but they were more likely to support him than open the door for Hillary Clinton to become elected. That is partisan politics at work.

There is increasing evidence that Democrats and Republicans tend to live in separate "worlds," and see issues and the nation in different ways. The media play a role in the continuing political divide in the nation. Selective exposure theory in Communication (Sears and Freedman 1967, Bryant and Davies 2006) posits that individuals tend to seek out and select information that reinforces and confirms their existing biases. The news media in the United States has been going through changes since the 1970s, and those changes have allowed consumers to have more control over their media choices (Carey 1993). This transformation of media has led to a return to a mainstream news model that is less objective and more likely to interpret events through a political lens. The new version is sometimes called hyperpartisan because of its heavy degree of partisanship, coupled with its relationship to alternative and social media. "This conceptual location distinguishes hyperpartisan news from older forms of partisan news, because hyperpartisan news is not just partisan, but also alternative. As non-mainstream media that eschew journalistic norms and routines, alternative media typically challenge or subvert mainstream narratives and establishment politics" (Barnidge and Peacock 2019). The rise of hyperpartisan online news outlets such as Newsmax, OAN,

Democracy Now!, and The Intercept demonstrate that is easier than ever for selective exposure to influence American society and politics, prompting individuals to divide into political "teams," even when they might not have a clear idea of their own "team's" ideology. In this era of mass media, content is king, and most consumers are drawn to the types of content that reinforce their core beliefs and ideas. An article in Psychology Today argues that "For much of the voting public, political affiliation isn't so much about the issues as it is about being part of 'Team Red' and 'Team Blue.' So opposed between 'us' and 'them,' 'liberals become 'libtards,' 'conservatives' become 'fascists,' and the possibility of finding common ground flies out the window" (Pierre 2018). So, what does this mean for possible outsider presidential candidates in the coming years?

FACTORS TO CONSIDER

While Americans seem to be looking for a candidate who can promote and bring about change in the nation, the two main political parties have differing ideas about what those changes should be. But many American voters are looking for someone who can unite the country. That seems to have been the case in the 2020 election, in which more than half of the voters rejected the chaos and bombast of Trump in favor of Biden, who vowed to unify the country in his inauguration speech. Biden presented himself as an approachable "common guy," but didn't utilize populist discourse. Many of Biden's issues—paid leave for parents, reforming the prison system, boosting teacher pay, expanding Medicare, and increasing taxes on upper-income Americans—can be traced back to Shirley Chisholm and the Rev. Jesse Jackson, who brought complex social issues to the forefront in the 1960s and 1980s.

The office of the president is highly idealized for most Americans (Powell and Cowart 2003), and it symbolizes power, strength, and international influence. The following are three areas of importance for future outsider candidates. These are areas that could provide opportunities for outsiders, or they could provide pitfalls, depending on how they are navigated.

DIVISION CAN CREATE OPPORTUNITY

Although voters in the United States see the nation as divided, that doesn't mean that they approve of such a division between those in the two main political parties. A Public Agenda/USA TODAY/Ipsos poll in December 2019 found a number of Americans longing for an end to the political squabbling in Washington, D.C. and in their own families and communities.

Those who participated in the poll blamed continuing division on national leaders, social media, and the news media. These groups were singled out for exaggerating or exacerbating political divisions, sometimes for their own benefit. More than nine out of ten respondents said that it is important to find ways to reduce the political divisiveness in the nation. Many Democrats and Republicans related that they view half of the members of the *other party* as too extreme, and even said a quarter of their *own party's* members were too extreme, which makes it hard to compromise (USA Today 2019).

Viewing the glass half empty might lead to despair about the country's political future. But it could also be viewed as a potential opportunity for an outsider candidate who can appeal to members of both parties who are look-ing for someone to bridge the gap. The tone of most recent presidential cam-paigns has been overwhelmingly negative and seemed to focus on aggressive rhetoric. But, as has been shown in previous chapters, populist candidates can often appeal to enough voters from both major parties to become a political contender. Populist rhetoric is oppositional, adversarial, and often quite jarring. Populist messages generally find more support during times of uncertainty and shifting economic and cultural norms (Gerteis and Goolsby 2005, Bonikowski and Gidron 2016, Brubaker 2020). The elections of 2016 and 2020 both featured divisive rhetoric, and the Trump presidency utilized populist discourse both in speeches and in social media. This exacerbated the political fissures in the nation, and a Pew Research Center study from 2019 found that many Americans at that time actually found it more comfortable to discuss religion—rather than politics—with those they didn't know well.

An outsider candidate with a compelling personal narrative and strong, consistent appeals on issues that a percentage of both Republicans and Democrats can agree on could forge an interesting path through the primaries. It is possible that this type of candidate might be viewed positively by those looking for a different political option. It would be very important for the person to have an authentic persona—one in which both positives and nega-tives are on display for voters—as this has become a salient characteristic for younger generations. A study from 2017 found that authenticity was the most important characteristic for Millennials, Baby Boomers, and Gen Xers in choosing a brand to support (Cassidy 2017). In late 2020, Millennials became a larger share of America's adult population than Baby Boomers, and they are interested in seeing more authenticity from political candidates, as opposed to the "pre-packaged" politicians who live by teleprompters and rote answers.

A genuine candidate would be one who is not seen as pandering to the electorate with rehearsed rhetoric, which is how many young people view traditional American politics. "Research on mediated talk in the public sphere has shown that 'being authentic' and 'being sincere' are interactional, discursive accomplishments, produced in specific contexts for particular audiences" (Ekstrom, Patrona and Thornborrow 2018). This would be absolutely necessary for a successful candidate in today's heavily mediated society. A reliance on public relations, rehearsed comments, and orchestrated events in politics has left many voters with a distrust for what they see in media. They are looking for a candidate who seems authentic—even rough or common at times—to take up their causes and work for change. Oftentimes, a populist approach is seen as more authentic, possibly because of the different type of discourse that is employed.

Some scholars have advocated for a new brand of leftist populism that can compete with the rise of right-wing populism to solve a variety of issues that include challenges in the environment, finance, international trade, and inequality. As Eklundh and Knott (2020) state: "The spread of these various crises and the intractability of core problems also point to a further crisis—the crisis of politics or, more specifically, the failure of the left to produce a sufficiently compelling response to our situation" (4). To be clear, Eklundh and Knott and their fellow scholars see populism as a way of doing politics, not as an ideology. It would be more of a rhetorical approach working to spark a grassroots movement that would target a wide swath of voters and unite various groups. The modern Democratic Party is populated by many different groups of people who have differing ideas about what issues are most important, as well as how far left the party should move in order to solve those challenges. The Republican Party, meanwhile, is in the middle of an ongoing identity crisis as those loyal to former President Trump dig in and prepare to do warfare with the internal "enemies" who they believe have been sabotaging his efforts to restore the country to greatness. It remains to be seen if Republican moderates will remain loyal to the party or look elsewhere for affiliation.

A 2012 study found that how those who affiliate with one party feel about those on the other side has been becoming more negative since the 1980s. The findings indicated that these negative judgments aren't related to issues as much as partisan identity (Pierre 2018). A study in 2018 found the best predictor of this behavior was not defined by what people believe about issues, but identity-based ideology, or how people identify themselves politically (Pierre 2018).

Given the extent to which Americans seemed entrenched in their own political parties, it would seem difficult to overcome the gulf separating them. But it must be remembered that not all members of a political party feel this way. Earlier, it was stated that those in both the Republican and Democratic parties feel that about 25 percent of their fellow party members are too extreme, which makes it difficult to reach a compromise or work together. A candidate who can span a bridge between those who are looking for change in both parties by addressing common issues and concerns might be able to have political success.

CHANGES IN MEDIA

Political candidates do not have control over how the mainstream media cover their campaigns. Candidates have traditionally railed against negative media coverage and cozied up to those who provide more positive stories. As campaigns have become more negative, mainstream media have also had more negative reporting, much to the chagrin of presidential candidates. For outsider candidates in third parties, there is often little to no coverage, and what is published usually points out the futility of running as something other than a Republican or a Democrat. This leads to third-party candidates using what Neville-Shepard (2019) calls "genre busting" rhetoric, or discourse that is seen as violating norms, to draw media attention. But the media can be finicky and unpredictable, which is why it has always been important for presidential candidates to have consistent messaging through various types of media, including television commercials, print, and radio. The days of television ads being king in a nationwide presidential campaign are probably over. (Local races might still see a good deal of broadcast advertising.) With the advent of social media, campaigns now have more opportunities to make an end run around the mainstream media and directly address voters.

The media landscape in the United States has been fragmenting for several years, making it more difficult to find the right advertising vehicles for political candidates. As Americans move into different media outlets and platforms, it becomes more of a challenge to match a political message to the appropriate groups of potential voters. For instance, while political candidates could once place ads around particular cable television shows that was shown to appeal to one party or another, many Americans no longer subscribe to cable, but spend more time streaming online content. This means the search for supporters has essentially moved online where they are often targeted through social media.

Because of this, outsider presidential candidates need to become proficient in using social media and invest more campaign funds in this platform. Some candidates, such as President Donald Trump, used social media to attack opponents, while others, such as Hillary Clinton, have used it to try to establish a more approachable persona. One thing that Trump managed to do was to rule the daily news cycle through the tweets he sent out multiple times a day. It would be hard for any other candidate to wield that much influence over the American media unless the candidate had already established a large social media following prior to a candidacy.

The adoption of new media technologies is a characteristic common to both populist and third-party candidates (Jager and Borriello 2020, Ekstrom, Patrona and Thornborrow 2018). While third-party candidates are often looking for less expensive ways to get their messages in front of the public, populists are always looking for ways to reach voters directly, without having to go through the mass media. For instance, Huey Long saw the potential of radio addresses when that technology was still evolving, and Ron Paul discovered that fundraising could be incredibly effective when done online. Although candidates had already embraced social media platforms, in 2016 Trump took voter messaging on social media to another level, utilizing digital strategies to directly address his supporters every day.

> This tactic has had a double effect. First, it has allowed them to neutralize opposition within their camp by establishing a seemingly direct communication line with their supporters. But it also shielded the party from outside forces, rewiring politics around a digital arena rather than a classical public sphere. (Jager and Borriello 2020)

Simply put, if candidates can control the messages that are being sent to supporters or potential supporters, then they have a better chance of success at the ballot box. "In the past, upsurges of populist sentiment have often coincided with innovations in communication technology that rendered the voices of the 'little people' more discernible and easier to mobilize" (Nash 2016). Mobilization is key to political success, and a digital culture is one in which social media and other digital outlets can be used to galvanize, organize, and mobilize.

Although candidates are shifting to more direct methods of conversation with their audiences, traditional media still wield some power. Modern American media outlets have been placed under extraordinary pressure, partially because of the COVID-19 pandemic. A drop in advertising revenue has been plaguing newspapers for several years, and the pandemic brought even more newsroom cuts and media closures, even to online news outlets. The national news media are shifting into a more interpretive and partisan form of reporting, harkening back to the earlier days of American print media. Some say Trump was the catalyst for this type of reporting, but it was already shifting before the 2016 campaign. However, his campaign style and rhetoric certainly accelerated the pace of this transition.

Many of those reporting and writing about politics in the United States are young reporters with less political experience, but with a great working knowledge of social media. Reporters now routinely find sources for stories through Twitter, and news outlets tease stories on Facebook and Twitter to lead readers to their websites. Young reporters might not know all of the history behind an issue, but they are very good at following a candidate's social media efforts.

Candidates who run less-than-professional social media campaigns will probably find themselves outpaced by opponents and even shamed in the media. Outside candidates must make an effort to publish messages that are professional but point the conversation to issues in their favor. Messages should be "share worthy," as many people will help spread a candidate's messages through social media if they have snappy headlines, interesting photos, and messages that relate to an audience. One of the most important aspects of social media is its visual content. People are more likely to share a message if it has effective visual content, which could be photos, graphs, or short videos. Outsider politicians should also not be afraid of using provocative headlines, although they must decide if they want to cross the line between shocking and insulting or angering. For candidates who might not be the odds-on favorite, social media can help them leverage trending topics or create news with their own messages, and it can drive potential voters and donors to share messages or donate funds. In short, outsider candidates must invest in quality online messaging, and doing that well can often lead to effective online fundraising, which is always of paramount importance to outsider candidates.

THE IMPORTANCE OF TECHNOLOGY

One thread that runs through an examination of modern presidential contests is how quickly campaigns adapt new technology for their needs. From Shirley Chisholm's vehicle equipped with a loudspeaker to Ron Paul's online money bombs to Ross Perot's television infomercials, technology can provide new ways of reaching large groups of potential voters more efficiently. This is especially true of digital media, which can establish a viable link between a candidate and his or her supporters (Jager and Borriello 2020).

Outsider candidates often fall back on technology to help provide opportunities to reach larger numbers of voters because they frequently have less funding for national travel than major candidates, and it is physically impossible to speak with every potential supporter in the nation. This is one reason that social media platforms have become so important for all candidates: it is a relatively inexpensive way to reach large numbers of people without the involvement of the American news media. Messages can be tailored to individual groups, similar to the way Trump's 2016 Facebook messages were tweaked for different audiences, and there is the added bonus that supporters will often share the messages, making them have an even wider dispersal.

Candidates should still have websites where they post and manage longer-form policy statements, campaign photos, schedules, donations, and various other types of information. Political websites have come a long way since the 1996 campaign between President Bill Clinton and Sen. Bob Dole, when Dole's website was constructed by two students at Arizona State University working out of a dorm room (LaFrance 2016). According to Campaigns and Elections, candidates should be aware that mobile traffic now accounts for half of the traffic on the web (Eastman 2019). This means that websites should be set up so that they display properly on mobile phones and other devices. Otherwise, it's a frustrating experience for users, and they might never come back. Other characteristics such as simple landing pages, tasteful design and photos, and quick load times are important to keeping a potential voter's attention. The ever-present candidate campaign shops—for selling T-shirts, hats, mugs, and other items—are also good ways to get out a simple message and make a few dollars at the same time.

One important shift for outsider candidates to keep in mind is that the American public is no longer a passive consumer of political messages. Because of technological advances in recent years and the fragmentation of media, we are now in the era of citizens constructing their own social media and online messages for candidates, sharing campaign messages, and becoming more active and vocal supporters through online platforms. A study by the Media Insight Project in 2017 found that how much Americans trust the content on social media is determined more by *who shares it* than *who actually creates it* (American Press Institute 2017). Those who share an article can even determine whether someone feels the article is accurate. "For instance, when the story is passed on by a trusted figure and the article is attributed to The [Associated Press], 52 percent of people think the article got the facts right. When the article is still attributed to The [Associated Press] but the person passing it on is less trusted, only 32 percent say the facts were right" (American Press Institute 2017). For political candidates, it's easy to spot the importance of having messages shared by individuals on social media in networks where they are trusted or liked. That greatly increases the chances of the messages being accepted and passed along again. This is why it is so important to customize social media messages for identifiable groups. The more variations that can be produced and targeted at smaller groups, the better the chances that a trusted individual will pass the message on to other people who will then accept it and also share the message.

This also applies to online advertising, where identifying target audiences is vitally important. A social media platform can usually provide information for advertisers that is vital to zeroing in on different audiences, and that is also available for other types of online advertising. Getting a candidate's message to the right groups of people is important because it not only saves time, but also money. "The key is to target 'persuasive' messages for the right niche. In addition to geographic and demographic targeting, the internet also allows targeting ads by key words or phrases. If someone is searching a specific word, a related ad is triggered" (Denton, Trent & Friedenberg 2020, 341). Candidates should not be looking for a one-time encounter with a potential voter, but actively requesting those who support them to pass along their campaign messages.

One might say that those sharing the messages are a type of social surrogate for a candidate. The chances of an individual having a one-on-one physical encounter with a presidential candidate is slim unless that individual is donating a large sum of money. But having trusted sharers' passing along a candidate's message increases the credibility of those messages and, by extension, the candidate.

Another technology that should be considered by outsider political candidates is YouTube. Most people are familiar with this platform, but few understand how impactful it can be. According to Statista, YouTube reaches 81 percent of Americans ages 15–25 years. It reaches 71 percent of those 26–35 years old, and of those in the 36–45 year demographic, 67 percent use YouTube. It is almost identical for those 46–55, with 66 percent of them using the social medium. It is said to have 126 million unique monthly viewers, it and has one of the most popular mobile apps in the United States. A candidate can have a specific channel on which to post campaign messages and videos, plus there are now very popular YouTube shows that are watched by millions of viewers each week. For candidates who don't have the name recognition to get invitations to cable news shows or "Meet the Press," this type of outlet can be greatly beneficial. For instance, "The Joe Rogan Experience" channel has more than six million subscribers, and former 2020 presidential outsider candidate Andrew Yang had his first interview on that YouTube channel. Yang's episode quickly reached a million views after only a few days, and Yang then saw an increase in his number of supporters and financial donations (Kelly 2019). It set him on a course that allowed him to qualify for several Democratic Party debates.

This type of messaging seems to resonate with younger voters and those looking for the all-important authenticity that outsider candidates can bring to an election. Joanna Rosholm, Michelle Obama's former press secretary and deputy communications director, said that YouTube shows are important to consider. "Whether it's on a creator's channel or their own social channels, candidates will need to strike the right balance between showing up somewhere interesting or unexpected, but in a way that is authentic to who they are and how their audience perceives them. What works for one candidate or political figure may not work for another. Millennials have an incredible read on authenticity" (Kelly 2019).

SUMMARY

In conclusion, the most successful outsider candidate will probably come from either the Republican or Democratic party and will need to address areas on which a slice of membership from both parties can reach some sort of agreement or compromise. Reaching across the current political bifurcation to find potential supporters will be of paramount importance, and candidates will need to relate to audiences in authentic ways. Outsider candidates must find ways to go around traditional news media and take their messages straight to potential supporters. That means investing in a good online and social media team and making a commitment to using professional social media that work to reach a continually fragmenting audience. Any successful political campaign will need to incorporate the latest technology into its messaging, including online advertising, social media, and YouTube channels and shows. An outsider candidate should be prepared for the challenge of locating and persuading potential voters in an era when many are suspicious of even formerly trusted sources of information. Finding trusted opinion leaders to share campaign information is important, as research shows who shares information is more important than who originally published the information.

However, simply knowing how to use media isn't enough. A political candidate cannot be successful without people's votes. As noted earlier, only about 11 percent of Americans now say they are not affiliated with or leaning toward either the Republican or Democratic parties. Persuading those voters, as well as attracting a significant slice of the major parties' members, is a difficult task. "The last five presidential elections have been a contest for the favor of a tiny percentage of the electorate. And this is a symptom of a larger shift from argument to other kinds of stimuli that do the work faster. Persuasion has come to seem an intricate and rare undertaking" (Bromwich 2021). This book does not argue that persuading individuals to vote for a particular candidate is a simple process. On the contrary, changing people's minds is difficult, and only one of the presidential candidates profiled here actually went on to occupy the White House.

Mounting a successful political campaign in the United States might seem to be easier now that social media allows candidates to speak directly to potential supporters. But the process of finding those potential voters, crafting persuasive messages, and continuing to attract supporters and money is an almost overwhelming challenge, even for those with major party support. For outsider candidates, the challenge is even greater, and it will require an investment of time, staffing, and expertise—all of which come at a high price.

REFERENCES

American Press Institute. 2017. "Who Shared It? How Americans Decide What News to Trust on Social Media." American Press Institute. March 20, 2017. https://www.americanpressinstitute.org/publications/reports/survey-research/trust-social-media/.

Barnidge, Matthew and Cynthia Peacock. 2019. A Third Wave of Selective Exposure Research? The Challenges Posed by Hyperpartisan News on Social Media. *Media and Communication* 7 (3): 4–7. https://doi.org/10.17645/mac.v7i3.2257.

Black, Earl and Merle Black. 2002. *The Rise of Southern Republicans*. Cambridge, MA: Harvard University Press.

Bonikowski, Bart and Noam Gidron. 2016. The Populist style in American Politics: Presidential Campaign Discourse, 1952-1996. *Social Forces* 94, no. 4 (June): 1593–1621. https://doi.org/10.1093/sf/sov120.

Bromwich, David. 2021. "The Dying Art of Political Persuasion: Education, like Elections, Depends on the Assumption that People Can Be Convinced." *The Chronicle of Higher Education* Jan 19, 2021. Accessed Jan. 19, 2021. https://www.chronicle.com/author/david-bromwich.

Brubaker, Rogers. 2020. Populism and Nationalism. *Nations & Nationalism* 26, no. 1 (January): 44–66.

Bryant, Jennings and John Davies. 2006. Selective Exposure Processes. *In Psychology of Entertainment, edited by Jennings Bryant and Peter Vorderer*, 19-33. Mahwah, NJ: Lawrence Erlbaum Associates.

Carey, James. 1993. The Mass Media and Democracy: Between the Modern and the Postmodern. *Journal of International Affairs* 47, no. 1 (Summer): 1–21. http://www.jstor.org/stable/24357082.

Carnes, Nicholas and Noam Lupu. 2020. The White Working Class and the 2016 Election. *Perspectives on Politics* 19, no. 1 (May): 1–18. https://doi.org/10.1017/S1537592720001267.

Cassidy, Peter. 2017. "Survey Finds Consumers Crave Authenticity - and User-Generated Content Delivers." *Social Media Today*. Nov. 21, 2017. https://www.socialmediatoday.com/news/survey-finds-consumers-crave-authenticity-and-user-generated-content-deli/511360/.

Denton, Robert E., Judith S. Trent and Robert C. Friedenberg. 2020. *"Political Campaign Communication: Principles & Practices."* Lanham, MD: Rowman & Littlefield.

Eastman, Bryan. 2019. "6 Campaign Web Design Trends to Watch in 2020." *Campaigns & Elections*. June 18, 2019. https://www.campaignsandelections.com/campaign-insider/6-campaign-web-design-trends-to-watch-in-2020.

Eklundh, Emmy and Andy Knott. Introduction. In *The Populist Manifesto*, edited by Emmy Eklundh and Andy Knott, 1-8. London: Rowman & Littlefield.

Ekstrom, Mats, Marianna Patrona and Joanna Thornborrow. 2018. Right-Wing Populism and the Dynamics of Style: A Discourse-Analytic Perspective on Mediated Political Performances. *Palgrave Communication* 4 (83). https://doi.org/10.1057/s41599-018-0132-6

Gerteis, Joseph and Alyssa Goolsby. 2005. Nationalism in America: The Case of the Populist Movement. *Theory and Society* 34, no. 2 (April):197–225.

Gronbeck, Bruce E. 1995. The Rhetorics of the Past: History, Argument, and Collective Memory. Paper presented at *Greenspun Conference on Rhetorical History: Rhetoric, History, and Critical Interpretation: The Recovery of the Historical-Critical Praxis, the University of Nevada Las Vegas, 1995.* https://clas.uiowa.edu/commstudies/sites/clas.uiowa.edu.commstudies/files/THE%20RHETORICS%20OF%20THE%20PAST.pdf.

Guerlain, Pierre. The Double Matrix of the 60s: Progressive and Reactionary Legacies of the Sixties. Alizes: *Revue angliciste de La Reunion*, Faculte des Lettres et Sciences humaines (Universite de La Reunion), Side Views: 164-177. Hal-01639860.

Jager, Anton and Arthur Borriello. 2020. Making Sense of Populism. *Catalyst* 3, no. 4 (Winter): 49–81. https://catalyst-journal.com/vol3/no4/making-sense-of-populism.

Jones, Jeffrey. 2019. "Democrats Hold Edge in U.S. Party Affiliation in 3rd Quarter." Gallup. Oct. 7, 2019. https://news.gallup.com/poll/267239/democrats-hold-edge-party-affiliation-3rd-quarter.aspx.

Kelly, Makena. 2019. "YouTube Shows Have Become a Secret Weapon For Rising Politicians: The Video Platform Reaches More Young Voters in an Average Week Than Every Cable Network Combined." *The Verge.* Aug. 20, 2019. https://www.theverge.com/2019/8/20/20812826/youtube-politics-voters-presidential-candi-dates-sanders-yang-gabbard-podcast-interview-2020.

LaFrance, Adrienne. 2016. "The First Campaign Websites: The Site Made for Bob Dole's 1996 Presidential Run is a Little Jewel in Internet History." *The Atlantic.* Feb. 19, 2016. https://www.theatlantic.com/technology/archive/2016/02/1996/470106/.

Lipset, Seymour M. (1959). Democracy and Working-Class Authoritarianism. *American Sociological Review* 24, 4 (August): 482–501. https://www.jstor.org/stable/pdf/2089536.pdf.

Murphy, John M. 2015. Barack Obama and Rhetorical History. *Quarterly Journal of Speech* 101, no. 1 (February): 213–224.

Nash, George H. 2016. American Conservatism & the Problem of Populism. *The New Criterion* 35 (1): 4–14.

Neville-Shepard, Ryan. 2019. Genre-Busting, Campaign Speech Genres and the Rhetoric of Political Outsiders. In *Reading the Presidency Advances in Presidential Rhetoric*, edited by Stephen J. Heidt and Mary E. Stuckey, 86–105. New York: Peter Lang.

Pew Research Center. 2019. "Partisan Antipathy: More Intense, More Personal." Oct. 10, 2019. https://www.pewresearch.org/politics/2019/10/10/partisan-antipathy-more-intense-more-personal/.

Pierre, Joe. 2018. "Why Has America Become So Divided? Four Reasons the United States Doesn't Seem So United Anymore." *Psychology Today.* Sept. 5, 2018. https://www.psychologytoday.com/us/blog/psych-unseen/201809/why-has-america-become-so-divided.

Powell, Larry and Joseph Cowart. 2003. *Political Campaign Communication Inside and Out.* Boston: Pearson Education Inc.

Sears, David O. and Jonathan L. Freedman. 1967. Selective Exposure to Information: A Critical Review. *Public Opinion Quarterly* 31, 2 (Summer): 194–213.

Serazio, Michael. 2016. Encoding the Paranoid Style in American Politics: "Anti-Establishment' Discourse and Power in Contemporary Spin. *Critical Studies in Media Communication* 33, no. 2 (May): 181–194.

Shermer, Elizabeth Tandy. 2018. Collapse or Triumph? American Conservative Movement at 60. *American Studies Journal* 65, https://doi.org/10.18422/65-01.

Strahan, Randall and Daniel J. Palazzolo. 2004. The Gingrich Effect. *Political Science Quarterly* 119, no. 1 (Spring): 89–114.

Theye, Kirsten and Steven Melling. 2018. Total Losers and Bad hombres: The Political Incorrectness and Perceived Authenticity of Donald J. Trump. *Southern Communication Journal* 83, no. 5 (November-December): 322–337.

USA Today Network Pressroom. 2019. "America is Dangerously Divided. USA Today and Partners Launch 'Hidden Common Ground to Find Solutions." *USA Today*. Dec. 5, 2019. https://www.usatoday.com/story/news/pr/2019/12/05/america-dangerously-divided-usa-today-and-partners-launch-hidden-common-ground-find-solutions/2617559001/.

Chapter 15

Final Thoughts

It's tough to be an outsider presidential candidate. You are often running as a third-party nominee, have limited finances, little media coverage, and you are written off as a loser before you even begin the campaign. Many states make it almost impossible to get on the ballot, and it can cost thousands of dollars to accomplish that task.

So why does the United States have a rich tradition of long-shot candidates trying to overcome the odds and become president? Earlier in this book, it was mentioned that anger toward the political system, a lack of party loyalty, and looming economic challenges often combine to create the conditions that lead to the emergence of an outsider candidate. Almost all outsider candidates are spurred to pursue the presidency because of ideological beliefs that cause them to want to share their ideas with the nation. Most of them display populist tendencies, and they often rage against the elites, against the establishment, against big corporations, against those outside the group, and they tend to present themselves as political mavericks.

Americans seem to have a soft spot for such mavericks. There is a sort of fascination with someone who is an outsider candidate, who has interesting ideas, and who also might be electable. Perhaps there is a degree of romanticism associated with the outsider candidate that harkens back to the American love of the underdog—the person who keeps going despite setbacks and defies overwhelming odds. Many outsiders begin a national campaign with support and enthusiasm for their ideas, but the grind of a campaign wears them and their money supplies down, and eventually they either drop out or scale back their campaigns in an attempt to keep their ideas or movements alive (Neville-Shepard 2019a). While Donald J. Trump is the only outsider who has actually been elected president so far, several have left their ideological marks on the national conversation, pushing the country toward a particular ideal or policy, while a handful nudged a political party closer to the left or the right of the partisan spectrum. Others pursued new technologies that have made direct access to voters easier and less expensive. Some hear echoes of their discourse in modern campaigns, while others acknowledge their ideas have been co-opted by recent candidates. A couple have been blamed for the losses of a Democratic presidential candidate, while others were left wondering why their ideas did not resonate more strongly with the American public.

The United States is at a peculiar moment in time. There is a great political chasm between Republicans and Democrats. Traditional political terms such as left and right or liberal and conservative seem less important than party labels (Shermer 2018). We have also seen the rise of celebrity candidates and political fandom (Street 2019). Despite the 2020 election of President Joe Biden, who has been a member of the U.S. Senate and a previous vice president, there are still many Americans who are longing to elect someone from outside the Washington, D.C. beltway. Polls show that a significant number of them also think that a president should have some degree of prior political experience, but that is not always true of a real outsider candidate. This seems to be more important to Democrats than Republicans, but both groups are now trying to determine the future of their parties. A substantial number of Democrats want the party to jog more to the left, while a substantial number of Republicans want to continue the right-ward motion of the GOP. As the only president ever elected without political or military experience, Trump exemplifies the outsider candidate, but has created a polarizing effect on the nation.

Because of the political bifurcation in the country, outsider candidates will probably be more successful if they run within the Republican or Democratic parties. There are simply not enough potential voters right now without ties (membership or preference) to one of the two main parties for a third-party candidate to be successful. There are also other factors to consider that come into play when there is a great deal of political polarization. Research has shown that polarization can lead to less control by the elites within an established political party. "Our framework shows that when polarization between parties is strongest, party establishments are most vulnerable to entry from outsiders, and elites have the least control over their nominating process" (Buisseret and Van Weelden 2020). This same research posits that if an outsider candidate secures the nomination from one party, that candidate will be stronger in a general election than the other party's more mainstream nominee. This proved true in 2016.

Of course, this all hinges on there being enough division within a party to allow an outsider candidate a window to discuss issues that resonate with the right audiences. For instance, Donald Trump found his audience in blue-collar workers who were losing manufacturing jobs, evangelical Christians, white males, and those without college degrees. Many people who share one or more of those characteristics reside within the Republican Party—and they formed an operating base for him—but there are substantial numbers within the Democratic Party, also.

Trump was able to gain support from some of those who had only four years earlier voted for President Barack Obama. That is the power an outsider candidate can wield within a party when the leadership either discounts a candidate's possibility of winning the nomination or doesn't have the power to stop that candidate early in the primary. Cleavages within parties create opportunities for outsider candidates, and those with the political acumen to take advantage of that knowledge could successfully navigate through a contested primary. This is essentially what happened in 2016 within the Republican Party. Shermer argues that a party outsider won because conservatives "were so divided amongst themselves—as they have always been— that primary voters couldn't agree on a candidate from their established ranks, much to the frustration of party and movement leaders" (2018). Because of their inability to agree and lead the party, it was easy for the populist Trump to paint them as the "elite" villains selling out to the establishment and standing in the way of returning America to greatness (Casullo 2020, 30–31). This points out the opportunities that can arise within parties when internal bickering and strife lead to fissures in leadership.

One thing that becomes clear after an examination of several outsider presidential candidates is that those who have come before often crack open the door for those after them. You can see some of George Wallace's rhetoric on display in 2016, and you can also hear strong echoes of Pat Buchannan's ideas and wording from Donald Trump. Some say that a strong outsider candidate within a party can weaken its response to those who come in the future. "Dismissed as a fringe character for rejecting Republican orthodoxy on trade and immigration and interventionism, Buchanan effectively weakened the party's defenses, allowing a more forceful messenger with better timing to finish the insurrection he started back in 1991" (Alberta 2017). It was similar for Rev. Jesse Jackson, whose campaigns in the 1980s planted the idea that African Americans could compete in local and national politics. President Barack Obama supposedly told Jackson that, after watching him take part in debates, he knew that it was possible for a black candidate to win (Cobble 2018). While many outsider candidates have attempted to win the presidency, perhaps few of them realized that they were, essentially, standing on the shoulders of those who came before.

Another key for outsider candidates is that they must be good communicators. In a society that is awash in news, corporate and political messages, and individually crafted videos and postings, it is imperative that outsider candidates be able to speak without sounding rehearsed, debate with clarity, and present themselves well on television and in videos. It also doesn't hurt if some of the messages are a bit controversial, or if they use activist tactics, as that will potentially spark news coverage and will penetrate through much of the information clutter surrounding Americans every day (Neville-Shepard 2019b). Perhaps that is one reason that voters are looking for authenticity in candidates. There are so many advertising messages in society that individuals often discount or ignore most of them. The traditional adage is that a television advertisement must be seen at least seven times before most of those in an audience begin to notice its message. A political candidate who seems to speak directly to people, and with simple, direct messaging, has a greater chance of connecting with voters.

The technology is now available to send a message to millions of potential supporters in seconds. So far, that technology allows candidates to locate and reach potential groups of supporters with their messages, but not necessarily to persuade large groups of people to change their minds about issues or candidates. What outsider presidential candidates can do is locate those potential supporters and craft messages that will resonate with those who already share the same ideas on issues. Candidates who believe that social media will convert large groups of people in the other party to their voters are mistaken. Research shows that "how individuals respond to messages to which they are exposed is often contingent on their political predispositions. Politically palatable claims are more readily accepted than claims that are less compatible with their political worldview. Thus, media effects often vary by users' political affiliation" (Garrett 2019). In other words, a message will be more effective if a person already agrees with some or much of the content.

Voters are looking for cognitive shortcuts, and the cues and symbols used in political communication can oftentimes provide "markers" for voters awash in a world of messages. The concept of identification is important in today's political environment and particularly for those who use populist rhetoric. Kenneth Burke (1969), an American literary theorist with influential ideas in the field of rhetoric, explained identification as a process that is fundamental to human beings—one in which individuals are persuaded that they share important qualities in common with a speaker. A presidential candidate who is able to persuade audiences that they share a certain background, ideas, or common enemies has accomplished a degree of identification with potential voters. The degree of that identification—or how much this candidate is like me—can be instrumental in persuading an individual to support or vote for a particular person.

Of course, as witnessed in the 2016 election, social media can be used to try to interfere with the American political process. Short of devising a way to avoid this, which hasn't been found during the writing of this book, candidates will have to expect misinformation to be a continuing part of the American electoral process.

By using social media, which allows for microtargeting of potential audiences, an outsider candidate can use like-minded voters to help persuade others to do the same. As noted earlier, people are often more likely to distribute and believe information that is shared by those whom they trust. Perhaps a good strategy is to craft messages that are targeted to small groups of voters—either supporters or undecided—and allow individuals to distribute them to their own groups of friends or followers on social media. Candidates can also help supply materials such as campaign logos, graphics, or photos to supporters who want to craft their own political messages. Those messages could potentially be more influential than the ones produced and distributed by a campaign.

The purpose of this book was to take a look at a number of recent outsider presidential candidates and their campaigns and communication styles. Several common themes emerged, including the use of populist rhetoric, the adoption of updated technology, and candidates having greater success within one of the two main parties. Many will argue that third-party candidates have been pulling more votes in presidential elections, and it is true that the Libertarian and Green parties have increased their number of votes. But the nation is still driven by the Republican and Democratic parties, and will probably continue to be unless some dramatic event happens. As Magee points out, "It is a rare occurrence for third-party candidates to play decisive roles in U.S. presidential outcomes" (575). The increase in political polarization will limit the impact of third-party outsider candidates, but it could provide opportunities for those who can campaign from within one of those two main groups.

The United States has a long history of contentious politics, and if the past tells us anything, it is that the future holds more political uncertainty. Outsider candidates may be uniquely positioned to take advantage of such uncertain times through their populist appeals and rhetoric.

REFERENCES

Alberta, Tim. 2017. "The Ideas Made It, But I Didn't: Pat Buchanan Won After All. But Now He Thinks It Might Be Too Late for the Nation He Was Trying to Save." *Politico Magazine*. May/June 2017. https://www.politico.com/magazine/story/2017/04/22/pat-buchanan-trump-president-history-profile-215042.

Burke, Kenneth. 1969. *A Rhetoric of Motives*. Berkeley: University of California Press.

Buisseret, Peter and Richard Van Weelden. 2020. Crashing the Party? Elites, Outsiders, and Elections. *American Journal of Political Science* 64, no. 2 (August): 356–370. https://doi.org/10.1111/ajps.12457.

Casullo, Maria Esperanza. 2020. Populism and Myth. In *The Populist Manifesto*, edited by Emmy Eklundh and Andy Knott, 25-38. London: Rowman & Littlefield.

Cobble, Steve. 2018. "Jesse Jackson's Rainbow Coalition Created Today's Democratic Politics." *The Nation*. Oct. 2, 2018. https://www.thenation.com/article/archive/jesse-jackson-rainbow-coalition-democratic-politics/.

Garrett, R. Kelly. 2019. "Social Media's Contribution to Political Misperceptions in U.S. Presidential Elections." *PLOS ONE*. March 27, 2019. https://doi.org/10.1371/journal.pone.0213500.

Magee, Christopher S. P. 2003. Third-Party Candidates and the 2000 Presidential Election. *Social Science Quarterly* 84, no. 3 (September): 574–595.

Neville-Shepard, Ryan. 2019a. Containing the Third-Party Voter in the 2016 U.S. Presidential Election. *Journal of Communication Inquiry* 49, no. 3 (January): 272–292.

Neville-Shepard, Ryan. 2019b. Genre-Busting, Campaign Speech Genres and the Rhetoric of Political Outsiders. In *Reading the Presidency Advances in Presidential Rhetoric*, edited by Stephen J. Heidt and Mary E. Stuckey, 86–105. New York: Peter Lang.

Shermer, Elizabeth Tandy. 2018. Collapse or Triumph? American Conservative Movement at 60. *American Studies Journal* 65, https://doi.org/10.18422/65-01.

Street, John. 2019. What Is Donald Trump? Forms of 'Celebrity' in Celebrity Politics. *Political Studies Review* 17, (1): 3–13. https://journals.sagepub.com/doi/full/10.1177/1478929918772995.

Index

233

About the Author

Melissa M. Smith is a professor of communication and holds the Gibbons Chair of Journalism at Mississippi University for Women. She has published and presented several articles in political communication, and she was co-author of *Campaign Finance Reform: The Political Shell Game* (Lexington Books, 2010) and *Dark Money, Super PACs and the 2012 Election* (Lexington Books, 2014). She received her doctorate in mass communication from the University of Alabama in 2003. Before attending graduate school, she worked in both newspaper and television journalism.

www.ingramcontent.com/pod-product-compliance
Lightning Source LLC
Chambersburg PA
CBHW050641280326
41932CB00015B/2730